Wild Knitting

Wild Knitting

A & W Publishers, Inc.
New York

Contents

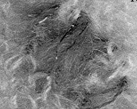

Executive Editor
Susannah Read

Art Editor
Linda Cole

Consultant Editor
Angela Jeffs

Assistant Art Editor
Ingrid Mason

Editor
Jane Garton

Technical Consultants
Sandy Carr
Jean Litchfield
Ena Richards

Editorial Assistant
Louise Egerton

Design Consultants
Debbie Hudson
Val Moon

Production
Martin Elliott

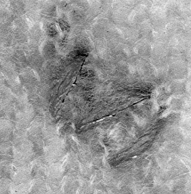

First published in the United States of America in
1979 by
A & W Publishers, Inc.
95 Madison Avenue
New York, New York 10016
By arrangement with Mitchell Beazley Publishers
Limited

Library of Congress Catalog Card Number: 79-51988
ISBN: 0-89479-054-4
Printed in Hong Kong

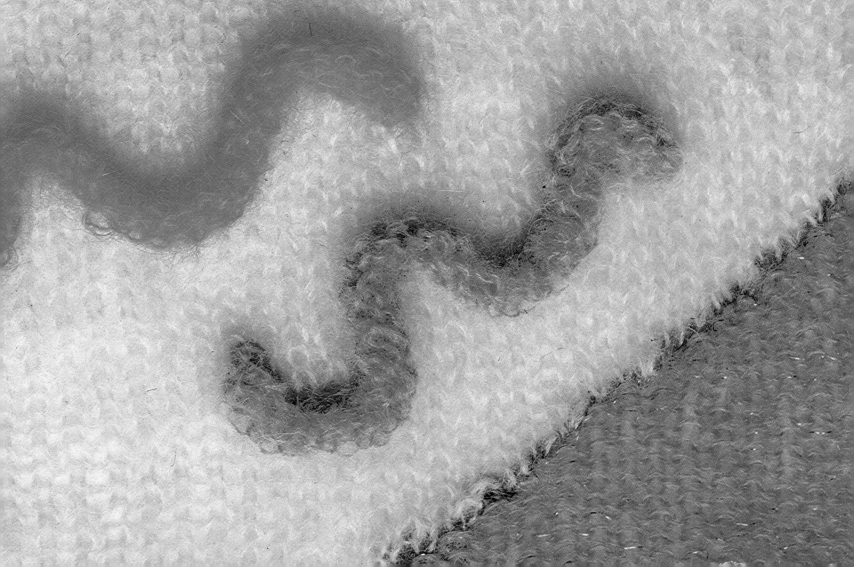

Introduction

For years knitting has had a dowdy image. An abundance of old-fashioned patterns, uninviting yarns and a surfeit of cheap, mass-produced knitwear have all contributed to a bleak, boring and uncreative outlook.

Now change is on the way. Beautiful, exciting yarns are appearing on the market; young designers are looking at the craft in a different light, suddenly hand-knitting is news. As a result, designs are becoming more inspired and simple shapes that are so much easier to knit are taking over.

This book sets out to reflect this revolutionary mood in an age-old craft and shows you how to acquire or make the most of existing knitting skills. It is planned in such a way so as to be of maximum use to the complete beginner and yet thought provoking enough in terms of color, texture and design to provide something for everyone.

The first section gives a straightforward introduction to all the basic techniques you may need. It starts with needles and yarns, casting on and binding off and the simple combinations of plain and purl stitches, then works through all the more advanced stages to adapting and designing patterns. Techniques are also given for making all those decorative extras that can transform a mundane piece of knitted fabric into something quite unique and full of fun.

There is also guidance on substituting yarns and stitch patterns – and this is where the stitch dictionary will prove useful. Located at the end of the book, it provides a selection of interesting patterns that you may prefer to use rather than those given in the instructions for individual designs. This follows the 50 or more patterns which undoubtedly form the most exciting part of the book and go a long way toward illustrating that there really is no limit to the materials that can be used, or to what can be made.

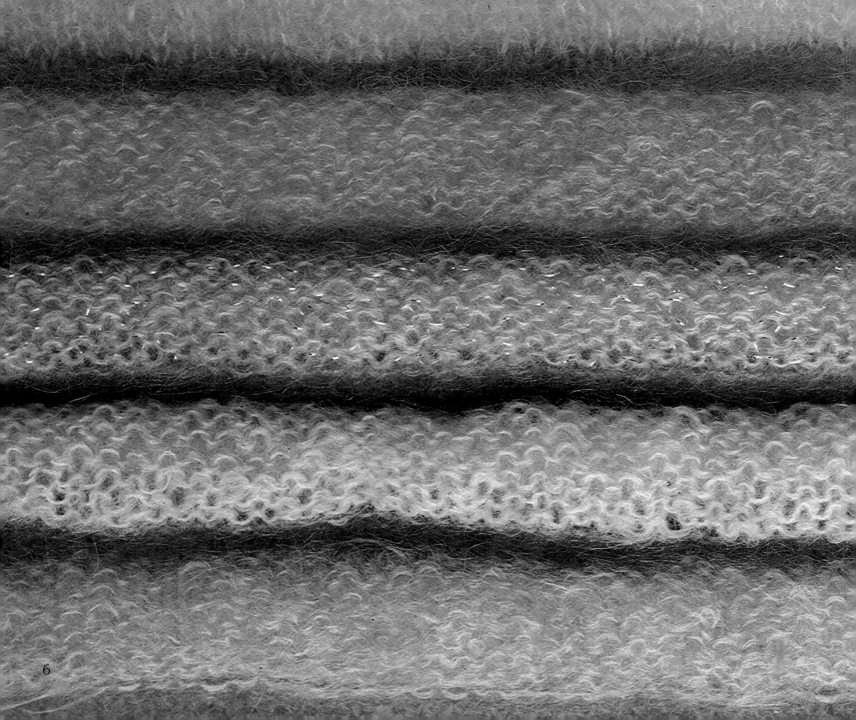

Taking up the challenge to produce designs that are wild in concept and yet simple to knit, 25 young designers have set out to prove that stunning clothes and accessories, objects and items for the home can be made at little cost and with the minimum of effort.

Try a daring bat hat or a zany all-weather indoor patio; go back to nature in a landscape sweater or sit things out on a pile of tropical fruit; face the music in a slinky silver tube of a dress or display super coordinated fashion sense in a simply spectacular wardrobe of warm winter woollies.

Each pattern, apart from being fully illustrated with color photographs, is backed with explanatory drawings showing the measurements of the main pieces. This means that you can see at a glance the size it should be and any alterations can be worked out before beginning on the pattern.

Measurements are given in metric with imperial in brackets. These are working equivalents rather than exact conversions and you should decide at the start which system you are going to use and follow it throughout. Each pattern specifies a general type or weight of yarn rather than a particular brand to encourage you to make your own choice from the wide range available. This does, however, make a tension check all the more important. Tension is specified wherever it is essential to the final success of the knitting. Techniques and projects are fully cross-referenced so that you can check back to a technique you have forgotten or check out an alternative stitch or extra detail that you might like to incorporate. For all those who like to have a straightforward pattern to follow, these patterns are ideal; and for those who want to explore and extend the craft of knitting even further, they provide an ideal starting-off point for experiment to see just how versatile this craft can be.

Abbreviations

alt	alternate(ly)		inc	increas(e/ing), p18–19
beg	begin(ning)		K	knit
BC	back cross: slip 1 stitch onto cable needle to back of work, knit 1 stitch, then purl stitch from cable needle		knitwise	insert needle as if to knit
			MB	make bobble, p39
			m1	make 1 stitch, p18
BKC	back knit cross: slip 1 stitch onto cable needle to back of work, knit 1 stitch, then knit stitch from cable needle		no	number
			P	purl
			purlwise	insert needle as if to purl
BPC	back purl cross: as BKC but purl both stitches		psso	pass slipped stitch over, p19
			p2sso	pass 2 slipped stitches over
CN	cable needle		rem	remain(ing)
dec	decreas(e/ing), p19		rep	repeat
DK	double knitting wool		rev st st	reverse stockinette stitch, p15
FC	front cross: slip 1 stitch onto cable needle to front of work, purl 1 stitch, then knit stitch from cable needle		sl	slip
			sl st	slip stitch
			st(s)	stitch(es)
FKC	front knit cross: slip 1 stitch onto cable needle to front of work, knit 1 stitch, then knit stitch from cable needle		st st	stockinette stitch, p15
			tbl	through back loop
			tog	together
foll	follow(ing)		yb	yarn back
FPC	front purl cross: as FKC but purl both stitches		yf	yarn forward, p18
			yon	yarn over needle, p18
g st	garter stitch, p15		yrn	yarn round needle, p19

Needles and yarns

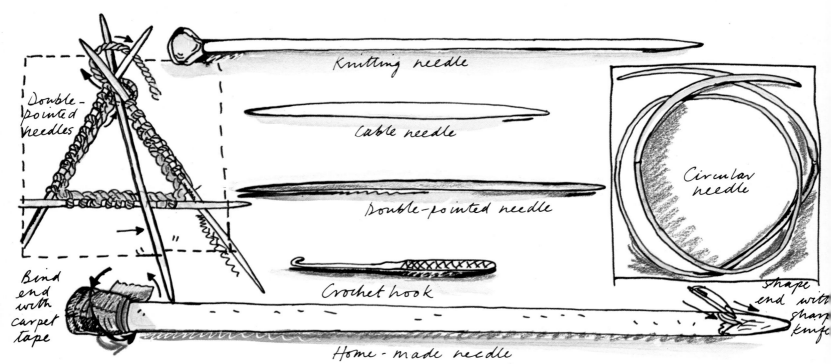

Double-pointed needles

Bind end with carpet tape

Knitting needle

Cable needle

Double-pointed needle

Crochet hook

Home-made needle

Circular needle

shape end with sharp knife

Needles

Knitting needles are the principal tools you will require. They come in various sizes and lengths and are sold in pairs. They used to be made from wood but are now usually made from more lightweight materials, such as coated metal or plastic. The length of needle is a matter of personal preference. If you are knitting a large item, you will need long needles, but these can be cumbersome, so for small articles use short ones.

Needles come in a wide range of sizes, from the finest of fine to the coarsest of jumbo. They are pointed at one end with a knob at the other to prevent the stitches from falling off. The needle size is usually marked on this knob. Sizes vary from country to country but are becoming standardized. The chart here gives the American size, the metric and the old British number for comparison. American sizes are given with the metric size in brackets in this book.

Home-made needles If you want to knit with bulky yarn or materials and cannot buy needles large enough, you can easily make them yourself. The simplest approach is to buy doweling, which comes in various sizes, from a lumber yard or hardwear store. Buy double the length required and cut in two for a pair of needles of equal length. Shape one end of each needle with a sharp knife or plane, then smooth with sandpaper. Aim for a rough point to begin with, then refine with finer grades of sandpaper until the ends are quite smooth and there is no danger of snagging the yarn or material with which you are going to knit.
Stick pieces of cork on the other ends of the needles to stop the stitches falling off. Alternatively you can bind the ends of the needles with carpet tape so that stitches slip no farther than the binding.
Cable needles These are short needles pointed at both ends. Stitches which are held at the front or the back of the work when cabling are slipped onto them.

Double-pointed needles These have a point at either end and usually come in sets of four. They are used for knitting in rounds for a circular fabric.
Circular needles These have two small needle sections, which are pointed at both ends and joined together by a piece of flexible nylon. They are easier to handle than four needles, but can only be used when the number of stitches being worked is sufficient to reach from one needle point to the other. They are available in various lengths and are also useful when working straight knitting in rows on a large number of stitches.
Crochet hook This is not really a needle but is useful for pulling through knots and tassels, picking up stitches and making simple edges.
Care of needles It is worthwhile caring for your needles. When you are not using them, keep them in a dry, clean place where they will not become bent. Smooth needles speed up knitting, so when working with home-made needles, be careful that there are no splinters.

Metric	British	American
2	14	00
$2\frac{1}{4}$	13	0
$2\frac{3}{4}$	12	1
3	11	2
$3\frac{1}{4}$	10	3
$3\frac{3}{4}$	9	4
4	8	5
$4\frac{1}{2}$	7	6
5	6	7
$5\frac{1}{2}$	5	8
6	4	9
$6\frac{1}{2}$	3	10
7	2	$10\frac{1}{2}$
$7\frac{1}{2}$	1	11
8	0	12
9	00	13
10	000	15

Yarns

Yarns are made from natural or man-made fibers, or a combination of both.

Natural yarns These are either protein or cellulosic in origin, depending on whether they come from animals or plants. They include lambswool, Botany wool, cashmere, mohair, alpaca and angora (protein fibers); linen, cotton, raffia and jute (cellulosic fibers).

Man-made yarns These are made by stimulating a chemical reaction between various basic substances and drawing out the fibers in continuous filament threads. They include Nylon, Acrilan, Tricel and Courtelle.

Construction Yarns are made up of different plys, a ply being a single strand of spun thread. Each single thread is combined with one, two, three or more similar strands to make up the ply of the yarn. Classic yarns such as 2 ply, 3 ply, 4 ply or double knitting are usually made up of non-textured strands and are the standard yarns used by the majority of the spinners. Much progress has been made

in the manufacture of fancy yarns, such as bouclé, metallic yarns, chenille and others, featuring slubs and knops. These often combine plain and textured strands of yarn twisted together. The twisting is important for it is this which gives a yarn its specific character and makes it workable for knitting. Without any twist it would easily break. A loose twist gives a soft yarn whereas a tighter one produces a more lasting and hard-wearing yarn.

Once the yarn has been spun into long lengths, suitable for knitting large areas of fabric without necessitating too many joins, it is formed into skeins or balls. They are sold in varying weights and are available from shops, or direct from the mill or bulk suppliers.

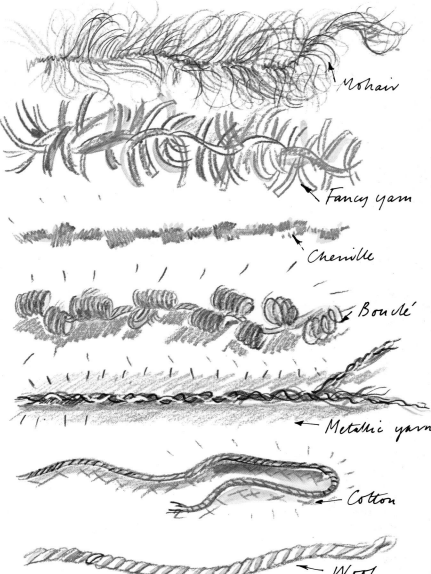

Materials

You do not have to confine yourself to knitting with yarn. There are many other materials which, although they are not usually used for knitting, will do just as well. These include such things as plastic, leather, shoelaces, string, ribbon, braid and any other kind of trimming such as felt, tinsel and wire. In fact you can knit with practically anything you want.

You can also incorporate into your knitting pipe cleaners, sequins, beads and any natural objects such as grasses, feathers, seeds, bark, stones and shells.

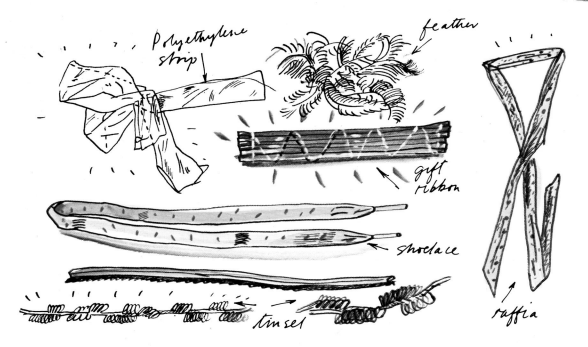

Casting on and binding off

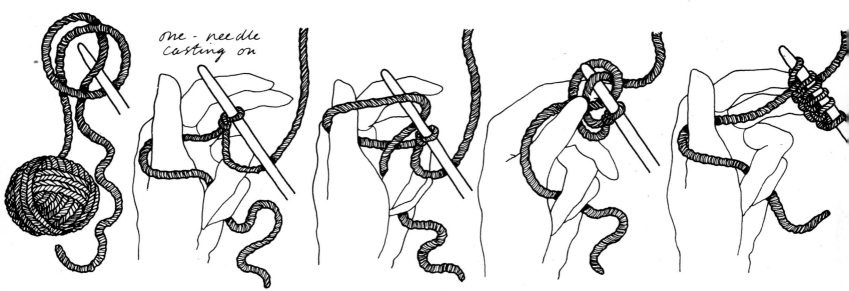

Casting on

There are three basic methods of casting on—the one-needle method, the two-needle method and the invisible method. Sometimes there are minor variations within these categories, but the final choice comes down to the type of edging required and the method which is the most comfortable to work and easiest to remember.

The one-needle method This produces an elastic, but hard-wearing edge.

1 Measure a length of yarn, allowing about 1m (1yd) for every 100 stitches. Make a slip loop at this point and tighten it onto the needle. Hold the needle in the right hand and work with the measured length in the left hand. All these instructions work in reverse if you are left-handed.

2 Pass the yarn round the left thumb as shown, holding the end against the palm with the third and fourth fingers. Never completely release these fingers but allow the yarn to ease through.

3 Insert the point of the needle under the loop on the thumb.

4 Pass the yarn from the ball round the needle and draw it through the loop.

5 To ensure an even tension, tighten the stitch on the needle by placing the left thumb under the measured yarn close to the needle and pull it away from the needle as the loop is released. In this way the yarn is now round the thumb ready for the next stitch.

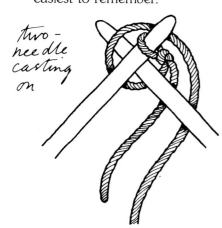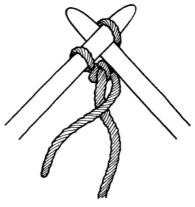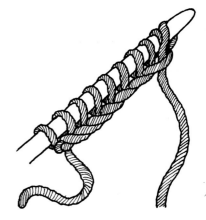

The two-needle method This is a general-purpose method which gives a firm edge and can be used within the garment where required as well as at the beginning. For an edge which is not quite so firm, insert the needle into the previous stitch knitwise or, to give this variation a twisted effect, into the back of each stitch. All instructions work in reverse if you are left-handed.

1 Make a slip loop, leaving a short length for finishing off, and place it on the left-hand needle. Holding on firmly to this short end with the fingers of the left hand, insert the right-hand needle to the left of the slip loop. Pass the yarn from the ball under and over the point of the right-hand needle.

2 Draw the yarn through to the front of the work. Pass this

new loop onto the left-hand needle and tighten in position.

3 Insert the right-hand needle between the two stitches on the left-hand needle, wind the yarn under and over the point of the right-hand needle and draw through the loop. Place it on the left-hand needle, as before.

4 Continue in this way until the required number of stitches have been cast on. If you are

intending to work in garter stitch or stocking stitch, knit the first row through the back of the loops which will twist the stitches and give a firm edge to the fabric.

12

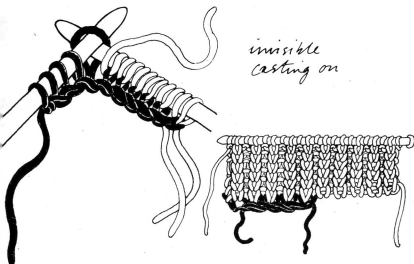

invisible casting on

The invisible method This gives a rounded edge on K1, P1 ribbing, similar to a hemmed or machine-made finish. It also gives a firm, elastic edge which, being hollow, can be used as a casing for elastic, ribbon, cord or any other materials.
1 Using a spare yarn in contrast colour and either of the previous methods, cast on half the required number of stitches, plus one extra.
2 Using the correct yarn,

continue in rib as follows:
1st row (Right side) K1, *yf, K1; rep from * to end.
2nd row Yf, sl 1, *yb, K1, yf, sl 1; rep from * to end.
3rd row K1, *yf, sl 1, yb, K1; rep from * to end.
4th–5th row As 2nd–3rd row.
6th row P1, *K1, P1; rep from * to end.
7th row K1, *P1, K1; rep from * to end.
Continue in rib for the required length then unpick the contrast yarn.

Binding off

There are two basic methods of binding off—the two-needle method and the invisible method. As with casting on the choice is up to you.
The two-needle method This is the most popular method.
1 On a knit row, knit the first two stitches in the usual way.
2 Insert the point of the left-hand needle into the front of the first stitch on the right-hand needle and lift it over the second stitch and off the needle, leaving only one stitch.

3 Knit the next stitch on the left-hand needle and pass the other stitch on the right-hand needle over it. Continue until only one stitch remains.
4 Break off the yarn and pull it through this last stitch. Slip the stitch off the needle and tighten the knot.
On a purl row, work as given for knit stitches but purling the stitches. On ribbing, bind off in the same way as before but knitting or purling the stitches so that they keep in line with the rib pattern.

two-needle binding off

invisible binding off

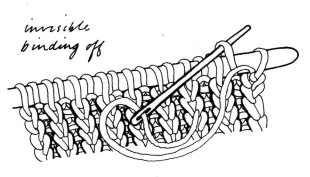

The invisible method This can be used on K1, P1 rib. There must be an odd number of stitches, the right-side rows beginning K1.
1 Work until two more rows are required for the completed depth, ending with a wrong-side row.
1st row K1, *yf, sl 1, yb, K1; rep from * to end.
2nd row Yf, sl 1, *yb, K1, yf, sl 1; rep from * to end.

2 Break off the yarn leaving an end of about three times the width of the edge to be bound off.
3 Thread the end through a blunt-ended wool needle and, holding the knitting in the left hand, insert the wool needle into the first stitch as if to purl it and draw the yarn through. Insert the wool needle into the next stitch as if to knit it and draw the yarn through, leaving

both stitches on the needle.
4 *Insert the wool needle into the first stitch again, this time as if to knit it, draw the yarn through and slip the stitch off the knitting needle.
5 Take the wool needle in front of the next stitch and into the following stitch as if to purl it and draw the yarn through.
6 Insert the wool needle into the first stitch now on the

needle as if to purl it, draw the yarn through and then slip the stitch right off the knitting needle.
7 Take the wool needle behind the next stitch and into the back of the following stitch as if to knit it, drawing the yarn through.
8 Taking the yarn under the point of the needle, repeat from *, until all the stitches have been worked. Fasten off.

13

Simple stitches

Knitting is a series of loops built into a fabric by drawing yarn through each loop in turn to create new loops. The original loops then drop down to increase the length of the fabric. The width is determined by the number of loops in the original series. Each loop, or stitch, has a knot which comes either at the front or the back of the work. However, each stitch is interlinked with all the others and the fabric is not finally secured until the last stitch is fastened off. Therefore the entire structure of a piece of knitting can be unravelled. Patterns are built into the design by using these two characteristics of the knitted stitch. The more complex patterns depend on the relation of any one stitch to the others.

A variety of fabrics, however, is the direct result of stitches having their knots either at the back or front of the work.

These are known as knit stitches and purl stitches, and when combined form the three basic patterns of knitting which are garter stitch, stockinette stitch and ribbing.

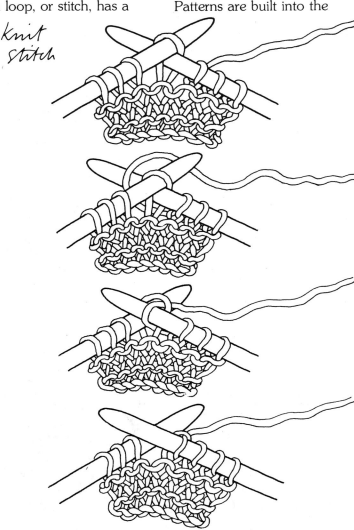

knit stitch

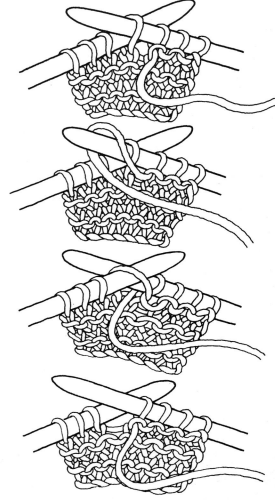

Purl stitch

The knit stitch When the knot is at the back of the knitting on the row in which it was worked, it is known as a knit stitch.
1 Hold the needle with the stitches in the left hand and keep the yarn at the back of the work. Insert the point of the right-hand needle into the first stitch from front to back, left to right. This is called inserting the needle "knitwise".
2 Take the yarn round the point of the right-hand needle, under, right to left; then over, left to right.
3 Draw this new loop through the stitch on the left-hand needle to the front of work.
4 Slip the stitch off the left-hand needle, leaving the new loop on the right-hand needle. At the end of the row when all the new stitches are on the right-hand needle transfer it to the left hand before beginning the next row.

The purl stitch When the knot is at the front of the knitting on the row in which it was worked, it is known as a purl stitch.
1 With the yarn at the front of the work, insert the point of the right-hand needle into the front of the first stitch on the left-hand needle, from right to left. This is called inserting the needle "purlwise".
2 Take the yarn round the point of the right-hand needle over the top and under from right to left.
3 Draw this new loop through the stitch on the left-hand needle to the back of the work.
4 Slip the stitch off the left-hand needle, leaving the new loop on the right-hand needle. Continue in this way until the row is completed when all the stitches will be on the right-hand needle. Transfer this needle to the left hand before beginning the next row.

Garter stitch

Stockinette stitch

Ribbing

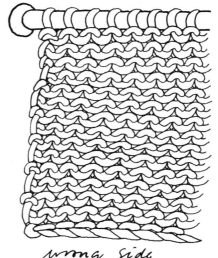

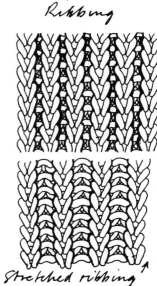

right side

wrong Side

Stretched ribbing

Garter stitch This is when the work is entirely made up of knit stitches. The knots form ridges on both sides of the work, making it reversible. It has a sideways stretch, hence the name because this meant it was originally particularly suitable for garters and stocking tops.

The same fabric would result from using all purl stitches, but it is easier to maintain an even tension with knit stitches.

Stockinette stitch This is formed by working one row knit, one row purl throughout. In this way all the knots form on the same side—the wrong side. The right side is a smooth chain stitch. The fabric has a lengthways stretch and, again, this made it particularly suitable for stockings, hence its name. Sometimes the purl, or ridged side is used as the right side and this is known as reversed stockinette stitch.

Ribbing This is formed by alternating knit and purl stitches across the same row. The knitted chain stitch forms a rib, which stands forwards from the purl knot. As a result the fabric "shrinks" inward but has a strong sideways stretch. This makes it particularly suitable where a garment is required to stretch when being put on and cling during wear, such as at cuffs or necks.

A one by one rib is when one knit stitch is alternated with one purl stitch throughout. This is the stretchiest rib, but the combination varies, such as two by two, three by two or five by three. In all cases the knit stitches of the previous row are purled and the purl stitches of the previous row are knitted.

Changing colors —
At the start
of a row

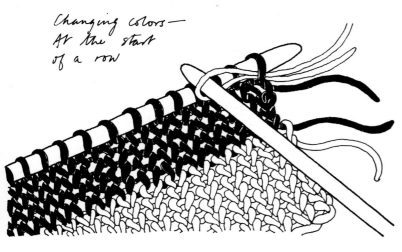

During a row

Color changes
These simple stitches can be worked in a variety of different colors to achieve a brightly striped fabric. Change color at the beginning of a row for horizontal stripes or during a row for vertical stripes.

At the start of a row To join in a new color, insert the needle into the first stitch and using the new color, make a loop over the right-hand needle. Pull this through to complete the stitch in the usual way and continue to the end of the row. Carry yarn up the side of the work for narrow stripes but break it off and rejoin it for wider stripes.

During a row To change color when working a row of narrow stripes simply twist the two colors together and carry the yarn not in use across the back of the work until you need it again.

It is important to carry the yarn loosely across to avoid a puckered appearance. This method produces a fabric of double thickness. To avoid this when working wider stripes of more than four or five stitches knit each color with a separate ball of yarn. Twist one color with the next at the back of the work when a change is made to avoid making a hole between stripes.

15

Tension

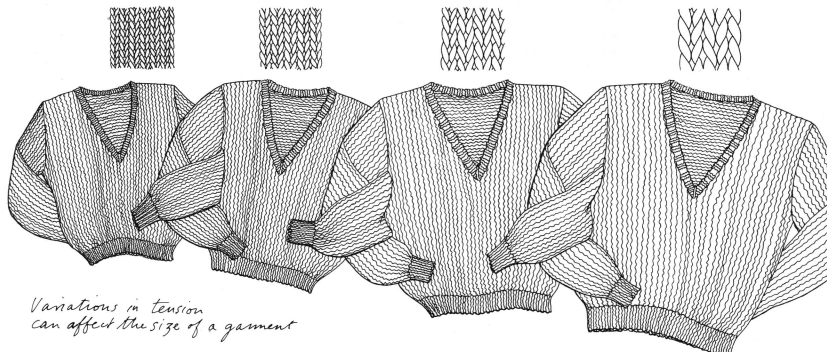

Variations in tension can affect the size of a garment

The basis of any knitting design is purely mathematical and is called tension. It refers to the number of stitches and rows which will fit into a given measurement. It is vital, for if ignored it can lead to disastrous results such as garments too large, garments too small, garments too wide, and so on.

Following a pattern
When working to a pattern, if you are to end up with the garment intended in the size desired, it is essential to have stitches and rows working to the same measurements as the designer's. You can be as little as a couple of stitches out on the given tension and the garment could come out a whole size larger or smaller. Tension is a personal thing and two people rarely knit to the same tension, therefore some adjustments are often necessary.

Tension check Before you start knitting you must do a tension check. Work a small square of at least 10cm (4in) and then measure it vertically and horizontally. Place the knitting on a firm surface so that it is lying flat without distortion. Using a rigid ruler mark the given measurement with pins and count the stitches and rows between the pins. If there are too many stitches or rows between the pins the knitting will be too tight and a larger size of needle should be used on a new tension square. If there are too few stitches or rows, the knitting will be loose and a smaller size of needle should be used. Continue making squares until the correct result is achieved.

Designing
When designing your own garment, or any other piece of knitting, first choose the yarn and then the size of needles you are going to use. This is important for on it depends the look of the garment and its practicability. If the stitches are too big and open for the structure of the yarn, or too close and tight, it will wash and wear badly, grow or shrink, lose its shape or simply not hang well. On some yarns the most appropriate size of needle is recommended on the ball band.

Sample square Once you have chosen the yarn and needle size knit up a small sample square to find out what tension it produces. That is how many stitches and rows there are to a certain measurement. The measurement normally used is 10cm (4in) square. When you have worked this out count the number of stitches to the centimeter or inch, multiply it by the width of the fabric required to give you the number of stitches to cast on. With these figures the entire garment can be planned on graph paper without a single stitch being knitted.

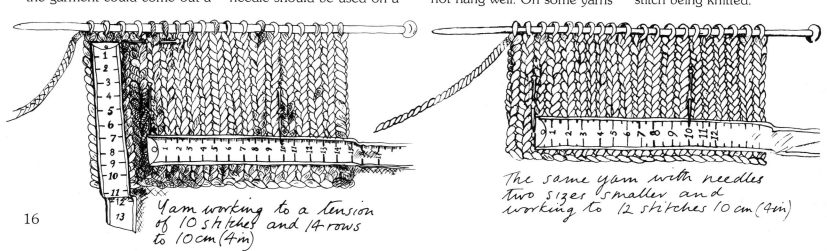

Yarn working to a tension of 10 stitches and 14 rows to 10cm (4in)

The same yarn with needles two sizes smaller and working to 12 stitches 10cm (4in)

Changing yarns

When mixing yarns for a one-off design, where you do not have to work out instructions for several sizes, tension becomes synonymous with balance. Mix thick yarns with thin ones for a textured effect, but remember, however many different yarns you are using they must still hold together as one garment. If you want to substitute a yarn when working to a pattern you must remember that the ply and weight of yarns are not standardized. A pattern may tell you to use 4 ply but individual brands vary in thickness. It is therefore essential to knit a tension sample to find out how many stitches you will need for the required dimensions.

Changing stitch patterns

Stitch patterns create their own tension, therefore if you decide to replace a basic stockinette stitch pattern with something more textured you must be careful. Don't assume that if a pattern in stockinette stitch tells you to cast on 34 stitches you will get the same measurements if you work in moss stitch. You must work a tension sample to find out how many stitches you will have to cast on for the stitch pattern chosen, in order to give you the required width of the garment. Some of the more complicated stitch patterns require a specific multiple of stitches and rows if an even number of repeats, both horizontally and vertically, is to be achieved. In such cases it is not always possible simply to add or subtract stitches to reach the required measurements and this must be taken into consideration when you are planning your design. It may well be quicker to adjust the size of your needles than to vary the number of stitches.

Design chart

Our chart offers you a quick way of working out the mathematics of a design without doing anything more difficult than joining up points on two of the columns with a ruler and reading off where it crosses the third.
1 If you have instructions for an 80cm (32in) garment and want to knit it in a 96cm (38in) size instead, simply place one end of the ruler at 48cm (19in)—half of 96cm (38in)—on the right-hand column and the other end at the number of stitches to 10cm (4in)—given as tension in the instructions—in the left-hand column.
2 The number the ruler crosses in the central column is the number of stitches required at the underarm on either the front or the back of the garment in the new size.
3 To find out how many stitches to cast on, place one end of the ruler on 40cm (16in)—half of 80cm (32in) —in the right-hand column and through the central column at the number of stitches given in the instructions for casting on.
4 The other end of the ruler passes through the left-hand column at an indeterminate point. Mark this place and keeping the left-hand end of the ruler at the mark, swing the other end to 48cm (19in) —half of 96cm (38in)—on the right-hand column.
5 Read off on the central column how many stitches to cast on for the new size.
6 The figures on the left of the outer columns are for inches, the figures on the right for centimeters. Decide whether you are going to work in imperial or metric measurements, and use the chart accordingly, but remember that it is not a conversion chart.

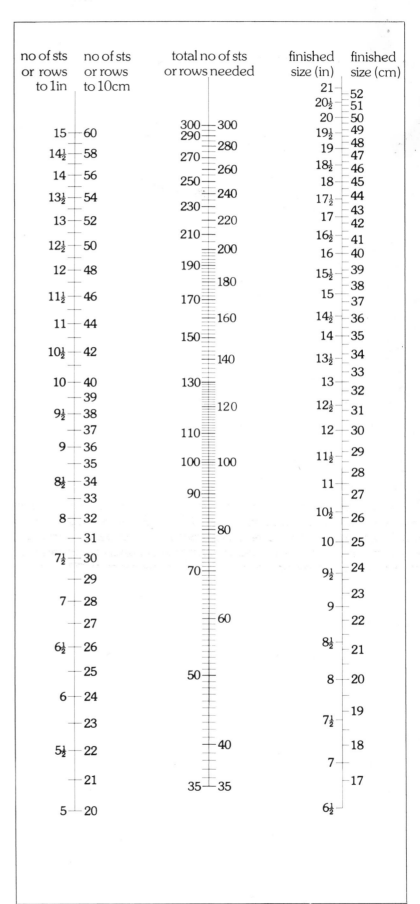

Increasing and decreasing

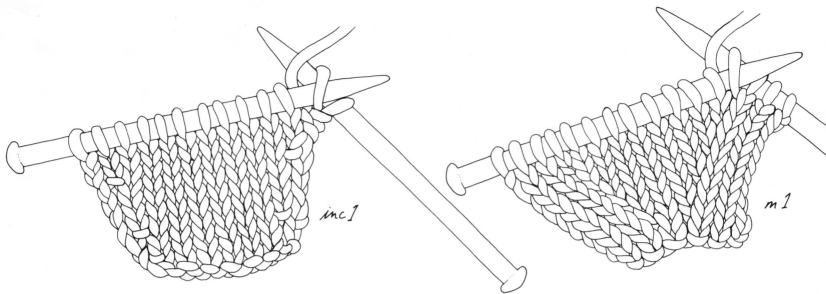

inc 1

m 1

Shaping in knitting is done by increasing or decreasing stitches at the edge of or during a row. The former changes the shape of the outline while the latter changes the shape within the work. The principles of increasing and decreasing are also the basis of the majority of lace and eyelet patterns shown on pp136–9.
There are two types of increasing and decreasing: one is simple and almost invisible while the other is more decorative and visible. There are various ways of carrying out both methods.

Simple increasing
The following methods leave no holes in the fabric and are therefore almost invisible.
Increase one stitch This is the simplest way of increasing a stitch and can be carried out anywhere during a row. It is generally used to shape side edges and gives a gathered effect if worked during a row. It is abbreviated as inc 1.
1 Insert the right-hand needle into the next stitch on the left-hand needle, knit or purl it but do not slip the original stitch off the needle.
2 Insert the right-hand needle into the back of the original

stitch and knit or purl into the stitch again, thus making two stitches. This method of increasing creates a lump on the left-hand side of the increased stitch. Therefore if the first and the last stitches of the row are increased, the right-hand edge of the work will be smooth with the lump lying inside the edge stitch, but the left-hand edge will be uneven as the lump will lie at the outer edge.
To achieve a smooth edge on both sides, increase into the first stitch at the beginning of a row, but into the second from last at the end of a row.

Make one stitch This method is generally used during rows rather than at the side edges of the knitting. It is more suitable to tailored shaping and is abbreviated as m1.
1 Pick up the loop lying between the stitch just worked and the next stitch.
2 Place the loop on the left-hand needle and knit into the back of it, thus making an extra stitch.
3 To form a neat line of shaping, keep the same number of stitches on one side of the made stitch and work all the new stitches on the other.

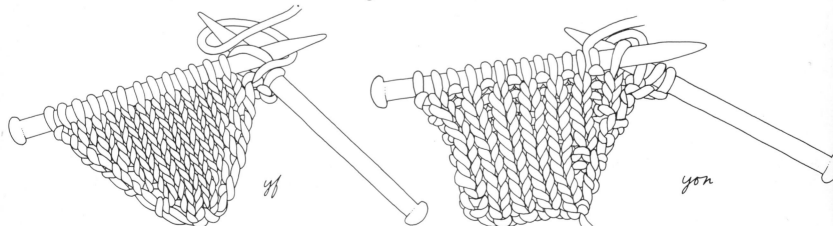

yf

yon

Decorative increasing
Increasing on an edge can be turned into a decorative feature of a design by creating a small hole with each increased stitch. This is formed by putting the yarn forward, over the needle or round the

needle. All three methods provide the basis for many other stitch patterns.
Yarn forward Use this method to increase a stitch between two knit stitches. It is abbreviated as yf.
1 Knit the first stitch, then

bring the yarn to the front of the work between the two needles.
2 Keep it in this position and knit the next stitch in the usual way.
Yarn over needle Use this method when you want to

increase a stitch between a purl and a knit stitch. It is usually abbreviated as yon.
1 Take the yarn from the front of the work over the top of the right-hand needle.
2 Knit the next stitch in the usual way.

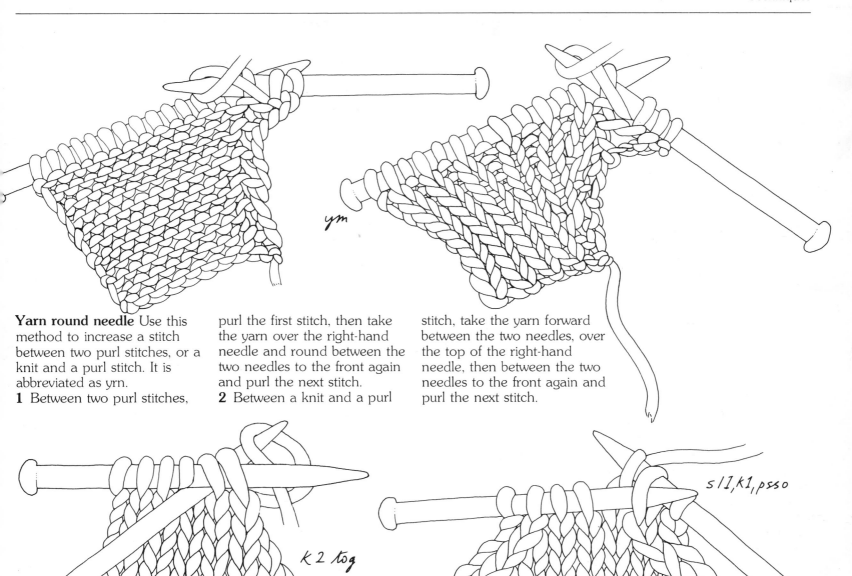

Yarn round needle Use this method to increase a stitch between two purl stitches, or a knit and a purl stitch. It is abbreviated as yrn.
1 Between two purl stitches, purl the first stitch, then take the yarn over the right-hand needle and round between the two needles to the front again and purl the next stitch.
2 Between a knit and a purl stitch, take the yarn forward between the two needles, over the top of the right-hand needle, then between the two needles to the front again and purl the next stitch.

Simple decreasing
This method is used at either end of or during a row. It is abbreviated as K2tog or P2tog.
1 On a knit row, insert the right-hand needle knitwise into the second stitch and then into the first and knit together.
2 On a purl row, insert the needle into the first stitch, then the second and purl together.

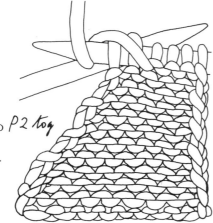

Decorative decreasing
If you want to make a feature of your decreasing use the slipped stitch method, which will produce a definite slant to the left. This is used when a smooth edge is required, for example when shaping the tops of raglan sleeves, and is worked inside the edge stitch. It is abbreviated as sl 1, K1, psso.
1 Slip the first stitch off the left-hand needle onto the right-hand needle without knitting it. Then knit the next stitch in the usual way.
2 Using the point of the left-hand needle, lift the slipped stitch over the knit stitch and off the needle.
3 If you want to do a similar decrease on a purl row, simply purl two stitches together through the back of the loops. It is abbreviated as P2tog-tbl.

Following patterns

Besides the actual working instructions, all knitting patterns contain other vital, basic information such as size, materials, tension and abbreviations. When the pattern involves working with several different colors it contains charts to save space and make it easier to follow. It is also important to read yarn wrappers carefully for information on how to look after garments once they are finished.

Size

Before you choose a pattern it is important to check that the size or the size range will fit your particular measurements. In this book, patterns are given in one size only but are basic and often loose enough to fit a wide range. Scale drawings show the main measurements of the garment. These are given in metric with the imperial equivalent in brackets. If the measurements are too large or too small refer to pp22–3 for information on adapting patterns. Other patterns often give instructions for several sizes and in this case the smallest size is usually first with the larger ones following in order in brackets.

Materials

All patterns specify the amount of yarn of a suitable weight and thickness required for the design. Any brand may be used as long as you do a tension square to make sure that it will knit up to the required size and weight. It is always advisable to buy a few extra balls of yarn for alterations and repairs. Patterns also list other items required for the design. This includes the size of needles suitable for the stated yarn, plus any haberdashery for finishing the garment such as zippers, buttons and so on.

Tension

All patterns give the tension you need to achieve with a specified weight of yarn, size of needle and stitch to end up with the correct size of garment. You will be told the number of stitches to cast on and the number of rows to work for a measured square of knitting. This must not be overlooked and it is vital to knit up as many tension squares as are required to get it exactly right. This is especially important when you have substituted a yarn or, as in this book, you are only given a generic name. Different types of yarn have characteristics of their own, which must be taken into account. For example, a 4 ply mohair may give more than an ordinary 4 ply yarn, causing your garment to drop in wear, so even if their tension is theoretically the same, always work a tension square beforehand.

Working instructions

Instructions for the different parts of a garment or object are usually given in separate sections under headings such as front, back, side and so on. It is important to knit them in the order given for there is usually a reason for it such as having to join pieces together before going on to the next stage. It often helps when following a pattern to place a ruler under the line you are working. One K1 looks exactly the same as any other K1 and you may find out all too late that you have missed out a whole chunk of instructions. It is also advisable to mark the point at which you have stopped before putting your knitting away. If you have to leave a number of stitches aside for any length of time slip them off the needle and on to a stitch holder.

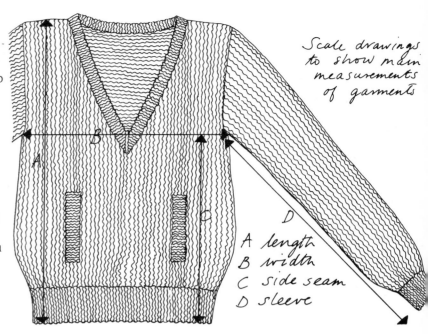

Scale drawings to show main measurements of garments

A length
B width
C side seam
D sleeve

Abbreviations

Knitting has its own technical terms and special abbreviations, which have been developed to save space and make patterns less lengthy and tedious to follow. Basically they enable the instructions for a long and complicated pattern to be conveyed simply and concisely. The abbreviations used in this book are listed on p9 and it is important to refer to them before beginning to knit any of the projects in this book. Most of them are as those generally used but some apply only to the patterns given here.
Asterisks (*) are used where it is necessary to save space and avoid repetition. A single * within a row means that you should repeat the stitches from that point as instructed. A single, double or triple * at the beginning and end of a section of a pattern mean that you will be instructed to repeat it later on. Similarly, for the right side of a garment you may be told to work as for the left, reversing all shaping. Specific instructions for a certain stitch or technique are

given in full the first time they are used with a suitable abbreviation in brackets. The abbreviation will be given each time when the same technique or stitch is to be worked again, or you will be simply told to work in pattern. In some cases you will be referred to another page, or to the stitch dictionary in this book, for the stitch pattern.

Working from charts

Charts are used to simplify knitting instructions involving Fair Isle, patchwork patterns and complicated shapes or motifs which, if written out in full, would be difficult and confusing to follow. Charts are usually set out on graph paper; one square represents one stitch and a horizontal line of squares represents a knitted row. Colors are either shown in blocks or denoted by symbols. For example, o would equal color one, x color two, and so on. A chart usually begins at the bottom right-hand corner, the odd-numbered rows are knit rows and the even-numbered rows, purl rows. Therefore read from right to left for a

Motif chart

Fair Isle chart

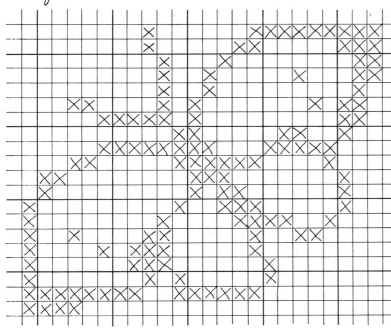

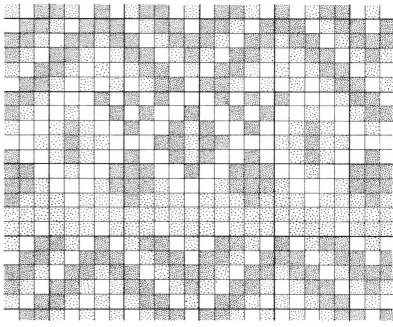

knit row and from left to right for a purl row. If working from a chart in circular knitting each round will begin on the right-hand edge of the chart. Most cross-stitch and canvas designs as used in embroidery can also be used for knitting, but remember a knitted stitch is not square and therefore a tension square must be worked first and a few lines added to the height of the design to ensure that it comes out to the right dimensions.

Reading yarn wrappers

Yarn wrappers bear more and more information nowadays, and should be read carefully when you purchase yarn. Many carry the size of knitting needle suitable for the yarn, and a suggested tension is often given in diagrammatic form. More important to the care and treatment of completed garments is the series of symbols used internationally to overcome language difficulties in reading labels on imported yarns. This code consists of four basic symbols, and gives guidance on washing, ironing, bleaching and dry cleaning.

The washing process A number or temperature in the wash tub indicates that the article can be washed safely either by machine or hand. The figure used above the waterline represents the full automatic washing process and appears on machine-washable yarns. The figure below the waterline gives the temperature of the water the yarn may be washed in. A hand in the tub indicates that the yarn can only be washed by hand and if the tub is crossed out this means it cannot be washed at all and should be dry cleaned instead.

Chlorine bleaching A triangle containing the letters CL indicates that the yarn may be treated with chlorine bleach. If the triangle is crossed out, this means that no household bleach should be used.

Ironing There are four variations of this symbol, the temperatures "cool", "warm" and "hot" being indicated by one, two or three dots within the iron. If the iron is crossed out, the yarn should not be pressed. When working with a mixture of yarns, remember to check all the yarn wrappers and set the iron at the lowest temperature given.

Dry cleaning Letters placed within a circle indicate that the yarn may be dry cleaned and the type of solvent to be used. The letters A, P and F refer to different solvents. If the circle is crossed out, this means that the yarn should not be dry cleaned.

Adapting and designing

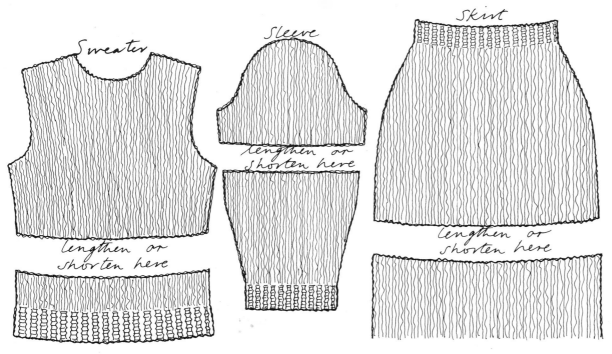

Sweater

Lengthen or shorten here

Sleeve

lengthen or shorten here

lengthen or shorten here

Skirt

lengthen or shorten here

Creating new trimmings and making minor adjustments to garments as suggested on pp36–9 are among the first steps toward adapting and designing your own patterns. You can then move on to adapting basic patterns in more complex ways and finally to designing your own garments completely from scratch.

Adapting patterns

Once you have chosen a knitting pattern you may find the given measurements need adjusting to suit your own body measurements. This is simple to do as long as you take the time to work out where the alterations should be made before beginning on any actual knitting. Working with the tension quoted on your pattern, calculate the amendments necessary to the stitches and rows and mark in the alterations on the pattern.

Measuring Always use a rigid ruler to measure a knitted piece of fabric. Knitting is an elastic fabric and therefore easy to stretch out of shape, thus giving inaccurate measurements. Take measurements from a straight line following the stitches and not from the curved sections of the garment, such as the slanting edge of the sleeve, or around the curve of the armhole.

Where to adapt It is vital to work out in advance the correct positioning of alterations and how this will affect the amount of yarn that is required.

Jacket or sweater length Add or subtract any change in length from the original given measurement from shoulder to hem. Make the alteration in the main body of the garment before reaching the armhole shaping. If the pattern is in a simple stitch pattern such as stockinette stitch the alteration is easy to make, but if you are working an intricate stitch pattern which involves a large repeat, the length can sometimes only be altered by adding or subtracting a complete pattern repeat.

Sleeve length The underarm measurement of the sleeve is taken from the wrist to the armhole along the straight line of stitches. Alter the length in the straight section after the sleeve shaping and before beginning the shaping of the sleeve head.

Skirt length Lengthen or shorten the skirt size in the straight section after the hem before any shaping begins to be done.

Fitting shoulders To ensure a well-fitting garment, modification of the shoulder width is often necessary. Decide on the finished width of the shoulder and calculate the number of stitches that need to be added or subtracted. Adjust your pattern by casting on or binding off more stitches under the arms and then work extra increases and decreases during the armhole shaping.

Changing the stitch When changing the stitch pattern it is essential to knit a tension square. All stitch patterns have a tension of their own, so the original measurements might be drastically different if worked in a different stitch on the given number of stitches and rows. A different stitch will also change the amount of yarn required and a tension square will help you make the necessary calculations. A textured stitch, for example, will use a lot more yarn than basic stitches like garter stitch and stockinette stitch.

Designing garments

Designing garments is fun and as long as you follow a few basic steps, as are shown in the drawings on the opposite page for a hypothetical V-neck sweater, it is not difficult. You can either work from a graph paper pattern or an ordinary paper pattern, drawn to scale.

Graph paper method First, work out the design in sketch form and decide on the final shape, colour and yarn. Then knit a tension square and, using graph paper, work out the shape of each piece of the garment. Each square represents a stitch and symbols are used to represent increases, decreases, knit rows and purl rows.

The graph is not drawn to scale and remember that stitches are not square and therefore the design will look out of proportion. Calculate how many stitches to cast on and then how many rows to work to reach required lengths. Remember to add several extra stitches for ease of movement and make sure that the multiples of stitches will work out correctly over the stitch pattern chosen. An extra measurement of 5cm (2in) gives sufficient room for movement to most garments.

Where to shape On basic garments, made up of rectangles and squares, it is not necessary to work any shapings on the main body of the garment until you reach the armhole shaping.

Armhole shaping Generally the armhole shaping is acute to start with, giving way to a gentle and more gradual curve. This acute shaping is usually carried out during the first 8cm (3in).

Shoulder shaping This should begin about 2.5cm (1in) below the finished length of the garment.

Basic steps in design — Choose a stitch and pattern

sketch design ↓

knit a tension square ↓

work out pattern on graph paper

```
\ = k
/ = P
o = Dec 1
x = Bind off 1
```

Neck shaping On a basic round neck, the front and back body shapings are the same except for on the front neck. The shaping should begin about 5cm (2in) below the back neck. The stitches should be divided at this point and each shoulder worked separately. On a basic V-neck the shaping usually begins at the same time as the armhole shaping. If a shorter V is required, start the shaping after the armhole section has been completed.

Each shoulder should be worked separately and stitches should be decreased evenly along the front neck edge until you have the same amount of stitches on your needles as for the back shoulder shaping.

Sleeve shaping This usually begins at the wrist and continues to about 4cm (1½in) below the armhole. The head shaping should be acute to begin with, giving way to a more gradual curve to match the armhole shaping.

Paper pattern method This involves working from a paper pattern. You can either make one yourself or work from a commercial pattern, provided the shaping is simple and does not involve darts or tucks. Work out from your tension sample how many stitches to cast on to achieve the required width and start to knit.

Check your work constantly against the pattern, increasing or decreasing where necessary. This method is not as accurate as the former one. Knitting is never as flat as paper and great care and precision are required.

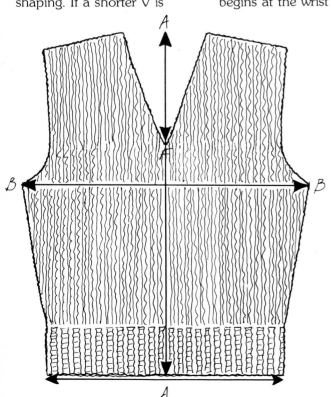

Take measurements allowing an extra 5 cm (2in) on width measurement for ease of movement

A — A *back length I*
B — B *half bust measurement*
A — F *depth of neck*
G — G *outer arm length*
I — I *upper arm width*
J — J *wrist measurement*

Basic shapes

Traditional knitting patterns often involve shaping instructions that are so complicated that the average knitter is understandably reluctant to vary them in any way. The tendency is to follow the pattern religiously and perhaps to try out a few adaptations for size, such as those described on pp22–3. Much of this shaping, however, is quite unnecessary unless a style is tailored or close-fitting. Most garments are based on a number of simple rectangular shapes and when you understand the underlying principles, it becomes possible to create an entire wardrobe using nothing but these basic shapes.

Sweater The pattern for this is given on p53. It is based on four rectangles – two for the body, two for the sleeves – and has no shaping whatsoever. It can be varied in numerous ways, some of which are shown here. Changing the colors or stitch pattern are obvious possibilities. The body can be made wider by increasing the number of cast-on stitches, or longer by adding more rows before the neck ribbing. A plain or picot hem, as shown on pp28–9, could be worked instead of ribbing on the sleeve and lower edges. The sleeves can be wider or narrower. The sweater can be worked in any type of yarn or combination of yarns twisted together. Knit a tension square to begin with to calculate the number of stitches required to achieve a given measurement. This basic pattern can be adapted to make cardigans, dresses and coats in several different styles, changing or adding design details like sleeves, collars, pockets and edgings as required.

Cardigan Make a cardigan by increasing the width of the

basic sweater, shaping the neck and adding a collar. Calculate the width of the fronts by halving the back measurement and then subtracting half the width of the front band. Omit the top ribbing on front and back and work a deep rib around the neck edge for the collar or a narrow rib for a round neck.

Vest Make a sleeveless cardigan or vest by leaving out the sleeves and working armhole bands with the rib at right angles to the row ends. Add vertical or horizontal pockets (see pp28–9). The vest on p50 has been made according to these principles and is worked in buttonhole stitch.

Dress Widen and lengthen the basic sweater to make a loose-fitting dress, with or without sleeves. Work a plain or picot hem at the lower edge instead of ribbing.

Coat Lengthen the basic cardigan and increase the width of the body. The sleeves must be made shorter by the same amount that the body is widened. Work a hem rather than ribbing along the lower edge. It can have a collar as on the coat on p48 or a plain round neck. A kimono coat or jacket can be made in the same way but make the fronts narrower so that there is no neck shaping. Knit the front band in one piece, long enough to go up one front, round the neck and down the second front. Make the sleeves wider, leave out the ribbing and add sleeve bands instead.

Skirt This basic skirt is made from one rectangular piece, the pattern for which is given on p51. Work a plain or picot hem at the top and bottom of the skirt and thread wide elastic through the top hem. Tier the skirt by changing to progressively smaller needles as you work upward.

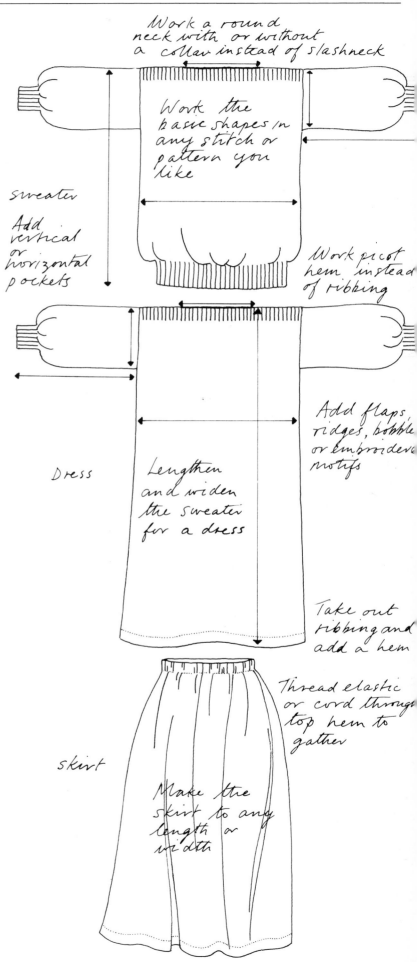

Work a round neck with or without a collar instead of slashneck

Work the basic shapes in any stitch or pattern you like

sweater

Add vertical or horizontal pockets

Work picot hem instead of ribbing

Dress

Lengthen and widen the sweater for a dress

Add flaps, ridges, bobble or embroidered motifs

Take out ribbing and add a hem

Thread elastic or cord through top hem to gather

skirt

Make the skirt to any length or width

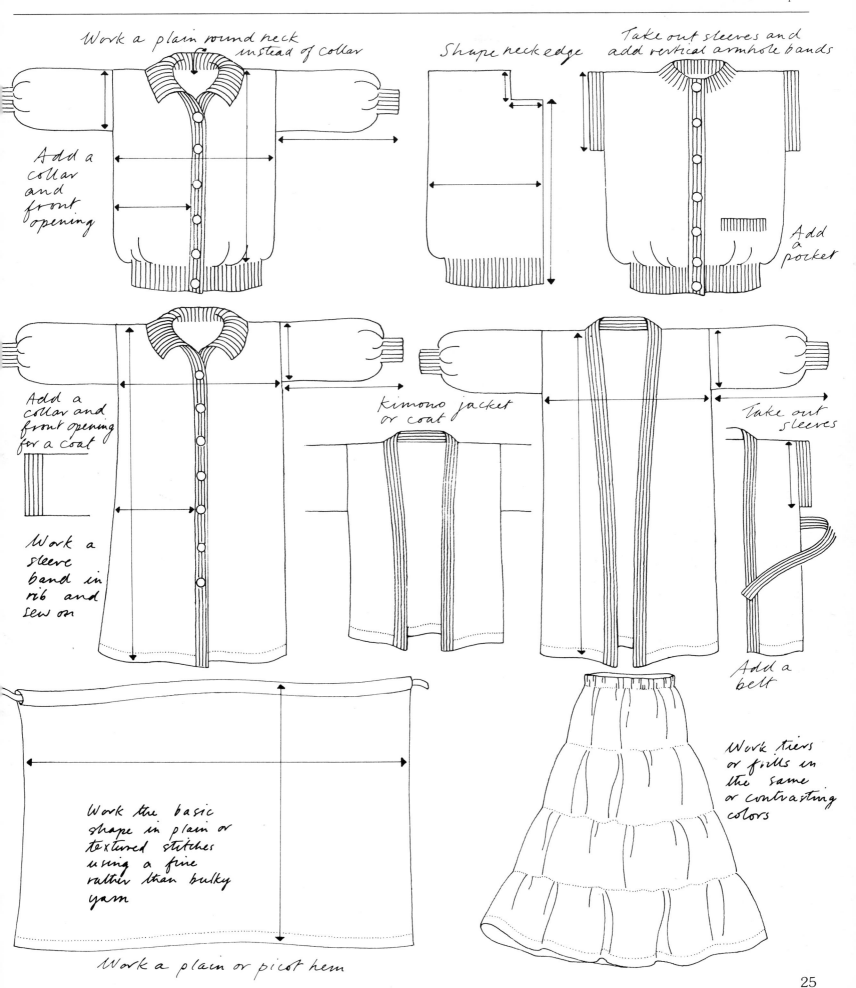

Work a plain round neck instead of collar

Add a collar and front opening

Shape neck edge

Take out sleeves and add vertical armhole bands

Add a pocket

Add a collar and front opening for a coat

Work a sleeve band in rib and sew on

Kimono jacket or coat

Take out sleeves

Add a belt

Work the basic shape in plain or textured stitches using a fine rather than bulky yarn

Work a plain or picot hem

Work tiers or frills in the same or contrasting colors

Making up

Finishing is often regarded as a chore. It is important however, to do it correctly as it can make all the difference to the final success of a garment or object.

Ends

Loose ends can look untidy, so leave a long enough end at the beginning and end of each ball of yarn to allow it to be neatened off at the back of the work.

Before finishing, thread each end in turn into a blunt-ended needle and darn it into the back of the knitting, taking two or three back stitches at various points along the darn. The end can then be safely trimmed close to the fabric. When working with different-colored yarns darn the ends into the same colored stitches for a neat effect.

Blocking

Individual pieces of a garment or object need to be blocked to ensure that they are the right size and shape and that they fit together.

1 Place each separate section on a clean, firm base—an ironing board for small pieces, a blanket folded and covered with a sheet for larger pieces—and pin it out to the correct measurements and shape.

2 Push each pin into the knitting and through to the base. If the garment is to be pressed, push the pins down right to the head, otherwise allow them to project a little to make the job of removing them easier.

Pressing

Before pressing, always check that the yarn is meant to be

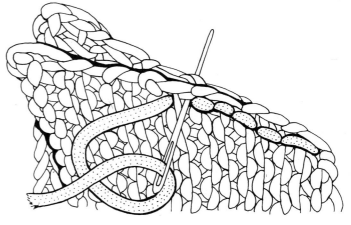

Block out to right measurements and press

pressed. This information, and a guide to temperature, is given on the wrapper (p47).

1 Many man-made fibers can be completely ruined by pressing, in which case simply cover the blocked knitting with a damp cloth and leave until completely dry. If the yarn is suitable for pressing, cover the knitted fabric with a damp or dry cloth, depending on what it says on the yarn

wrapper and gently lower the iron onto the fabric without moving it across the surface. Press lightly, lift the iron and lower it on to the next part of the fabric.

2 Continue in this way until the entire section has been pressed. Leave the knitting pinned out until completely dry. Never press ribbing because it will lose its elasticity and become out of shape.

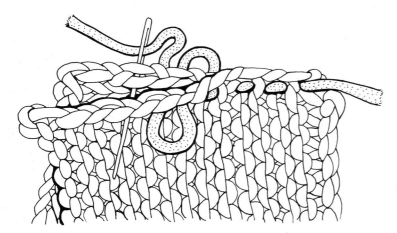

Seaming

There are different methods of seaming knitting, and the one you use depends on what you are seaming. The correct choice makes the job easier as well as neater. Always use a blunt-ended needle and take care not to split the stitches. When following a pattern it is advisable to make up a garment in the sequence given in the instructions; there is usually a good reason for it, such as having to join certain seams before joining others.

Flat seam As the name implies, this seam avoids bulk such as on ribbing, highly textured knitting, or when joining on a button band.

1 Place the edges right sides together and secure the end of the yarn.

2 Pass the needle through the first edge stitch and through to the first edge stitch on the other side.

3 Turn the needle and pass it back through the next edge stitch. Continue in this way along the seam.

Back-stitch seam Use this wherever the seam runs across the grain of the fabric, such as on the shoulder line or along a shaped edge.

1 Place the knitting right sides together and secure the yarn at the right-hand end at the back of the work.

2 Working toward the left and covering only one knitted stitch at a time, bring the needle to the front of the work, take it back to the right the same distance and then through to the back again.

3 Take the needle along to the left over two knitted stitches and bring it through to the front, back to the right and through to the back at the same place as the left-hand end of the previous stitch.

4 Continue in this way along the seam.

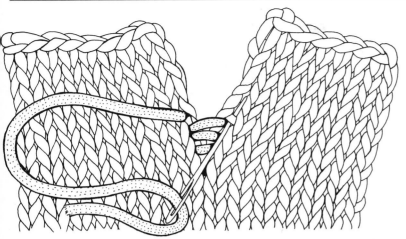

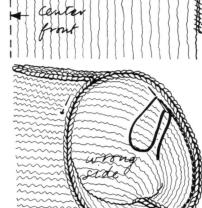

Setting in sleeve flat

center back

shoulder seam

center of sleeve

center front

setting in shaped sleeve

wrong side

wrong side

Invisible seam This gives an extremely smooth join, particularly on stockinette stitch, and is best worked on a straight edge or when any shaping has been worked in from the edges.
1 Place the edges side by side, with the right sides facing each other. Secure the yarn at the bottom right of the seam.
2 Pass the needle under one thread between the first and second edge stitches on the left side of the seam and pick up the thread.
3 Pick up the next thread on the right-hand side of the seam and draw the edges closely together, firmly enough to hold them in place, but take care that they remain flat and do not gather.
4 Continue in this way along the length of the seam.

Sleeves
When setting in sleeves use loose stitches and gently ease in any fullness around the sleeve head.
1 Pin the centre top of the sleeve head to the shoulder seam and the sleeve seam to the side seam of the garment.
2 Join the two edges together between these points with the pins at right angles to the edge and sew.

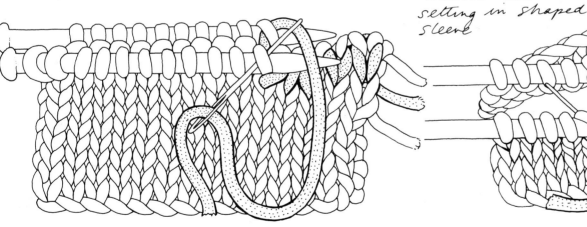

Grafting
This is a seamless method of joining knitting. It looks neat on a shoulder line or anywhere where the bulk of a seam would give an uneven line. Instead of binding off stitches, transfer them onto a spare needle.
1 To graft stockinette stitch, place the two sets of stitches one behind the other on their needles, wrong sides together, needles pointing to the right.
2 Using a blunt-ended needle, draw a length of yarn through the first stitch on the front needle purlwise, leaving the stitch on the knitting needle.
3 Taking the yarn under the knitting needle points, pass the wool needle through the first stitch on the back needle purlwise, draw the yarn through and slip the stitch off the knitting needle.
4 Pass the wool needle through the next stitch on the back needle knitwise and draw the yarn through, leaving the stitch on the knitting needle.
5 Making sure that the wool needle passes over the yarn coming from the back needle, insert the wool needle into the first stitch on the front needle knitwise, draw the yarn through and slip the stitch off the knitting needle.
6 Insert the wool needle into the next stitch on the front needle purlwise and draw the yarn through, leaving the stitch on the knitting needle.
7 Continue in this manner along the row, until all the stitches have been worked off the knitting needle.

Finishing touches

Buttonholes, hems, collars, zippers, sleeves and pockets add the finishing touches to the appearance of a knitted garment or item and have a decorative as well as practical function. All finishing touches are easy to achieve as long as you use the correct method. Before you embark upon them you need to know how to pick up stitches.

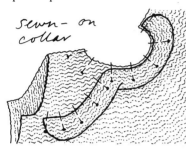

sewn-on collar

Collars
Collars can either be knitted in by first picking up stitches around the neck edge or made separately and sewn on.
Picked-up collar Divide the neck edge into sections to space the picked-up stitches evenly. When working a nonreversible stitch such as stockinette stitch remember to pick up stitches from the correct side to ensure that the pattern is on the right side when the collar is turned over.
Sewn-on collar Divide the neck edge and the inner collar edge into the same number of equal sections and mark them with a pin. With the right side of the collar facing the wrong side of the garment, pin the two edges together, matching up the marker pins and sew.

Pockets
Pockets can either be inserted horizontally or vertically, or made separately and sewn on.
Sewn-on pocket Knit a shape to the required size and sew it in place when the garment is completed. If knitting in stockinette stitch, work a few rows of rib before binding off.

Picking up stitches
To pick up a large number of stitches, divide the edge into equal sections and mark them with pins. Then divide the total number of stitches to be picked up by the number of sections. By working out the number of stitches to be picked up in each section you can make sure that they are spaced evenly.

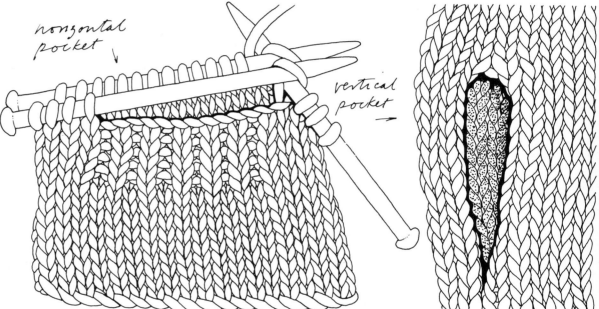

horizontal pocket

vertical pocket

Inserted horizontal pocket
The lining is knitted separately and then inserted behind a horizontal slit in the main fabric.
1 Using your tension square work out the number of stitches and rows you will need for the pocket size.
2 Make the lining first, using a smooth fabric stitch such as stockinette stitch. Leave the stitches on a spare needle.
3 Work the main fabric to five rows before level of pocket top, ending on a right side row. Work four rows in rib.
4 On the next row (wrong side) work to position of the pocket and bind off pocket-top stitches. Then work to the end of the row.
5 On the next row (right side) work to within one stitch of

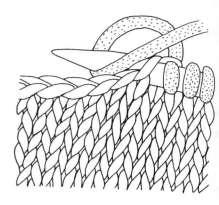

1 With the right side of the knitting facing, insert the needle into a row end on a vertical edge or stitch on a horizontal edge.
2 Wind the yarn round the needle point, draw the loop through to the front of the work and continue to knit up the required number of stitches, picking up one loop for each stitch.

the pocket top. Knit the next stitch together with the first stitch of the pocket lining. Work to the last stitch of the pocket lining and knit this stitch together with the next stitch of the main fabric. Knit to the end of the row.
6 Once the garment is completed, slip stitch the lining into place.
Inserted vertical pocket The lining should always lie toward the center front of the garment so make sure that there is enough room for it to lie flat within the front edge.
1 Using your tension square work out the number of stitches and rows you will need for the pocket size.
2 Make the lining first and bind the stitches off.
3 Work the main fabric until

you reach the position for the pocket, ending on a wrong-side row.
4 On the next row work to position of opening, turn and knit each side separately until opening is required depth, ending on a wrong-side row.
5 Rejoin yarn and work across all stitches so as to close the opening.
6 When the garment is completed, pick up stitches across the first section worked for a right-hand pocket and the second section worked for a left-hand pocket and knit a few rows in rib to give the pocket a neat edge.
7 With the right side of the lining facing the wrong side of the main fabric, join along the other edge of the opening and slip stitch the lining in place.

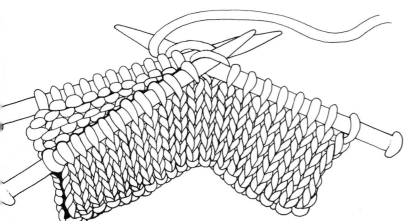

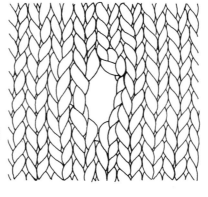

Hems

Hems can either be sewn up with slip stitch or actually knitted in with the garment. For a sharp edge to plain hems always work the fold line as a knit row on the wrong (purl) side of the fabric. Work the underside of the hem on needles one size smaller than those for the lower edge of the garment.

Knitted-in hem This produces a firmer edge than the sewn-in hem which is worked in exactly the same way except that it is sewn up afterwards rather than knitted in.

1 Cast on, using the two-needle method and knit for the required length, ending with a right-side row.
2 Work the fold line then changing to the correct size needles, work one row less than before, ending with a wrong-side row.
3 Using a spare needle, pick up all the stitches along the cast-on edge.
4 Fold up the hem and, holding the spare needle behind the left-hand needle, knit together one stitch from each of the two needles across the row.

Buttonholes

Buttonholes may be vertical or horizontal or when a small button is required a simple eyelet stitch, as shown on p136 may be used.

Vertical buttonholes These are worked on narrow bands and can also be used on the main fabric.

1 Work to the position of the buttonhole, turn and knit each side separately.
2 When you have worked both sections to the required length continue knitting across the whole row. Finish off the buttonhole by working round it in buttonhole stitch.

Horizontal buttonholes

These may be worked on the main fabric or on a separate narrow band.

1 Work to position of the buttonhole and bind off the number of stitches required for the width of the button and knit to the end of the row.
2 Work to within one stitch of the bound-off stitches and knit twice into it. Then cast on one stitch less than was bound off and work to end of the row.
3 Once the garment is complete, finish off the buttonhole by working round it in buttonhole stitch.

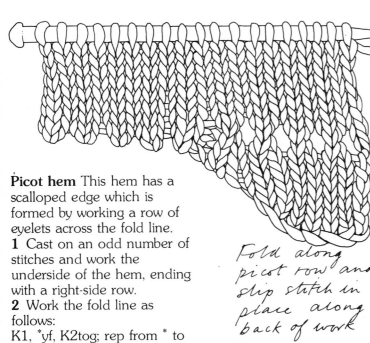

Picot hem

This hem has a scalloped edge which is formed by working a row of eyelets across the fold line.

1 Cast on an odd number of stitches and work the underside of the hem, ending with a right-side row.
2 Work the fold line as follows:
K1, *yf, K2tog; rep from * to end.
3 Complete the hem either sewn-up or knitted-in.

Fold along picot row and slip stitch in place along back of work

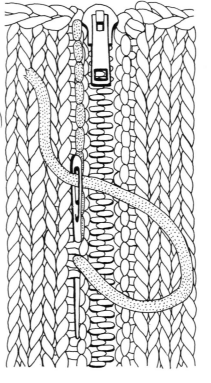

Zippers

Before inserting a zipper it is advisable to reinforce the edges. Either work a row of double crochet or pick up a row of stitches and bind them off. Always insert an open-ended zipper with the fastener closed to ensure that both sides match.

1 Pin the zipper in position, taking care not to stretch the knitting. Use an ordinary sewing needle and thread that matches the yarn.
2 With the right side of the work facing, sew in the zipper with a back-stitch seam, keeping as close to the knitted edge as possible. Always work from top to bottom and take care not to cover the zipper teeth. Slip stitch down the zipper edges on the inside.

Edges and insertions

Knitted edgings and insertions can be used practically and decoratively to join two parts of a garment or object together or to finish off the edges neatly. They are most effective when they are worked in a different stitch or pattern to the main body of knitting. They may also be worked in a different color.

Make them separately and sew them on afterward or pick up the correct number of stitches along the edge of the finished work and knit for the required length. When picking up stitches, to ensure that the pattern forms on the right side of the work, you may need to purl one row before beginning on the first pattern row. You can find out how to pick up stitches on p28.

Edgings

These may be used to trim practically any object or garment you can think of. They may be plain or decorative. The latter often have a curved or wavy outer edge. You can continue in the same yarn as the main fabric or choose a different one. Eyelet edgings are useful for threading with cords or ribbons of various kinds to draw up knitted fabric. Frilled or lacy edgings look best on fine knitting and can effectively be decorated with beads or sequins. An edge incorporating ridges adds real dimension to a border especially if each ridge is knitted in a contrasting color. The ridges can also be slightly padded to enhance the three-dimensional effect.

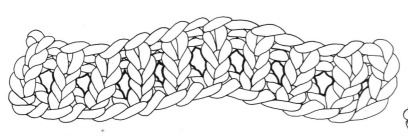

Ribbed eyelet Pick up or cast on an odd number of sts.
1st row (Wrong side) K1, *P1, K1; rep from * to end.
2nd row *K2tog, yf; rep from *, to last st, K1.
3rd row As 1st row.

4th row P1, *K1, P1; rep from * to end.
Rep 1st–4th row until edging is required length.
Bind off in rib.

Feather and fan Pick up or cast on a multiple of 11 sts, plus 2 extra.
1st–2nd row K.
3rd row (Right side) K1, *K2tog twice, (yf, K1) 3 times, yf, (sl 1, K1, psso) twice; rep

from * to last st, K1.
4th row P.
Rep 3rd–4th row until edging is required length, end with a 3rd row.
Rep 1st–2nd row.
Bind off.

Frills Cast on a multiple of 10 sts, plus 3 extra.
1st row (Right side) P3, *K7, P3; rep from * to end.
2nd row K3, *P7, K3; rep from * to end.
3rd row P3, *sl 1, K1, psso, K3, K2tog, P3; rep from *.
4th row K3, *P5, K3; rep from * to end.
5th row P3, *sl 1, K1, psso,

K1, K2tog, P3; rep from * to end.
6th row K3, *P3, K3; rep from * to end.
7th row P3, *sl 1, K2tog, psso, P3; rep from * to end.
8th row K3, *P1, K3; rep from * to end.
9th row P3, *K1, P3; rep from * to end.
Bind off.

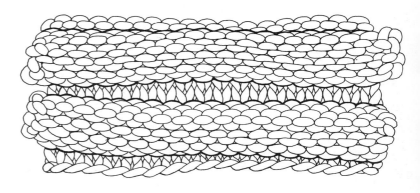

Ridges Pick up or cast on required number of sts.
1st row (Right side) K.
2nd row P.
3rd–9th row Work in rev st st, beg with a P row.
10th row P.
11th row *With right-hand needle, pick up loop from the first st of 2nd row and place on left-hand needle and K tog

with next st on needle*. Rep from * across row.
12th–16th row Work in st st, beg with a P row.
Rep 11th–16th row until edging is required length, end with a P row instead of 5 rows st st.
Bind off.

Insertions

Strips of knitting may be inserted between two pieces of fabric to great decorative effect. Whereas edgings often have curved outer edges, insertions usually have two straight parallel edges to enable them to fit neatly between the two pieces of fabric. Like edgings they can be knitted separately or picked up from the main piece of knitting. The following patterns for insertions may also be used as edgings.

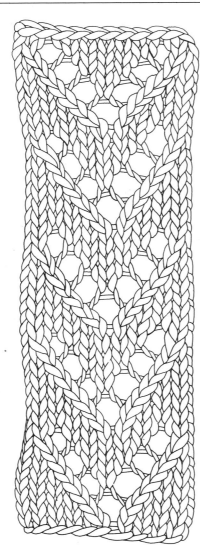

Chevron lace Pick up or cast on a multiple of 11 sts.

1st row (Right side) *K5, yf, sl 1, K1, psso, K4; rep from *.

2nd row (Wrong side) and all wrong side rows P.

3rd row *K3, K2tog, yf, K1, yf, sl 1, K1, psso, K3; rep from *.

5th row *K2, K2tog, yf, K3, yf, sl 1, K1, psso, K2; rep from *.

7th row *K1, K2tog, yf, K5, yf, sl 1, K1, psso, K1; rep from *.

8th row P.

Rep 1st–8th row until work is required length.
Bind off.

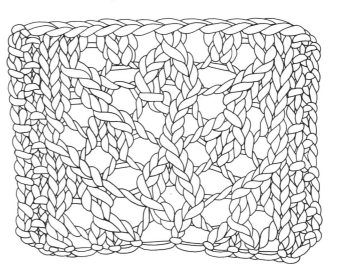

Lacy openwork Pick up or cast on a multiple of 4 sts, plus 2 extra.

1st–4th row K.

5th row (Right side) K1, K2tog, *(yrn) twice, (K2tog) twice; rep from *, end (yrn) twice, K2tog, K1.

6th row P2, *K first made st, P second made st, P2; rep from * to end.

7th row K1, yf, (K2tog) twice, *(yrn) twice, (K2tog) twice; rep from *, to last st, yf, K1.

8th row P4, *K1, K first made st, P second made st, P2; rep from *, to last 2 sts, P2.
Rep 5th–8th row until insertion is required length, end with 6th or 8th row. Bind off. For a horizontal insertion, work 1st–4th row once more before binding off.

Lacy diamond Pick up or cast on a multiple of 10 sts, plus 1 extra.

1st–3rd row K.

4th row P.

5th row K1, *yf, K2tog; rep from * to end.

6th–8th row Work in st st.

9th row K5, *yf, sl 1, K1, psso, K8; rep from *, end last rep K4.

10th and every alt row P.

11th row K3, *K2tog, yf, K1, yf, sl 1, K1, psso, K5; rep from *, end last rep K3.

13th row K2, *K2tog, yf, K3, yf, sl 1, K1, psso, K3; rep from *, end last rep K2.

15th row K1, *K2tog, yf, K5, yf, sl 1, K1, psso, K1; rep from * to end.

17th row K2, *yf, sl 1, K1, psso, K3, K2tog, yf, K3; rep from *, end last rep K2.

19th row K3, yf, sl 1, K1, psso, K1, K2tog, yf, K5; rep from *, end last rep K3.

21st row K4, *yf, sl 1, K2tog, psso, yf, K7; rep from *, end last rep K4.

23rd row As 9th row.

24th–26th row Work in st st, beg with a P row.

27th row As 5th row.

28th row P.

29th–31st row K.
Bind off.

Renovating

It is easy to miscalculate when knitting and to end up with something quite unwearable. Fashions also change; designs quickly become out-of-date and the garment gets pushed to the back of the drawer. There are, however, ways of giving new life to these apparently useless garments. Either unpick the seams, unravel the yarn and recycle it so that you can begin again, or alter and renovate garments for a more up-to-date look.

Recycling yarn
Knitted yarn intended for reuse must be in fairly good condition. If it is matted or worn it will be difficult to unravel. It must also be steamed or washed to remove the kinks which, if left, will prevent it from forming a smooth fabric when it is knitted up again.

Altering a garment
A badly fitting or worn garment need never be discarded; there is usually a way to solve the problem. Alterations such as lengthening and shortening can often be anticipated, especially in the case of children, so to be on the safe side always buy several extra balls of yarn in the same dye lot.
If when you come to make the alteration you find you are short of yarn, rather than trying to match the original color exactly, use a yarn of similar weight in a contrast color. Tension also changes with wear and washing so it is advisable to work alterations in a contrasting stitch to cover up any discrepancy. Seams are often difficult to detect, so if you anticipate unpicking them at a later stage, run a

Unravelling yarn Unpick the seams and starting at the bound-off edge, undo the final stitch and begin to unravel, working slowly and evenly, row by row. Continue to the end of the piece, winding the unravelled yarn onto a frame such as a bent wire coat hanger. Always wind loosely so that the steam can penetrate.

different-colored yarn under the stitches as you join the seam. This will not show on the right side but will show the exact position of the stitches when it comes to unpicking.
Replacing ribbing Ribbing tends to wear more round the wrists than anywhere else and if it needs replacing it is advisable to reknit it around the neck and bottom as well so as to give the garment a coordinated look.
1 Unpick the side seams and sleeve seams to about 15cm (6in) above the ribbing and open up one shoulder seam.
2 Unravel the ribbing, pick up the stitches and reknit either to the original length, or shorten or lengthen as required. At the neck edge it is quite possible to add a polo neck or collar, or to replace such styles with a crew or turtle neck.

Steaming yarn Hold the frame with the yarn over a pan or kettle of boiling water until all the kinks have been steamed out. Remove the yarn from the frame and tie it with a figure of eight loop to prevent the threads tangling. Then leave it to dry away from direct heat before winding it loosely into balls for reuse.

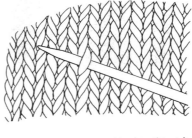

Altering the length There are quite a number of reasons why you may want to add or take away a section of knitting: to repair some damage, to extend the life of a favorite sweater or jacket or to shorten or lengthen a skirt. Whether lengthening or

Washing yarn Wind the yarn from the frame into bundles and secure with lengths of yarn or thread tied into a figure of eight to prevent the yarn tangling. Gently wash the bundles by hand in warm water to remove the kinks. Then hang them to dry before rewinding into loose balls ready for reknitting.

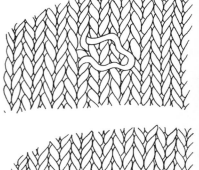

shortening, the method is always the same.
Never cut stitches and only alter garments which are in a plain stitch such as garter stitch or stockinette stitch. Picking up stitches in a complicated pattern can become a nightmare. Decide

exactly where you are going to make the alteration and unpick the relevant seam above, until you have enough room in which to maneuver the knitting needles. Count the number of rows below the alteration point and add to or subtract from this amount when making calculations.

1 Mark the point at each end of the row where you intend to start unpicking and, with the right side facing, pick up a loop just above one of the markers.

2 Pull on this loop tightly to form a long loop of yarn as you tighten the stitches across the row.

3 Cut the loop and carefully separate the pieces of knitting until you have two sets of stitches. Continue to pull the fabric apart gently until it is in two complete pieces.

4 Pick up the original number of stitches along the edge of the main piece, taking care not to twist them. Rejoin the yarn at the beginning of the row and complete the

alterations as required, remembering to bind off as loosely as possible.

5 Alternatively you may need to graft two sections together. In this case do not bind off, but pick up the stitches from the second section on another needle and graft the two sections carefully together as shown on p26.

Altering sleeves Sleeves can be altered from long to short or vice-versa. The latter is more difficult and you must work out the shaping

beforehand as shown on p22. If you want to alter the length by only a few centimeters or inches, do it above the cuff or wrist welt using the method above. If elbows are worn beyond repair, undo the seam to just above the new length and unravel the knitting to the point required. Then pick up the stitches and work a band of ribbing in the same yarn or a contrasting one.

Renovating knitwear

Give a new look to an old favorite and bring it back into fashion by taking out the sleeves, adding some fabric or by decorating with interesting accessories as shown on pp36–7.

Removing sleeves Unpick the seams, take out the sleeves and trim with leather, braid, fabric cut on the bias or add knitted bands. To do the latter, pick up all the stitches around the edge, knit a band approximately 2.5cm (1in) wide, bind off and sew up the seam neatly.

Adding fabric Combining knitted fabric with a woven fabric can completely transform the look of a garment.

1 Take the knitting to pieces and carefully block and press the individual pieces.

2 Make a pattern of the area you wish to replace with fabric and unravel the equivalent area of knitting, binding off the edge neatly.

3 Stitch the fabric in place and sew the garment back together again.

4 Alternatively fabric can be added to knitting to cover worn patches in a decorative way. Using techniques such as appliqué and quilting, make elbow and shoulder patches.

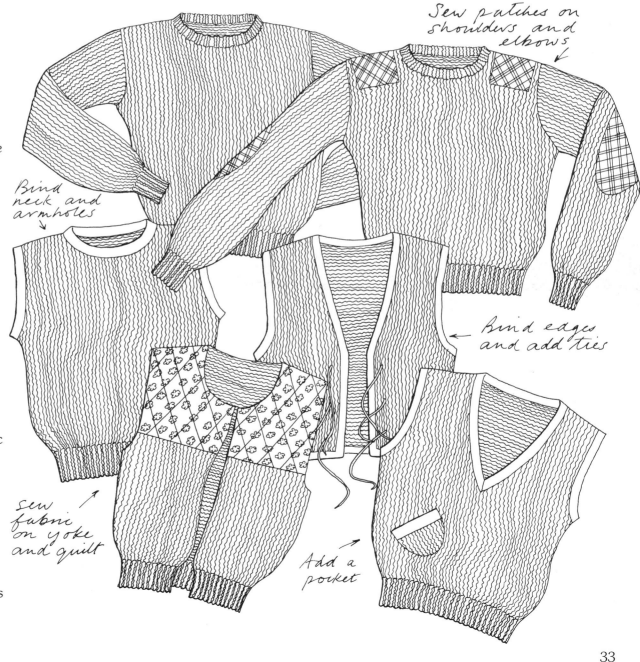

Sew patches on shoulders and elbows

Bind neck and armholes

Bind edges and add ties

sew fabric on yoke and quilt

Add a pocket

Patchwork

Patchwork knitting is the skill of joining together a selection of colorful shapes to form a whole fabric. It is economical because it enables you to use leftover scraps of yarn, old tension squares and to re-cycle the yarns in unwanted garments. It is also exciting, the results being as random or planned as you choose. The combinations of yarns, color and texture within a piece of patchwork can be endless and the possibilities of creating an individual and colorful fabric are unlimited. Some examples of what can be achieved may be seen on pp62–5, 112–13.

Methods
There are two basic methods of creating knitted patchwork. The first, known as joined patchwork, is the simplest and involves knitting separate pieces of fabric and then sewing them together to form a single length or shape. The second technique, known as collage patchwork, involves working the patchwork as a single piece. It is not difficult but does require some experience of handling a number of colored yarns at the same time within a single piece of knitting.

Before you start knitting, work out on a piece of graph paper the basic shapes and colors you are going to use and where you are going to place them. This will help you to sort out your ideas and to make sure that all the patches fit together in a colorful and coordinated way.

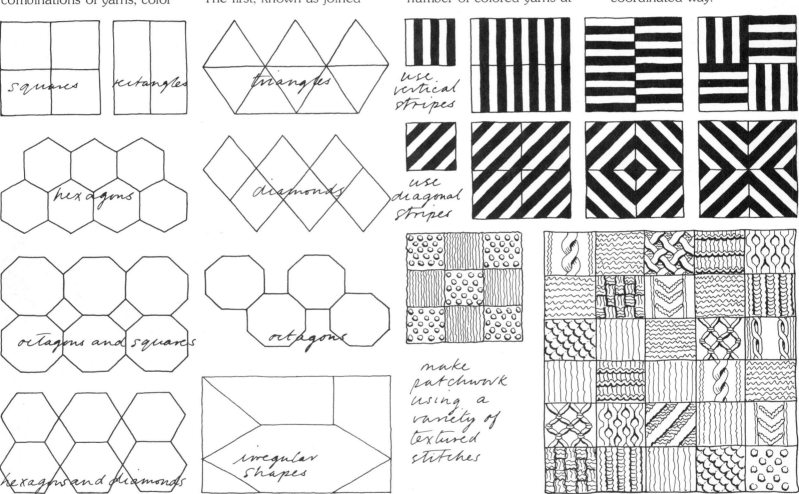

squares   rectangles   triangles   use vertical stripes

hexagons   diamonds   use diagonal stripes

octagons and squares   octagons   make patchwork using a variety of textured stitches

hexagons and diamonds   irregular shapes

Joined patchwork
A simple and easy form of patchwork can be achieved by sewing all your old tension squares together. The next step is to work out your own patchwork design on paper, marking in the colors and stitches that you intend to use. Patches can be of any size or shape – square, rectangular, triangular, hexagonal, octagonal, and so on. But the shapes need not necessarily be regular; the only thing to remember is that all the shapes or pieces have to join together to make a single piece of fabric in exactly the same way as a jigsaw fits together. Use a thin yarn for sewing shapes together and join them with a back-stitch seam as shown on p26. Alternatively, overlap and embroider edges (pp44–5).

Color themes Either make your patchwork a riot of color or choose a subtle theme to run through the design. For example, select a color like green and find as many shades of green yarn as you can of roughly the same weight and knit them up into patches. Another idea which is most effective is to knit up all the patches in the same color but in a variety of textured stitch patterns. These can be assembled in a completely random way or more carefully to a preplanned, balanced design.

Weight Weight is something to be considered. If you want a patchwork of even weight, choose yarns of similar weight. If you are not worried about an uneven fabric, use any or all of the yarns and materials at your disposal.

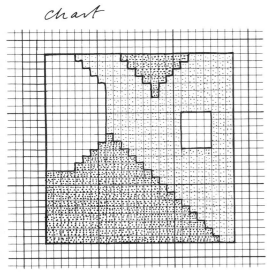

chart

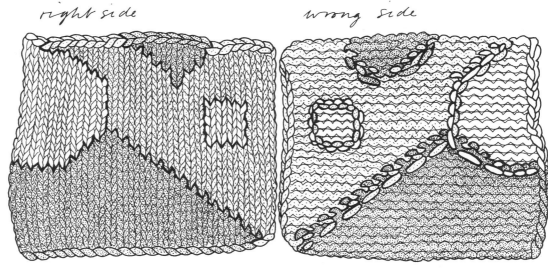

right side   wrong side

Collage patchwork

Work out your design in the usual way on graph paper. Draw the outline of the patchwork first, then fill in the patchwork shapes. Instead of working all the patches separately, calculate the number of stitches required for the first row or block of patches, then using your chart for reference, start to knit the patchwork as one piece.

Separating colors The major problem in collage patchwork is keeping the different colored yarns separate at the back of the work. The yarns have a habit of tangling which tends to slow down progress. Another problem is that of having to carry the yarn along behind the work. This is a waste of yarn and often a nuisance. The best way to work large areas of color is to use a small separate ball of yarn for each one. This means that if you have several colors in one row, each will have its own ball of yarn.

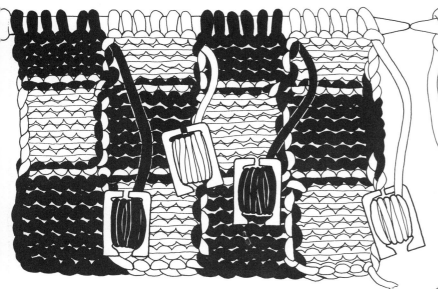

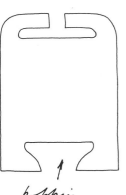

bobbin

Bobbins To keep the separate yarns from tangling wind small amounts of each color onto bobbins. If you are using the same color more than once in a row, it should have a separate bobbin for each time it is used.

You can buy bobbins or make them yourself. If you want to do the latter, simply trace the shape onto some stiff card. This size is suitable for fine to medium weight yarns. For bulky yarns, make the bobbins twice as large.

Before beginning to knit, wind the yarn around, making sure the working end passes through the narrow opening. Hang the loaded bobbins at the back of the work on the wrong side and this will stop the yarns from tangling.

By changing the color as you work along the row in this manner the fabric remains of single thickness and there are no clumsy strands at the back of the work.

To prevent holes appearing in your knitting make sure that when you change color you twist the yarns around each other. If you forget, there will be gaps between each patch of color.

All the extras

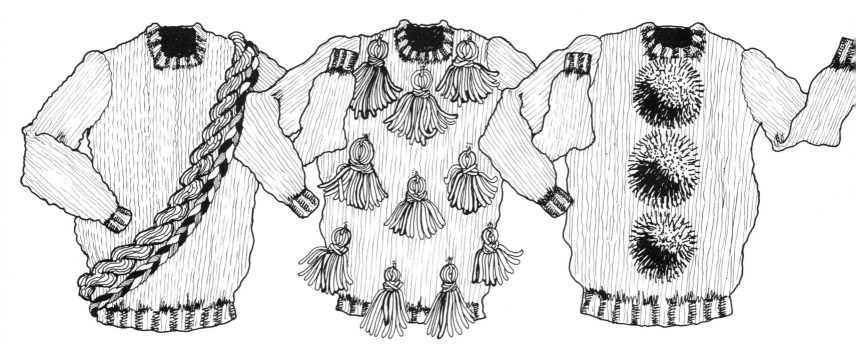

Accessories such as cords, tassels and pompons add great decorative interest to knitting. They can transform the most basic garments or objects into something unique.

Cords

There are two ways to make simple cords: by twisting or braiding. They can either be made from lengths of one yarn or from a mixture of several. Try incorporating unusual materials such as ribbons, raffia or wire. A length of the latter will enable you to twist the finished cord into a necklace, belt or abstract shape that can then be stitched, pinned or twisted into the knitted fabric.

Twisted cords These are easy to make but require two people for the speediest and most even effect. If a second person is unavailable, attach one end of the cord to a hook or some other firm object. The number of strands of yarn required will vary according to the thickness of the yarn that you are using.

1 Cut equal lengths of yarn to three times the length of the finished cord.

2 If working with a second

person, each take hold of one end and knot the strands of yarn together. Insert a pencil into each knot.

3 Twist the pencils to the right until the entire length is tightly twisted.

4 Holding the strands taut, fold the length in half and knot the two ends together.

5 Hold the knotted end and give the length a good shake. Then smooth out any unevenness, working from the knot toward the folded end.

6 Tie a knot at the folded end, cut through the folded loops, tease out the ends as required and trim if necessary.

Braided cords Cut strands

of yarn rather longer than the length required for the cord and knot them together.

1 Divide the strands into three parts and get someone to hold the knot or attach it to something secure.

2 Braid the three groups together, tie a knot at the end and trim if necessary.

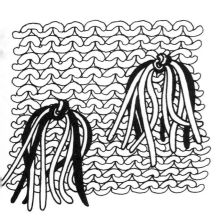

Tassels

Tassels can be inlaid directly into knitted fabric, either as surface decoration or to fringe the edges of garments and household furnishings. Alternatively you can make individual tassels and attach them in any way you like.

Inlaid tassels Short or long lengths of yarn can be inserted into knitted fabric to great decorative effect.

1 Cut several lengths of yarn and, using a crochet hook, pull them from the front of the fabric through to the back and then gently out to the front again.

2 Knot the ends together as close to the fabric as possible.

Fringing This is another technique which also involves hooking through lengths of yarn. These can either hang free or be tied in interesting ways. Tassels look good when plaited or when divided into groups and tied to give a latticework effect.

1 Cut strands of yarn to double the length of the required tassel. Fold them in half and, using a crochet hook, pull the looped ends through to the right side.

2 Pull the ends of the yarn through the loop on the right side and pull to tighten.

Individual tassels These can be as bulky as the knitted fabric will allow, and look most effective when made from different colored yarns.

1 Cut a piece of cardboard to the width required for the length of the tassel. Wind the yarn loosely round the card for the thickness required.

2 Thread a blunt needle with yarn and pull under the strands along the edge of the card. Pull up the yarn tightly and fasten securely, leaving an end long enough to tie around the top of the tassel.

3 Using a sharp pair of scissors, cut through the strands at the other end of the cord and trim if necessary.

4 Wind the long end of yarn tightly round the tassel a short way from the uncut end.

Pompons

Pompons can be used singly or attached to the surface of a knitted fabric. Work different-colored yarns together for a multi-colored pompon or, for a striped effect, work around the circle in one color and then another. You can even achieve a patchwork design by working blocks of color, one after the other.

1 Using a pair of compasses or the edge of a circular object for shape, cut out two cardboard circles. The size of the finished pompon will be equal to the diameter of the circle. Cut a smaller circle from the center of each piece. The size of this inner circle determines the amount of yarn required and the weight of the finished pompon.

2 Place the two circles together and wind the yarn as evenly as possible around the frame and through the center. When the hole is almost full, break the yarn, leaving a long end. Thread this through a blunt needle and use to fill the hole completely.

3 Take a sharp pair of scissors and cut through all the layers of yarn between the two edges of cardboard, taking care not to cut the cardboard.

4 Ease the two pieces of cardboard apart. Double a piece of yarn and tie between the two pieces, leaving an end long enough to attach the pompon to a knitted garment or object.

5 Pull or cut away the cardboard completely, fluff up the surface and trim to whatever shape and size you require.

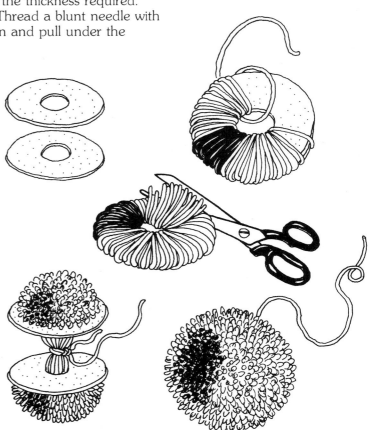

Textured effects

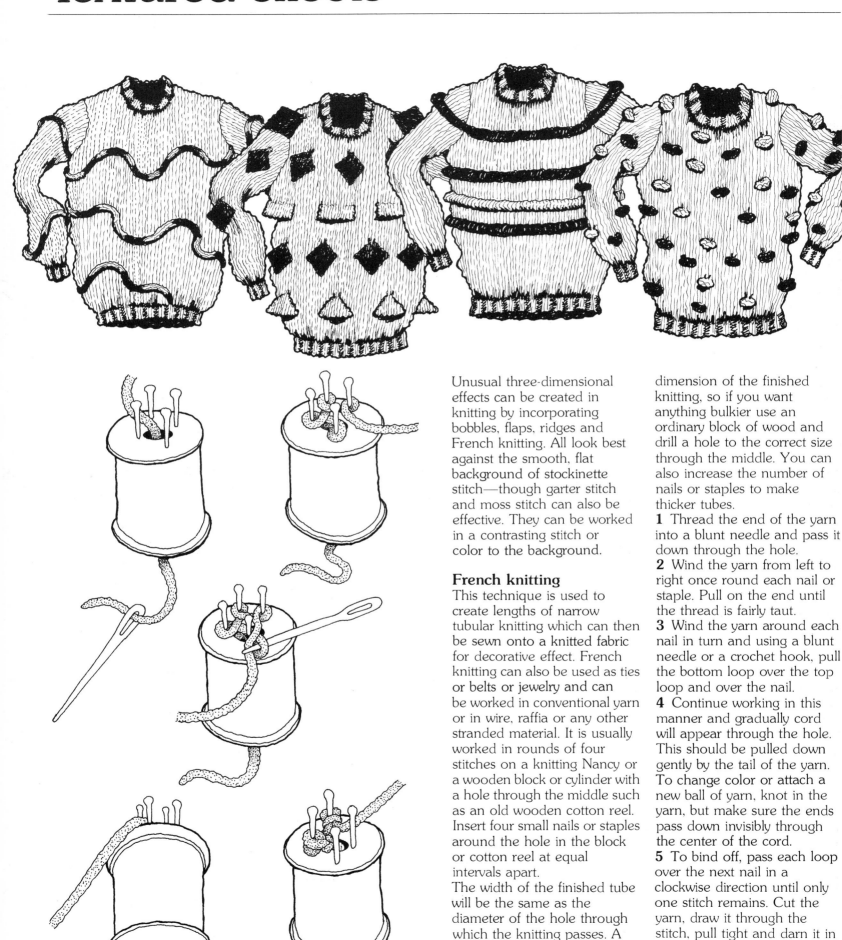

Unusual three-dimensional effects can be created in knitting by incorporating bobbles, flaps, ridges and French knitting. All look best against the smooth, flat background of stockinette stitch—though garter stitch and moss stitch can also be effective. They can be worked in a contrasting stitch or color to the background.

French knitting

This technique is used to create lengths of narrow tubular knitting which can then be sewn onto a knitted fabric for decorative effect. French knitting can also be used as ties or belts or jewelry and can be worked in conventional yarn or in wire, raffia or any other stranded material. It is usually worked in rounds of four stitches on a knitting Nancy or a wooden block or cylinder with a hole through the middle such as an old wooden cotton reel. Insert four small nails or staples around the hole in the block or cotton reel at equal intervals apart.

The width of the finished tube will be the same as the diameter of the hole through which the knitting passes. A cotton reel restricts the dimension of the finished knitting, so if you want anything bulkier use an ordinary block of wood and drill a hole to the correct size through the middle. You can also increase the number of nails or staples to make thicker tubes.

1 Thread the end of the yarn into a blunt needle and pass it down through the hole.
2 Wind the yarn from left to right once round each nail or staple. Pull on the end until the thread is fairly taut.
3 Wind the yarn around each nail in turn and using a blunt needle or a crochet hook, pull the bottom loop over the top loop and over the nail.
4 Continue working in this manner and gradually cord will appear through the hole. This should be pulled down gently by the tail of the yarn. To change color or attach a new ball of yarn, knot in the yarn, but make sure the ends pass down invisibly through the center of the cord.
5 To bind off, pass each loop over the next nail in a clockwise direction until only one stitch remains. Cut the yarn, draw it through the stitch, pull tight and darn it in through center of cord.

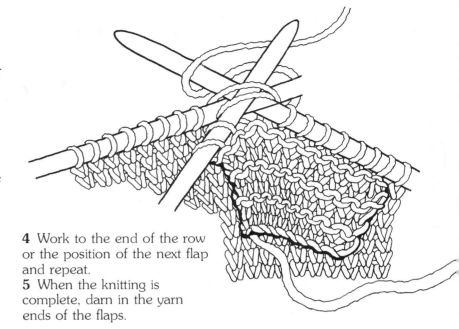

Flaps

Flaps can be incorporated as you knit, or sewn on afterward. Sewing on is sometimes easier as it is often difficult to decide where to place them while you are knitting. They can be of any size or shape but square, rectangular or triangular flaps are the easiest to make. Use garter stitch or moss stitch as the knitted fabric is less likely to curl up.

1 Before beginning on your main fabric, make as many separate flaps as you require. Finish them on a wrong-side row but do not bind them off.

2 Slide all the stitches of your flaps onto a spare needle, leaving a length of spare yarn on each.

3 Work the background knitting until you reach the position for the flap on a knit row. With the right side of the flap and the knitting facing you place the needle with the flap in front of the left-hand needle and knit together one stitch from each needle until you have worked all the flap stitches and incorporated them into the background knitting.

4 Work to the end of the row or the position of the next flap and repeat.

5 When the knitting is complete, darn in the yarn ends of the flaps.

Ridges

Ridges can be knitted to any depth simply by working more or fewer rows, but remember to work at least five rows before the joining row, or the ridge will not stand out sufficiently. Work the ridges in the basic color or one that contrasts with the background fabric. You can use the same stitch as the background or one that is complementary. Here instructions are for a stockinette stitch ridge, in a contrasting color. The basic color is A and the contrast, B.

1 With A, work in stockinette stitch to position of ridge, ending with a purl row.

2 Take up B and work an odd number of rows ending with a knit row.

3 With the wrong side facing, take a smaller spare needle and pick up the loops of the first row of B, starting at the left-hand edge.

4 With B, purl together one stitch from each needle to end of row.

5 Break off B and continue working with A until the position of the next ridge.

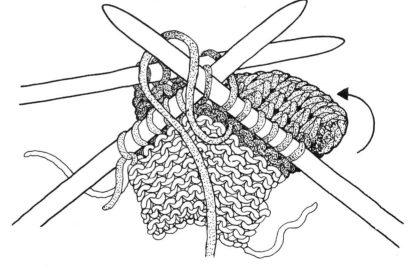

Bobbles

Bobbles can either be made separately or incorporated into your knitting as you go along. You can place them singly, at random or to form a pattern anywhere on the surface of a fabric. Their size can be varied by increasing the number of stitches worked from three upward. They can be worked in the same color as the background or for a different effect in a contrasting color.

Knitted-in bobbles You will get neater results if you knit in bobbles as you go along, but preplan your design carefully.

1 Knit to the position of the bobble. Make five stitches out of the next stitch in the following way: knit into the front and the back of the next stitch twice, then knit into the front again, turn, (knit five, turn, purl five) twice.

2 Using the left-hand needle lift the second, third, fourth and fifth stitch in turn over the first stitch and off the needle.

3 Continue knitting to the position of the next bobble.

Individual bobbles Starting with a loop on the needle, these can be made to the same pattern as knitted-in bobbles. Darn in any ends and sew them in place.

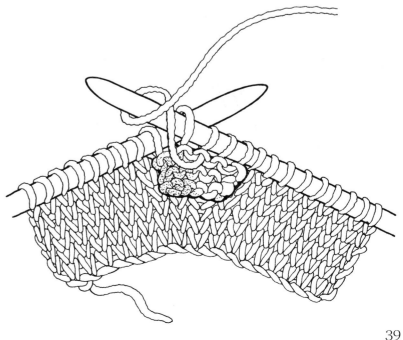

Beads and objects

Almost any object can be incorporated into a piece of knitting as long as it is, or can be, pierced or is shaped in such a way that it can be held securely.

Beads and sequins These are the most commonly used objects. They can be obtained in such a vast range of types, colors and sizes that they offer great potential for creating dazzling effects, especially when they are imaginatively combined with different kinds of yarns and threads. Notions counters are the obvious source of supply, but toy shops can also be relied upon to provide unusual beads as well as other interesting objects such as small plastic toys and doll's-house accessories, many of which are suitable for working into knitted articles.

Jewelry Odds and ends of junk jewelry such as plastic brooches, earrings and colored rings may well provide other possibilities.

Shells and nuts Some things like shells or hazel nuts will need to be pierced before they can be used. Nuts can be pierced with a fine hand drill. Most of the smaller shells which are suitable for incorporating in knitting are rather fragile and need careful handling. Rest the shell on a thick cork. Place the point of a fine needle on the inside of the thinnest part of the shell and tap it gently with a small hammer. Alternatively, use a fine drill.

Feathers and grass Dried flowers, plants, grass and feathers also make beautiful additions to knitted designs. Plait them into ties or cords and use them as accessories or take advantage of the eyelets and holes in lacy stitches and weave them in and out of the knitted fabric.

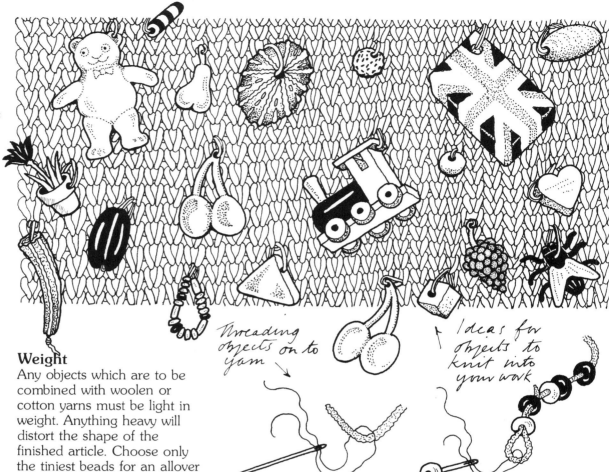

Weight
Any objects which are to be combined with woolen or cotton yarns must be light in weight. Anything heavy will distort the shape of the finished article. Choose only the tiniest beads for an allover beaded pattern, as even the finest can drag the fabric out of shape. If there are too many in a small area of work, the fabric could pucker badly.

Cleaning
Make sure that the objects can be cleaned by the same process as the yarn. Knit up a small sample before beginning on the main article and wash or dry clean it as appropriate.

Threading on to yarn
The easiest and neatest way of incorporating a large number of objects into knitting is to knit them in as you go along. Some objects have holes large enough to take the yarn direct. If they do not, use the following method:
1 Take a length of sewing thread about 25cm (10in) long. Fold it in half and thread both ends through the eye of the needle together. Thread

the yarn through the loop.
2 Slip the beads, sequins or other objects down the needle, over the doubled thread and on to the yarn.
If a definite pattern involving a particular sequence of different types of object is desired, some advance planning will be required. Once the beads have been threaded their order of appearance in the article is fixed and cannot be changed. Work out the order carefully beforehand, using graph paper if necessary, remembering that the last beads to be threaded will be the first to be worked. Before you begin knitting try to estimate the amount of wool that will be needed to complete the beaded part of the garment. Then divide the beads required among the right number of balls of wool.

Placing beads
The following methods describe the placing of beads, but they are equally appropriate for any of the objects which have been suggested. Stockinette stitch is usually used for beading as it provides a smooth, plain background. There is no reason, however, why any stitch cannot be used provided that it contains sequences of two or three knit stitches at a time to allow for the correct positioning of the beads while not interfering with the rest of the pattern. Beading is usually carried out on knit rows, but in some cases, for example where dense beading is required, it may be necessary to bead on purl rows also. The tension on bead rows must be kept as tight as possible.

Method 1

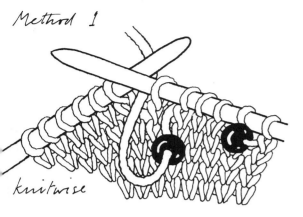

knitwise

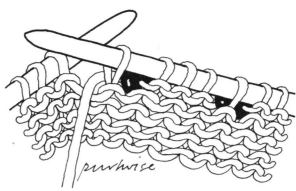

purlwise

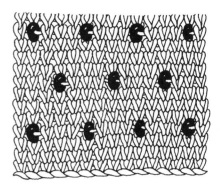

Method 1 By this method the beads are placed in front of the stitches on the right (knit) side of the work. It is most suitable for small beads or objects which might otherwise slip through to the back of the fabric.

1 On knit rows, knit to the position of the bead. Bring the yarn forward to the right side of the work. Slide the bead down the yarn close to the last stitch knitted. Slip the next stitch from the left-hand needle to the right-hand needle, return

the yarn to the back of the work and knit to the position of the next bead.

2 On purl rows, purl to the position of the bead. Take the yarn to the back (right side) of the work. Slip the next stitch from the left-hand needle to

the right-hand needle and slide the bead up as close to the right-hand needle as possible. Bring the yarn forward to the front of the work and purl to the position of the next bead.

Method 2

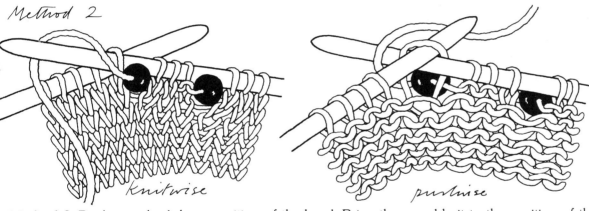

Knitwise   *purlwise*

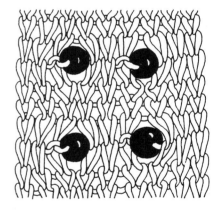

Method 2 By this method the beads are placed between stitches on the right (knit) side of the work.

1 On knit rows, work to the

position of the bead. Bring the yarn forward and push the bead as close as possible to the previous stitch. Purl the next stitch, take the yarn back,

and knit to the position of the next bead.

2 On purl rows, purl to the position of the bead. Take the yarn to the back (right side) of

the work and slide the bead up as close as possible to the right-hand needle. Knit the next stitch, bring the yarn forward and purl to the next bead.

Method 3

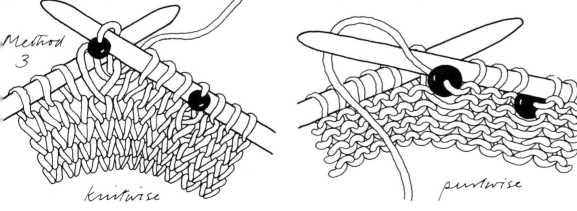

knitwise   *purlwise*

Method 3 This method is suitable for pendulous objects such as droplet beads and sequins which have holes close to the edge.

1 On knit rows, knit to the position of the bead and slide the bead down the yarn. Knit the next stitch through the back of the loop, bringing the

bead through the stitch as you do so. Knit to the position of the next bead.

2 On purl rows, purl to the position of the bead and slide

the bead up close to the right-hand needle, placing it on the right side of the work. Purl the next stitch as usual and purl to the position of the next bead.

Shaping and stuffing

Knitting used to be purely functional. People knitted to make clothes that were cheap and warm, or to create blankets and simple furnishings. Now the craft has gone beyond the purely practical and fashionable and all kinds of decorative items are being devised to accessorize both wardrobe and home. Some are perfectly sensible, while others are more imaginative and even border on the realms of fantasy.

Many of these objects need to be placed over a mold, or wired or stuffed to help them retain their shape. Once you know how, all the techniques are easy to do and some of the creative possibilities open to you can be seen later in the book on pp108–10, 120–1.

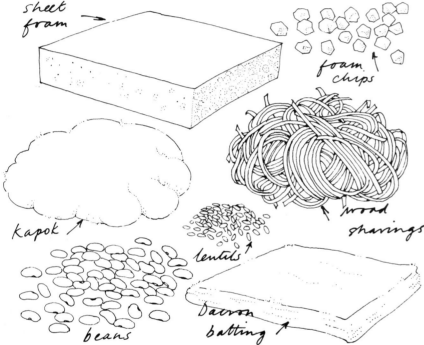

sheet foam

foam chips

wood shavings

kapok

lentils

beans

Dacron batting

Stuffings

A stuffing stick is an essential tool. Use a knitting needle, the handle of a wooden spoon or a length of doweling. Push in a small amount of stuffing at a time, pressing it in evenly and lightly. It is generally better to stuff too lightly than too hard. Foam and kapok are the two most practical and hard-wearing materials for stuffing, but there are also some others to consider.

Foam rubber This is either sold in solid blocks, sheets or as small chips. Foam rubber has the advantage of being washable and if a precise, solid shape is required it is best to get it cut professionally. Chips can be irritating to work with as the small fragments of foam tend to stick to yourself and the fabric. They are however an efficient and inexpensive method of stuffing knitted fabric.

Kapok This stuffing is easier to control than chips of foam. It molds well and is light and clean. Its main disadvantages are that it cannot be washed and that it is rather expensive.

Dacron batting Usually sold by the meter or yard in a variety of widths, this is useful for emphasizing an outline and for padding quilted articles. Cut it to the shape required and if any further stuffing is necessary, use kapok.

Wood shavings Use a combination of kapok and wood shavings to stuff large objects such as floor cushions and seating units. Wood shavings are obtainable in grades. The finest are the most suitable as they are easier to work with. Before using shavings, line the object with kapok or cotton flock. This makes the finished item softer and prevents the small pieces of wood shavings working their way out through the knitted fabric and onto the surface.

Wood shavings are dusty materials so work outside in the open air or on paper, away from drafts.

Pulses Use dried beans or lentils for small items that are required to "sit" rather than stand.

Wool scraps Use scraps of wool shredded into tiny pieces to stuff very small articles.

Papier-mâché

A papier-mâché mold produces a solid but lighter and more precise form of shaping than foam, kapok or any of the other suggested stuffings. It produces a rigid base over which knitting can be stretched. There are two methods of making papier-mâché.

Pulp papier-mâché This is easy to make and all you need is a plastic bucket, flour, water and a large quantity of torn or shredded newspapers.
1 Mix flour and water together to produce a sticky paste. As an alternative you can use wallpaper paste, which should be mixed according to the instructions supplied by the manufacturers.
2 Add the strips of newspaper to the paste, stirring and mashing it to a thick pulp. Leave it to stand for a day.
3 Mold the pulp as you would clay or plastic clay and then allow to dry out.
4 The mold is now ready to be covered with knitting.

Pulp papier-mâché

Papier-mâché over a base

You will need strips of newspaper, flour, water and clay, plastic clay or plaster of paris as a base.

1 Mold the base to shape, then oil the surface.

2 Lay strips of pasted newspaper over the entire surface until it is evenly and completely covered.

3 Repeat until several layers have been built up and there is a smooth finish.

4 Stand in a dry, warm place and allow to dry out. If using clay, try baking it in a medium hot oven, but make sure it does not burn.

5 When the papier-mâché is completely dry, remove it from the base.

6 To make a complete shape, make two halves and then assemble them together by pasting strips of newspaper over the join and allowing them to dry.

Wire

Wire is flexible and therefore useful for shaping knitted objects because it can be bent at acute angles if necessary. However, this flexibility does have disadvantages in that many finished items incorporating wire can all too easily be bent out of shape. There are three main grades of wire, fine, medium and thick. The type you choose depends on what you want to use it for.

Fine to medium wires Picture hanging and millinery wire can be used to give an object a delicate and precise shape. Fine wire has the advantage of being easy to thread through knitting and also does not show through the fabric. It can also be oversewn with embroidery thread for a neater and firmer edge.

Thick wire If you want to make a more permanent

shape, use galvanized wire, which is reasonably flexible but strong and hard enough not to bend out of shape.

On some items, you will find it practical to use wire in conjunction with another material. For example, on such things as leaves of plants, cut the shape from foam and then sew a wire of medium gauge around the edge.

Soldering If you want to attach one wire to another and twisting them together proves inadequate you will need to use a soldering iron. These are available from electrical stores and though the method may sound difficult it is in fact quite easy and safe to follow. Place a small bit of solder on the spot where a second piece of wire is to be attached. Direct the tip of the iron to solder all three together.

Plaster of paris

Plaster of paris provides an ideal support for items like plants or free-standing figures. Blocks of plaster of paris can also be carved with a chisel into shapes after they have set. They can then be filed and rubbed with sandpaper for a smooth finish.

1 Fill a plastic bucket with enough water to make a sufficient amount of plaster

for the job in hand. Add the plaster slowly and carefully until it breaks the surface of the water.

2 Mix together quickly with your hands to break any lumps and stir until the mixture is completely smooth.

3 The plaster should be thin enough to pour easily into a pot or a container suitable for a base. Use it immediately after mixing as it sets quickly.

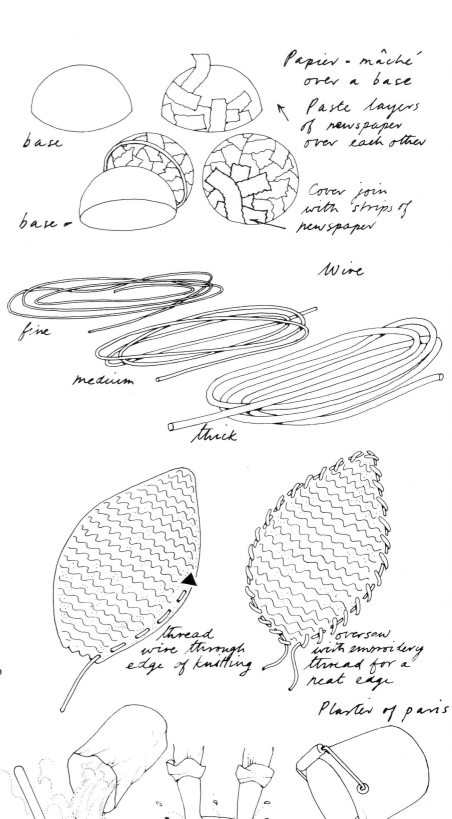

Papier-mâché over a base

Paste layers of newspaper over each other

base

base

Cover join with strips of newspaper

Wire

fine

medium

thick

thread wire through edge of knitting

oversew with embroidery thread for a neat edge

Plaster of paris

43

Embroidery

Embroidery adds an exciting, extra dimension to knitting in terms of texture, color and design. Stitches should be loose and can be used in direct contrast to the knitted fabric or in complete sympathy with the basic yarn and pattern. They can be applied in a totally free way but it is advisable to plan the position of the design before you start working. Alternatively you can work from a chart, counting the stitches and working as in counted thread embroidery. For example, if you want a regular effect in cross stitch or herringbone stitch, bring the yarn out at the beginning of a knitted stitch and take it across the required number of stitches. Likewise, count down for the required depth of the embroidery stitch and repeat across the row. It is important to remember when working from charts that are not specifically prepared for knitting that knitted stitches are not square so that the design will always come out slightly flattened. To avoid this, make a tension measurement and add extra rows of embroidery to the height as necessary.

Surface stitches

There are a large number of surface stitches from which to choose and the basic ones are often the most effective. Stitches are based on the simple techniques of running, looping and knotting and can be used to follow the line of a design, to fill in a shape or to produce random decoration. For adaptations and ideas on how to use them, refer to pp84–5 for inspiration.

Running stitch This is the easiest stitch of all and forms the basis of many others. Simply bring the needle through to the right side, carry the thread or yarn to the length of stitch required and through to the wrong side again. Remember the longer the stitch, the more likely it is to snag and catch.

Chain stitch Use for straight or curved lines, or as a filling.
1 Bring the needle through to the right side and hold the thread or yarn with your thumb. Insert the needle where it last emerged and bring it out a short way from where it entered.
2 Pull the thread or yarn through, keeping it under the needle and repeat for next stitch.

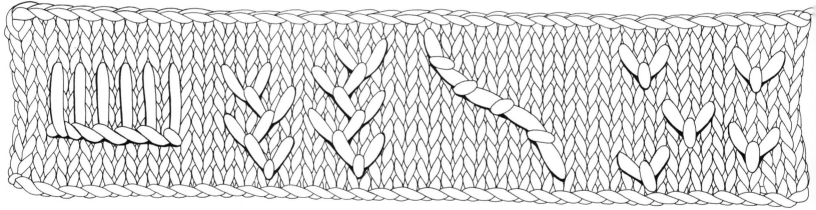

Blanket stitch Use to decorate and to neaten edges or as a surface stitch.
1 Working from left to right, with the edge facing you, insert the needle a short way away from the edge and take a straight downward stitch with the thread or yarn under the point of the needle.
2 Pull up the stitch to form a loop on the edge and repeat for the next stitch.

Feather stitch This is useful for borders or outlines and can be worked in straight or curved lines.
1 Bring the needle out at the center top of required position and hold the thread or yarn with your thumb.
2 Insert the needle a little to the right on the same level and take a small stitch down to the center, keeping the thread under the needle.
3 Insert the needle a little to the left on the same level and repeat above.
4 Continue in the same way, alternating from left to right.

Couching This stitch enables you to lay threads—even lengths of French knitting, ribbons and cords on the surface of a fabric by catching them down at regular intervals with small stitches.
1 Lay one thread on the surface of the fabric and stitch over it at intervals with another thread.
2 Continue in this manner along the thread to be couched.

Fly stitch This can be worked singly or in vertical or horizontal rows and is a most effective border stitch.
1 Bring the yarn or thread through at the top left of required position and hold it down with your thumb.
2 Insert the needle to the right of where you brought the thread through and take a small stitch down through the center with the thread or yarn below the needle.
3 Insert the needle just below the edge of the stitch and bring it through to the front to start a new stitch.

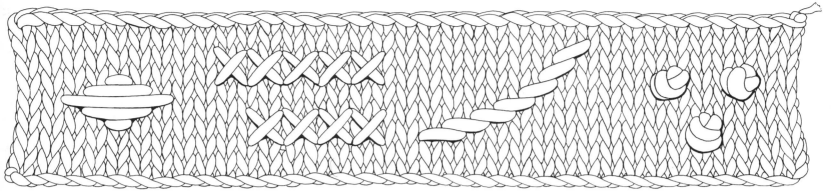

Satin stitch Use this stitch to embroider a shape of solid color. It is formed by working straight stitches parallel to one another. Keep the stitches short so that they do not pull the knitting out of shape and try to keep a hard edge.

Cross stitch This can be worked singly or in blocks to great effect.
Work a row of diagonal stitches from left to right, and complete the crosses by working diagonal stitches back across the row from right to left, always making sure that the tops of the crosses lie in the same direction.

Stem stitch Use for flower stems, to outline a shape or as a filling by working rows of stitches close together. Working from left to right, take regular slanting stitches along the line of the design. The thread or yarn should always emerge on the left side of the previous stitch.

French knot Scatter French knots at random or group them together in clusters.
1 Bring the needle out at required position and wind thread or yarn round the needle twice, or three or four times for a larger knot.
2 Holding the thread or yarn taut, reinsert the needle and pull the thread to the back.

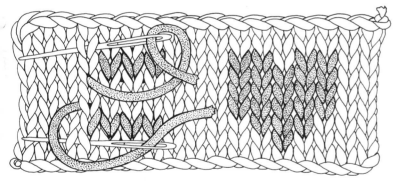
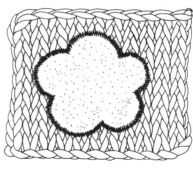

Swiss darning
This form of embroidery is an alternative to motif knitting in that a motif can be embroidered on to a plain piece of knitting to look as though it has been knitted in. It can only be worked on stockinette stitch, covers each stitch with a new color of yarn and results in a double thickness of fabric. Any yarn or embroidery thread can be used although it is advisable to use one of comparable thickness and weight to the main yarn to cover the knitted stitch completely.
1 Working from the back, insert the needle at the bottom of the stitch to be covered and pull the yarn or

thread through to the front.
2 Pass the needle from right to left under the two loops of the same stitch one row above and bring the yarn or thread through to the front.
3 Reinsert the needle into the base of the original stitch.
4 Continue working in this manner, taking care to keep the stitches at the same tension as the knitting.
5 At the end of the row insert the needle into the base of the last stitch worked and up through the center of the same stitch.
6 Insert the needle from left to right under the two loops of this stitch on the row above and continue working along the row.

Appliqué
This refers to the technique of applying one surface to another by means of machine-stitching, hand-sewing or embroidery. This means that you can decorate knitted garments and objects with shapes or designs cut from fabric, felt, fur, leather or any other suitable material. These can then be stuffed for added dimension or applied flat. By using close machine-stitching, it is also possible to cut out areas of knitting once the appliquéd shapes are securely in place. It is advisable to work small samples first to make sure that the knitted stitches will not run once they have been cut.

Quilting
Knitting can be quilted for added warmth and decorative interest. The technique involves sandwiching some form of batting which should be washable between the knitted fabric on top and a fabric lining underneath. Tack all the layers together around the edge, then along the lines or shapes to be quilted; this prevents them slipping during the quilting process. Then stitch the three layers together either by machine or by using stab stitch which is done by placing one hand above the work and the other below and by passing the needle up and down from one to the other.

45

Coping with disasters

Disasters do happen in knitting and the temptation to pull the stitches off the needle is often great. It is easy to drop a stitch or to become distracted and lose your place in a pattern. Difficulties also arise when it comes to caring for garments after they are finished. But with a little time and patience most mistakes can be rectified or avoided.

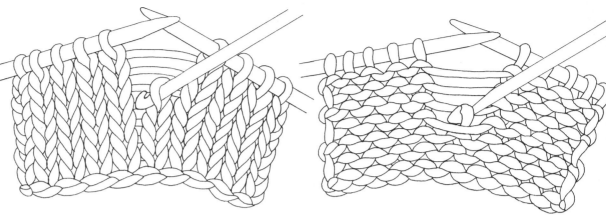

Dropped stitches

You may not realize you have dropped a stitch until you have knitted several more rows. When you are working some stitch patterns it is necessary to unpick the work only as far as the row where the accident occurred. When working really simple patterns the stitch can be picked up without undoing any knitting. A crochet hook is ideal for picking up stitches.

On a knit row When picking up stitches work with the right side facing you.
1 Insert a crochet hook from the front to the back of the dropped stitch.
2 Place the hook under the thread lying between the two stitches just above the dropped stitch and pull this thread straight through the dropped stitch.
3 Continue in this way, working upward until the dropped stitch is level with the row last worked.
4 Transfer the stitch to the left-hand needle and continue knitting in the usual way.
On a purl row The technique for picking up stitches is slightly different. Work with the wrong side facing you.
1 Insert a crochet hook into the dropped stitch, working from the back to the front.
2 Place the hook over the thread lying between the two stitches above the dropped stitch and pull it through the dropped stitch.
3 Slip the stitch onto a spare needle, remove the hook and prepare to insert it into the dropped stitch from the back to the front as before.
4 Continue working in this way until the dropped stitch is level with the last row worked.
5 Transfer the stitch to the left-hand needle and continue knitting in the usual way.

Unpicking stitches

Stitch patterns are often complicated and it sometimes happens that you end up with too few or too many stitches. To rectify the error, the work will have to be unpicked, but there is no need to pull the stitches right off the needle.
Knit stitches To take back stitches on a knit row make sure that the knit side is facing you.
1 Insert the right-hand needle into the stitch below the next stitch on the left-hand. needle, working from the front to the back.

2 Withdraw the left-hand needle from the stitch above and pull the yarn with the right hand. This will unravel the stitch, keeping the yarn at the back of the work.
3 Continue working in this way until you have unpicked the required number of stitches.
Purl stitches To take back stitches on a purl row work with the purl side facing you. Use the same method as for knit stitches but when the stitch is unravelled the yarn will be at the front of the work as opposed to the back.

Running out of yarn

Try to avoid running out of yarn in the middle of the row. It is better to join in yarn at the beginning where the end can be darned into the edge of the knitted fabric. A length of yarn about four times the width of the knitting is usually enough to complete a row. If you have underestimated the amount of yarn needed and you do not want to unpick the stitches to the beginning of the row, splice the ends of the yarn together.
Splicing This is an invisible method used for joining yarn

anywhere during a row.
1 Unravel the ends of the new and old yarn, separate the plys and cut away about half the strands.
2 Overlap the ends from opposite directions and twist them together until secure. Removing strands from the ends should ensure the thickness of the join is comparable with the rest of the yarn.
3 Splicing is not strong so knit gently until the join has been incorporated into the rest of the knitting and then trim any loose ends.

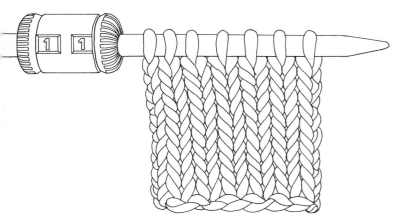

Losing track in a pattern

There are several ways of keeping your place in a pattern. Put row counters on the end of your knitting needle to keep track of the rows by the turning of a numbered dial. Alternatively, tick off each row as you go along or insert a pin in the place you have reached on the pattern if called away unexpectedly. If, despite all these tricks you still lose your place, the only thing to do is count the number of rows already worked. This is simple on a plain piece of knitting, but tricky on a complicated pattern repeat. If you lose your place within a pattern row, unpick the stitches to the beginning of the row. Take care if you have to do this on anything lacy or textured for it is often difficult to keep track of loops, eyelets, twisted stitches, and so on.

Aftercare

A symbol denoting how a yarn should be washed, pressed and dried is given on most yarn wrappers, so if you are knitting a garment with one yarn, a look at the yarn wrapper will tell you how to care for it. If a variety of yarns is being used together in one piece of knitting, aftercare becomes more of a problem. If one yarn should be dry cleaned and the other washed by hand, always dry clean. If the yarn wrapper gives no advice on aftercare, wash your tension square to see the effect that water and soap have on the yarn. Watch out for shrinkage and stretching and if you are satisfied with the results, go ahead and wash by hand. Never wash knitted fabric in hot water. Matting is one disaster that can never be rectified.

Washing Handle the knitting carefully and never lift the garment by the shoulders as the weight of the wet wool will drag the knitting out of shape. Squeeze out excess moisture gently but never wring the garment. It is important to support the overall weight with both hands and to make sure that you rinse every particle of soap out of the knitting before putting it to dry. If you do not it could cause matting.

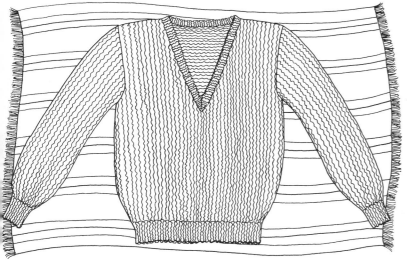

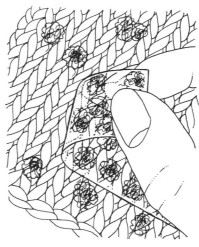

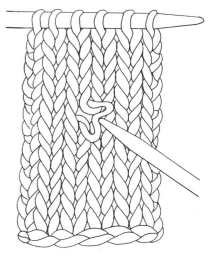

Drying Knitting should be dried away from direct heat. Dry the garment flat on a suitable surface. Spread the knitting out gently on a towel, and smooth out any creases. Leave the knitting until completely dry and then place over a line for final airing. Never hand knitting to drip dry. The weight of the wet fabric will pull the garment out of shape.

Pressing If a garment is properly dried it should not need pressing. If it does, check the instructions on the yarn wrapper and refer back to the basic finishing instructions on p26. Some yarns may need steaming or pressing over a damp cloth. Never use a heavy hand when pressing knitted garments as this could distort the shape badly, and never press ribbing.

Care in wear

It is important to look after your knitting when wearing it. Pilling and snagging often occur but they are easy and quick to remedy.

Pilling Some yarns are prone to pilling during wear. This means that loose fibers gather into balls of fluff on the surface of the knitting. These can either be picked off, brushed or combed away, or go over the surface with a strip of sellotape, sticky side down.

Snagging If a snag occurs never cut it off; if you do the whole garment will eventually unravel. Take a blunt needle and push the snag through to the wrong side of the work. Gently tighten the yarn until the stitch is the right size and then knot the end on the wrong side.

Beautiful basics

Take a few simple shapes, a range of pretty yarns in strong and pastel shades and make yourself a complete, coordinated wardrobe with a warm coat, an easy-to-wear vest and skirt with lots of texture and trimmings, a lacy frilled dress and a couple of happy-go-lucky sweaters that will see you through every occasion, formal or informal. All the patterns are based on the ideas and shapes given on pp24–5 and are quick and easy to knit. The garments are all medium sized.

Mohair coat
Knit yourself an extra warm coat in soft mohair and decorate with circular shapes of Swiss darning worked in a contrasting color or shade and then embroidered with bobbles or French knots.

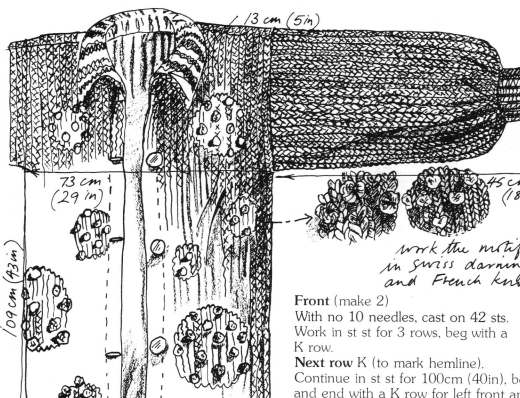

work the motif in Swiss darning and French knots

Materials
625g (25oz) mohair
1 pair no 8 (5½mm) needles
1 pair no 10 (6½mm) needles
25g (1oz) mohair in each of 4 contrasting colors for surface embroidery
5 buttons

Tension
12 sts and 15 rows to 10cm (4in) over st st on no 10 needles.

Back
With no 10 needles, cast on 90 sts.
Work in st st for 3 rows, beg with a K row.
Next row K (to mark hemline).
Continue in st st for 105cm (42in), beg with a K row.
To shape shoulders
Bind off 15 sts at beg of next 4 rows.
Bind off rem sts.

Front (make 2)
With no 10 needles, cast on 42 sts.
Work in st st for 3 rows, beg with a K row.
Next row K (to mark hemline).
Continue in st st for 100cm (40in), beg and end with a K row for left front and a P row for right front.
To shape neck
Bind off 8 sts at neck edge, then continue in st st for 5cm (2in), end at side edge.
To shape shoulder
Bind off 15 sts at beg of next and foll alt row.
Work 1 row.
Bind off.

Sleeves
With no 8 needles, cast on 30 sts.
Work in twisted rib until work measures 8cm (3in).
Change to no 10 needles.
Next row P.
Next row Inc 1 in every st across row (60 sts).
Work in st st until work measures 38cm (15in), beg with a P row.
Bind off.

Left front band
With no 8 needles, cast on 12 sts.
Work in twisted rib until work measures 98cm (39in).
Slip sts on to stitch holder.

Right front band
With no 8 needles, cast on 12 sts.
Work in twisted rib until work measures 30cm (12in).
To make buttonhole
Next row Rib 6, bind off 2 sts, rib to end.
Next row Rib 4, cast on 2 sts, rib to end.
Continue in rib making 4 more buttonholes at intervals of 14cm (6in).
Continue in rib until work measures 98cm (39in).
Slip sts on to stitch holder.

Collar
Join shoulder seams.
With no 8 needles, rib left front band sts from stitch holder, pick up and knit 56 sts from neck edge, then rib right front band sts from stitch holder (80 sts).
Work in twisted rib until work measures 13cm (5in).
Bind off.

Finishing
1 Block and press all pieces lightly over a damp cloth.
2 Match center of bound-off edge of sleeves to shoulder seam and sew sleeves in flat.
3 Join underarm and side seams as one continuous seam.
4 Fold hems along K row and slip stitch in place.
5 Sew on front bands stretching them slightly to fit.
6 Sew on buttons.
7 Work circular shapes in Swiss darning as shown on p45.
8 Decorate with small bobbles as shown on p39 or large French knots as shown on p45.

Mohair hat

Make a hat to match the coat and decorate with similar surface shapes. You can sew a pompon on the top or make a wide brim by extending the ribbing at the bottom.

Materials

50g (2oz) mohair
Scraps of mohair for surface embroidery.
1 pair no 8 (5½mm) needles
1 pair no 10 (6½mm) needles

Tension

12 sts and 15 rows to 10cm (4in) over st st on no 10 needles.

HONEYCOMB VEST

This vest is knitted in buttonhole stitch with double knitting yarn and stripes of mohair in contrasting colors. It can be decorated with beads, sequins and crystals and can be made up inside out for a stripy effect.

Materials

125g (5oz) DK in main color (A)
25g (1oz) mohair in each of 3 contrasting colors (B,C,D)
1 pair no 5 (4mm) needles
1 pair no 8 (5½mm) needles
Beads, sequins and crystals
6 buttons

Tension

40 rows and 18 sts to 10cm (4in) over buttonhole st on no 8 needles using A.

Back

With no 5 needles and A, cast on 80 sts.
Work in twisted rib as shown on p129 until work measures 9cm (3½in).
Change to no 8 needles.
Next row *P3, inc 1 purlwise; rep from * to end (100 sts).
Next row Inc 1, K to last st, inc 1.
Next row P.
Work in buttonhole st for 170 rows as shown on p141. Work 1st–5th and 11th–15th row of pattern in A and 6th–10th and 16th–20th row alternately in B, C and D.
With A, work in st st for 3 rows, beg with a P row.

With no 8 needles, cast on 76 sts.
Work in twisted rib for 2.5cm (1in).
Change to no 10 needles.
Work in st st for 9cm (3½in) beg and end with a P row.
Next row *K2, K2tog; rep from * to last 4 sts, K4 (58 sts).
Continue in st st for 2.5cm (1in).
Next row *K2, K2tog; rep from * to last 2 sts, K2 (44 sts).
Continue in st st for 2.5cm (1in).
Next row K2tog to end (22 sts).
Next row P.
Next row K2tog to end (11 sts).
Next row P.
Next row K2tog to last st, K1 (6 sts).
Break off yarn and thread through sts.

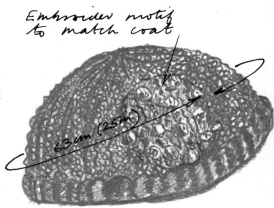

Embroider motif to match coat

Finishing

1 Join seam and sew in loose ends.
2 Embroider large circles using Swiss darning as shown on p45 and decorate with bobbles (p39) or French knots (p45).

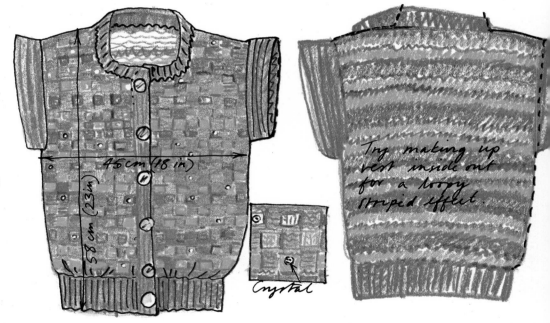

45cm (18 in)

58 cm (23in)

Crystal

Try making up vest inside out for a loopy striped effect.

Right front

**With 4mm needles and A, cast on 32 sts.
Work in twisted rib until work measures 9cm (3½in).
Change to no 8 needles.
Next row *P3, inc 1 purlwise; rep from * to end (40 sts).
Next row Inc 1, K to last st, inc 1 (42 sts).
Next row P.
Work in buttonhole st as for back for 140 rows.**
To shape neck
Next row With A, K.
Next row P.
Next row Bind off 20 sts, K to end.
Continue in buttonhole st for 27 rows, beg with 4th row of pattern.

With A, work in st st for 3 rows, beg with a P row.
Bind off.

Left front

Work as for right front from ** to **.
To shape neck
With A, work in st st for 3 rows.
Next row Bind off 20 sts, P to end.
Continue in buttonhole st for 26 rows, beg with 5th row of pattern.
With A, work in st st for 3 rows, beg with a P row.
Bind off.

Armhole band (make 2)

With no 5 needles and A, cast on 12 sts.
Work in twisted rib for 46cm (18in).
Bind off.

Thread elastic through picot hem

170 cm (67 in)

68 cm (27 in)

Stripy skirt

Make a skirt to match the vest. The pattern can be adapted to make a tiered skirt by changing to progressively smaller needles as shown on p24.

Materials

200g (8oz) DK in main color (A)
25g (1oz) mohair in each of 3 contrasting colors (B,C,D)
1 pair no 8 (5mm) needles
Elastic

Tension

18 sts and 22 rows to 10cm (4in) over st st on no 8 needles.

Main piece (make 2)

With A, cast on 150 sts.
Work in st st for 6 rows.
Picot row K1, *K2tog, yf; rep from * to last st, K1.
**With A, work in st st for 19 rows, beg with a P row.
Next row With B, K.**
Rep from ** to ** using B, C and D alternately on the single K row until work measures 68cm (27in) from picot row, end with a P row.
Next row Work picot row as above.
Work in st st for 6 rows.
Bind off.

Finishing

1 Press both pieces lightly.
2 Join side seams matching stripes.
3 Fold hems at top and bottom on picot rows and slip stitch in place.
4 Thread elastic through top hem.

Right front band

With no 5 needles and A, cast on 12 sts.
Work in twisted rib for 3 rows.
To make buttonhole
Next row Rib 6, bind off 2, rib to end.
Next row Rib 4, cast on 2, rib to end.
Continue in twisted rib making a buttonhole every 8cm (3in) until work measures 44cm (17in).
Slip sts onto stitch holder.

Left front band

With no 5 needles and A, cast on 12 sts.
Work in twisted rib until work measures 44cm (17in).
Slip sts onto stitch holder.

Neckband

Join shoulder seams.

With no 5 needles and A, rib the 12 sts from right front band stitch holder.
Pick up and knit 76 sts around neck edge, then rib 12 sts from left front band stitch holder (100 sts).
Work in twisted rib for 4cm (1½in).
Bind off.

Finishing

1 Press fronts and back.
2 Sew on armhole bands, matching center of bands to shoulder seam.
3 Join side seams.
4 Sew on front bands stretching bands slightly to fit.
5 Sew on buttons.
6 Sew beads, sequins and crystals into the "holes" formed by the buttonhole stitch pattern.

Flappy sweater

Knit a basic slash-neck sweater and turn it into something special by adding flaps and sequins. Make the flaps separately and sew them on afterwards as it is sometimes difficult to know where to place them as you knit.

Materials

About 300g (12oz) mohair
1 pair no 8 (5½mm) needles
1 pair no 10½ (7mm) needles

Tension

16 sts and 20 rows to 10cm (4in) over st st on no 10½ needles.

Back and front (alike)

With no 8 needles, cast on 60 sts.
Work in twisted rib as shown on p129 for 8cm (3in).
Change to no 10½ needles.
Next row P.
Next row K, inc 1 in every 4th st (75 sts).
Work in st st for 46cm (18in).
Change to no 8 needles.
Work in twisted rib for 5cm (2in).
Bind off.

Sleeves

With no 8 needles, cast on 30 sts.
Work in twisted rib for 8cm (3in).
Change to no 10½ needles.
Next row P.
Next row K, inc 1 in every st across row (60 sts).
Work in st st for 43cm (17in).
Bind off.

Flaps

These can be of any size or shape. Make them by casting on any number of stitches and increase or decrease as required. The shapes can then be beaded or embroidered.

Finishing

1 Darn in all loose ends neatly and press all pieces on the wrong side.
2 Sew together 13cm (5in) at each side for shoulder seams.
3 Matching center of sleeve to shoulder seam, sew sleeves in flat.
4 Sew underarm and side seams as one continuous seam.
5 Sew on flaps.
6 Press all seams lightly on wrong side of garment.

Some ideas for decorating flaps

Try buttons and beads

Make flaps in any size or shape and sew on afterwards

51cm (20in)

59cm (23in)

48cm (19in)

Lacy dress

This lacy dress is knitted in four pieces in traveling vine stitch. The top edge is folded over to form a collar and threaded with ribbon.

Materials

575g (23oz) mohair
1 pair no 8 (5½mm) needles
1 pair no 10½ (7mm) needles
1m (1yd) ribbon
Beads, sequins or crystals

Tension

12 sts and 14 rows to 10cm (4in) over st st on no 10½ needles.

Main piece (make 2)

With no 10½ needles, cast on 84 sts.
Work in st st for 3 rows, beg with a K row.
Next row K (hemline row).
Work in st st for 2 rows, beg with a K row.
Work in traveling vine pattern as shown on p139.
Rep 1st–12th row of pattern 14 times.
Continue in st st until work measures 114cm (45in) from hemline row, beg with a K row and end with a P row.
Next row K1, *yf, K2tog; rep from * to last st, K1.
Next row *P2, inc 1 purlwise; rep from * to end (112 sts).
Continue in st st for 8cm (3in), beg and end with a K row.
Next row K1, *yf, K2tog; rep from * to last st, K1.
Next row P.
Next row K2, *yf, K2tog; rep from * to end.
Next row P.
Rep last 4 rows 6 times.
Next row P.
Continue in rev st st for 8cm (3in), beg with a K row.
Bind off.

Sleeves

With no 8 needles, cast on 30 sts.
Work in twisted rib as shown on p129 until work measures 8cm (3in).
Change to no 10½ needles.
Next row P.
Next row Inc 1 in every st across row. (60 sts).
Next row P.
Work in traveling vine pattern, rep

1st–12th rows of pattern 5 times.
Work in st st until work measures 53cm (22in), beg with a K row.
Bind off.

Finishing

1 Press all pieces lightly over a damp cloth.
2 Join front and back collar at side seams.
3 Sew sleeves in flat, matching center of bound-off edge of sleeve to shoulder point (collar side seam).
4 Join side and underarm seams in one continuous seam.
5 Fold hem along hemline row and sew in place.
6 Thread ribbon through eyelet holes at neck edge.
7 Decorate dress with beads and sequins.

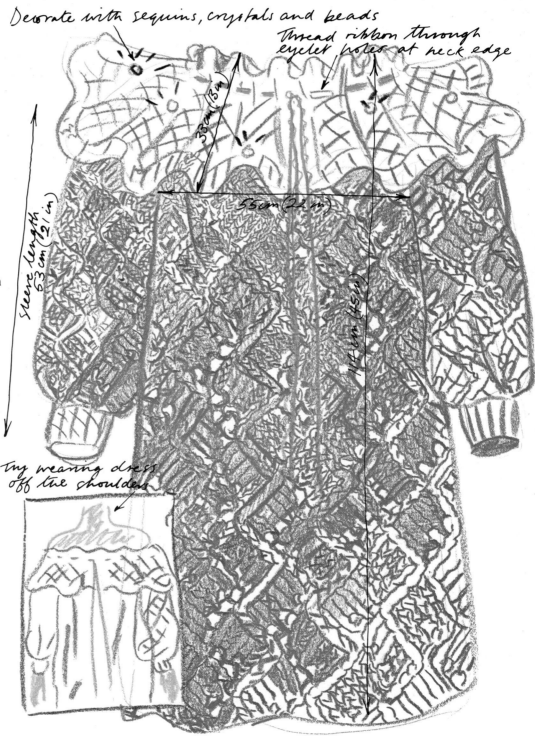

Decorate with sequins, crystals and beads

Thread ribbon through eyelet holes at neck edge

35cm (13in)

55cm (22in)

Sleeve length 53cm (21in)

114cm (45in)

Try wearing dress off the shoulders

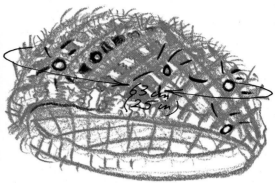

Lacy hat

This hat, designed to match the dress, is knitted with mohair in reverse stockinette stitch and a simple lacy stitch.

Materials

50g (2oz) mohair
1 pair no 8 (5½mm) needles
1 pair no 10½ (7mm) needles
Beads, sequins or crystals

Tension

12 sts and 14 rows to 10cm (4in) over st st on no 10½ needles.

With no 8 needles, cast on 76 sts.
Work in twisted rib as shown on p129 until work measures 2.5cm (1in).
Change to no 10½ needles.
Work in rev st st for 2 rows, beg with a P row.
Next row K1, *yf, K2tog; rep from * to last st, K1.
Next row P.
Next row K2, *yf, K2tog; rep from *.
Next row P.
Rep last 4 rows 3 times.
Next row P.
Next row *K2, K2tog; rep from * to last 4 sts, K4 (58 sts).
Continue in rev st st for 2.5cm (1in), beg and end with a P row.
Next row *K2, K2tog; rep from * to last 2 sts, K2 (44 sts).
Continue in rev st st for 2.5cm (1in), beg and end with a P row.
Next row K2tog to end (22 sts).
Next row P.
Next row K2tog to end (11 sts).
Next row P.
Next row K2tog to last st, K1 (6 sts).
Break off yarn and thread through sts.

Finishing

1 Join side seam and sew in loose ends.
2 Decorate with beads and sequins.

Forget-me-not bikini

Three simple flowers scattered strategically form the basis of this tiny bikini. The top consists of two six-petaled flowers wired for shape and lined for comfort; if the idea of wire does not appeal, a little padding will achieve the same effect. Their stems have been anchored safely to the bottom half. The bikini will fit small sizes but can easily be made larger by working more increases and decreases on the petals and creating additional ties wherever necessary. This bikini has been worked in garter stitch with the yarn doubled throughout—if you want to substitute stitches or yarns remember that the success of the garment depends on creating a relatively firm fabric. Alternatively you could make the top based on the poppy pattern on p110, lining and wiring the petals and attaching them with thin strands of French knitting as shown on p38.

13 cm (5 in) wire the petals and line with felt

back view

Materials
100g (4oz) metallic yarn in main color (A)
50g (2oz) in each of 2 contrast colors (B and C)
1 pair no 3 (3¼mm) needles
0.5m (½yd) felt
Thick fuse wire
Beads and artificial flower stamens

Tension
25 sts and 50 rows to 10cm (4in) over g st on no 3 needles using yarn double.

Top
Flower centers (make 2)
With B doubled, cast on 6 sts.
1st row K.
2nd–7th row Work in g st, inc 1 at beg of each row (12 sts).
8th row K.
9th–14th row Work in g st, dec 1 at beg of each row (6 sts).
15th row K.
Bind off.

Petals (make 12)
*With A doubled, pick up 6 sts on one side of flower center.
1st–4th row Work in g st.
5th row K2, (inc 1) twice, K2.
6th row and all other alt rows K.
7th row K3, (inc 1) twice, K3.
9th row K4, (inc 1) twice, K4.
11th row K5, (inc 1) twice, K5.
13th row K6, (inc 1) twice, K6.
15th row K7, (inc 1) twice, K7.
17th row K9, m1, K9.
19th row K9, inc 1, K9 (20 sts).
20th row K.
Bind off.*
Rep from * to * on all sides of flower centers to make 6 petals around each.

Bottom
With A doubled, cast on 54 sts and start at back.
1st–10th row Work in g st.
11th–54th row Work in g st, dec 1 at beg of each row (10 sts).
Continue in g st for 22 rows.
Continue in g st, inc 1 at beg of next 12 rows.
Continue in g st, dec 1 at beg of next 12 rows.
Next row K.
Bind off.

Petals (make 3)
**With A doubled, pick up 8 sts on one side of front (right dec edge).
1st–4th row Work in g st.
5th row K3, (inc 1) twice, K3.
6th row and every foll alt row K.
7th row K4, (inc 1) twice, K4.
9th row K5, (inc 1) twice, K5.
11th row K6, (inc 1) twice, K6.
13th row K7, (inc 1) twice, K7.
15th row K8, (inc 1) twice, K8.
17th row K9, (inc 1) twice, K9.
19th row K10, (inc 1) twice, K10.
21st row K12, m1, K12.
23rd row K12, inc 1, K12.

25th row K13, m1, K13 (27 sts).
26th row K.
Bind off.**
Rep from ** to ** on rem two sides of front (bound-off sts and left dec edge).

Finishing
1 Press all pieces with a cool iron.
2 With C, make four twisted cords about 50cm (20in) long as shown on p36. Attach them to center of top petal and at join of two petals at one side of flowers.
3 With C, make two cords about 15cm (6in) long and attach to join of petals at other side of flowers. Tie two short cords

together to join both halves of bikini top.
4 With A, make four cords about 33cm (13in) long. Attach one pair to each side of back.
5 With C, make two cords about 33cm (13in) long. Attach one end of each cord to center front of bottom and the other ends to center of bottom petal at lower edges of bikini top.
6 Embroider stamens on each flower petal and front of bottom and decorate with beads and artificial stamens.
7 To make lining for bikini top, cut two flower shapes in felt using knitted flowers as pattern.

8 Cut six pieces of fuse wire about 15cm (6in) long, three for each flower. Lay wire on back of flower as shown.
9 Bend over wire ends and sew to petal tips. Bind center join of wire pieces with thread and attach to back of flower center. Oversew wire in position.
10 Lay felt lining over backs of flowers and oversew around edges. Then mold flowers into required shape.

Ragbag top

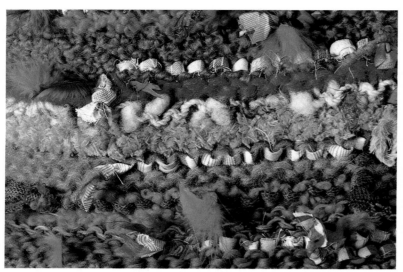

Let your imagination run wild and make this ragbag top, using up any scraps of fabric and leftover lengths of yarn. The effect will be random and personal but if it is to work well, plan ahead carefully. Collect all your materials together: color and texture themes will suggest themselves and your selection will emphasize these. Unless you particularly want an uneven texture it is advisable to aim for a fairly constant weight in your yarns. Bulky wools are ideal or you can work with two or more strands of a thinner yarn. When working with fabrics stick to cotton ones that are not too heavy. Cut the fabric into strips, about 2.5cm (1in) wide and use these on their own or twisted in with other yarns. Push all the knots through to one side of the work and you have the choice of wearing it rough or smooth side out. The garment will fit most sizes.

Materials
About 400g (16oz) assorted yarns and strips of fabric
1 pair no 7 (5mm) needles
1 pair no 15 (9mm) needles
Beads

Tension
You will have to work this out according to the fabrics and yarns you decide to use.

Back
With no 7 needles and DK doubled, cast on 68 sts.
Work in K1, P1 rib for about 4cm (1½in). Change to no 15 needles and use bulky yarns and fabric strips twisted together.
Next row (K2tog, K1) to last 2 sts, K2tog (45 sts).
Work in g st for about 43cm (17in), changing yarn and materials as often as possible.
To shape shoulders
Bind off 4 sts at beg of next 6 rows.
Bind off rem 21 sts.

Front
Work as back for 29cm (11½in), continuing to change colors as required but not necessarily matching up stripes with back.
Divide for neck
Next row K22 and leave on spare needle or stitch holder, bind off 1, K to end.
Work straight on 22 sts until same length as back, end at inner edge.
To shape neck and shoulders
Bind off 10 sts at beg of next row, then 4 sts at beg of next and foll 2 alt rows. Work other side to match, reversing all shaping.

Finishing
1 Put smooth sides together and join side and shoulder seams about 1cm (½in) from the edge.
2 Make two braided cords as shown on p36, sew beads on to the ends and attach to neck edges.

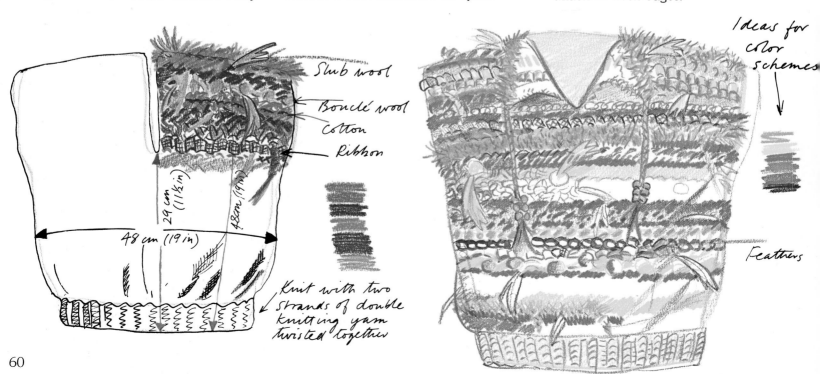

Slub wool

Bouclé wool

Cotton

Ribbon

29 cm (11½in)

48cm (19in)

48 cm (19 in)

Knit with two strands of double knitting yarn twisted together

Ideas for color schemes

Feathers

Clowning with color

This balloon dress and dungarees lend themselves to a free and easy way of working and can be made as subtle or as dazzling as you like. Much of the pleasure to be gained from knitting comes from the tremendous potential for working with color. Yarns come in such a wide range of beautiful colors that almost any scheme can be satisfied. If you cannot find the shade you want, buy white or natural colored yarn and dye it to your own specification as some of the yarns here have been. The information on pp82–3 tells you how to use chemical and vegetable dyes. You do not even have to decide in advance which colors you are going to use. Just join in a new one as the mood takes you.

Balloon dress
The body is made up of eight large triangles knitted sideways, four on the front and four on the back. Each may be divided into stripes by joining in a new color whenever you please. The sleeves and yoke are also knitted sideways in stripes of varying width and hues.

Materials
125g (5oz) brushed mohair in each of 6 contrasting colors
1 pair no 4 (3¾mm) needles
1 pair no 6 (4½mm) needles
1 no 4 (3¾mm) circular needle

Tension
18 sts and 28 rows to 10cm (4in) over st st on no 6 needles.

Body
With no 6 needles and 1st color (A), cast on 100 sts.
*Work in st st for 2 rows.
Next row With 2nd color (B), K2, K to end in A.
Next row P98A, P2B.
Next row K4B, K96A.
Next row P96A, P4B.
Continue dec the A sts by 2 and inc the B sts by 2 on every alt row until all sts are in B*.
Using different colors, rep from * to * 3 times.
Bind off.

Sleeves and yoke
With no 4 needles, cast on 48 sts.
Work in K2, P2 rib for 15 rows.
Next row P twice into each st (96 sts).
Change to no 6 needles.
Work in st st until work measures 78cm (31in) from beg, end with a P row.
Divide for neck
Next row K48, bind off rem 48 sts.
Next row Cast on 48 sts, P across 96 sts.

Work in st st for same length as first sleeve, end with a P row.
Change to no 4 needles.
Next row K2tog to end.
Work in K2, P2 rib for 15 rows.
Bind off.

Neckband
With no 4 needles, pick up 88 sts around neck edge.
Work in K2, P2 rib for 6 rows.
Bind off.

Welt
With a no 4 circular needle, pick up 400 sts around bottom edge of body.
Work in K2, P2 rib for 6 rows.
Bind off.

Clowning with color

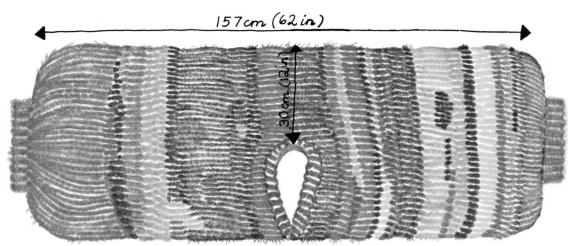

157cm (62in)

30cm (12in)

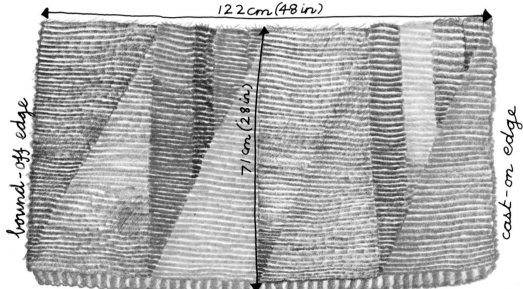

122cm (48in)

bound-off edge

71cm (28in)

cast-on edge

Finishing

1 Fold body in half and join side seam.
2 Fold sleeves and yoke lengthwise. Place so that divide for lower neck edge matches center front of body and join back and front yoke seams.
3 Join sleeve seams.
4 Overlap ends of neck edge and sew down.
5 Press seams and embroider dots here and there as required.

Dungarees

The trousers are made up of eight strips of fabric, four to each leg. Four are straight and four are shaped to fit inside the leg. The bib is gathered at the top.

Materials

450g (18oz) cotton/rayon gimp in a selection of bright colors
1 pair no 0 (2¼mm) needles
Elastic

Tension

30 sts and 40 rows to 10cm (4in) over st st on no 0 needles.

Left inner front strip

Cast on 30 sts and beg at waist edge.
1st–86th row Work in st st.
87th row Inc 1, K to end.
88th–92nd row Work in st st.

93rd row Cast on 2, K to end.
94th–96th row Work in st st.
97th row As 93rd row.
98th–105th row Rep 94th–97th row twice.
106th row P.
107th row Cast on 3, K to end.
108th row P.
109th row Cast on 4, K to end.
110th row P.
111th row As 109th row.
Work in st st without shaping until work measures 100cm (40in) from beg. Bind off.

Right inner front strip

Work as for left inner front strip but reverse all shapings.

Right inner back strip

Cast on 30 sts and beg at waist edge.

1st–104th row Work in st st.
105th row Inc 1, K to end.
106th–110th row Work in st st.
111th row Cast on 2, K to end.
112th–114th row Work in st st.
115th row As 111th row.
116th–118th row Work in st st.
119th row As 111th row.
120th row P.
121st–126th row Rep 119th–120th row 3 times.
127th row Cast on 3, K to end.
128th row P.
129th row Cast on 4, K to end.
Work in st st without shaping until work measures 100cm (40in) from beg. Bind off.

Left inner back strip

Work as for right inner back strip but reverse all shapings.

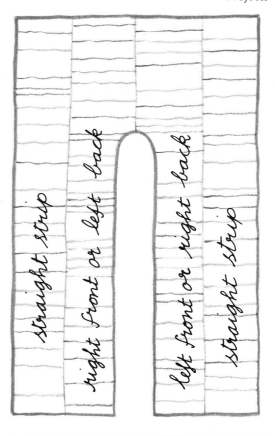

thread long cord through bib hem

back of bib

hem inside waist for elastic

Straight strip (make 4)
Cast on 50 sts.
Work in st st for 100cm (40in).
Bind off.

Bib strip (make 2)
Cast on 50 sts.
Work in st st for 110 rows.
Bind off.

Ankle cuff (make 2)
Cast on 32 sts.
Work in st st for 170 rows.
Bind off.

Finishing
1 Make three braided cords, two 30cm (12in) long and one 180cm (72in) long following instructions on p36.
2 Press strips on wrong side.
3 Join strips as shown and join side seams to complete trousers. Turn under a 2.5cm (1in) hem around waist and gather bottom edges of trouser legs to width of about 40cm (16in).
4 Fold ankle cuffs in half lengthwise and sew to bottom edges of trousers.
5 Join bib strips together to form a square and sew to center front of trousers along hem-stitching.
6 Turn under a 2.5cm (1in) hem along top of bib. Thread long cord through bib hem so that it is centrally placed. Stitch it in position at center seam of bib.
7 Gather bib top to width of about 20cm (8in) and sew cord in place at top corners of bib.
8 Attach short cords about halfway down either side of bib top.
9 Thread elastic through waist hem of trousers and adjust to fit. Press seams.

straight strip

right front or left back

left front or right back

straight strip

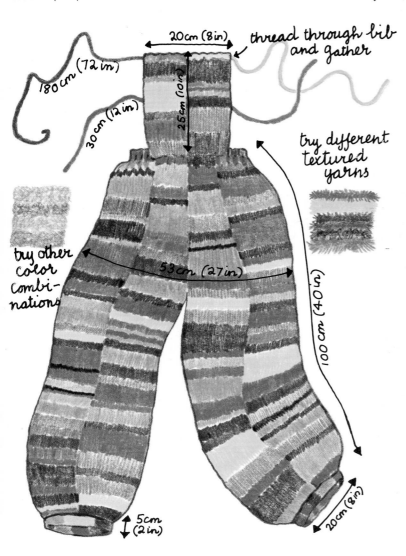

20cm (8in)
thread through bib and gather
180cm (72in)
30cm (12in)
25cm (10in)
try different textured yarns
try other color combinations
53cm (27in)
100cm (40in)
20cm (8in)
5cm (2in)

Winged traveler

Take off in any direction in a beautiful batwing jacket worked in a rainbow of colors. Alternate bands of stockinette stitch and reversed stockinette stitch, in single and double yarn respectively, form the ridges. A stripe of color consists of a band of each. Pastel colors have been chosen here, but it would look equally good in a bolder combination. Ties can be made by attaching braided cords with colorful pompons at the ends. The jacket is knitted in one piece and will fit most sizes. Just start knitting on straight needles and change to circular needles as the number of stitches increases.

Materials
200g (8oz) mohair and acrylic mixture in each of 5 colours
1 pair no 5 (4mm) needles
1 pair no 8 (5½mm) needles
1 no 5 (4mm) circular needle 100cm (40in) long
1 no 8 (5½mm) circular needle 100cm (40in) long
3 buttons

Tension
14 sts and 20 rows to 10cm (4in) over st st on no 8 needles using yarn double.

Main piece
With no 8 needles and double yarn, cast on 26 sts and start at right sleeve edge.
1st–5th row Work in rev st st, beg with a P row.
6th row K, working 3 times into first and last st.
7th row With single yarn, K.
8th row P.
9th row Change color and with double yarn K, working 3 times into first and last st.
10th–13th row Work in rev st st, beg with a K row.
14th row As 6th row.
15th–16th row As 7th–8th row. Rep 9th–16th row until 16 stripes of color have been worked.
*****Next row** Change color and with double yarn K, working 4 times into first and last st.
Next row K.
Next row P.
Rep last 2 rows twice.
Next row K, working 4 times into first and last st.
Next row Change to single yarn and K.
Next row P.*
Rep from * to * 3 times (198 sts).
Rep from * to * 4 more times without shaping.
Sl first 99 sts on to spare needle to divide for neck.

Rejoin yarn and continue on rem 99 sts for back.
Rep from * to * 5 times without shaping. Break off yarn.
For second sleeve, reverse colors to match first sleeve and with single yarn cast on 99 sts, joining first st on to last row of knitting.
With double yarn, rep from * to * across all 198 sts 4 times without shaping.
******Next row** Change color and with double yarn (K2tog) 3 times, K to last 6 sts, (K2tog) 3 times.
Next row K.
Next row P.
Rep last 2 rows twice.
Next row (K2tog) 3 times, K to last 6 sts, (K2tog) 3 times.
Next row Change to single yarn and K.
Next row P.**
Rep from ** to ** 3 times.
*******Next row** Change color and with double yarn (K2tog) twice, K to last 4 sts, (K2tog) twice.
Next row K.
Next row P.
Rep last 2 rows once.
Next row (K2tog) twice, K to last 4 sts, (K2tog) twice.
Next row Change to single yarn and K.
Next row P.***
Rep from *** to *** 14 times.
Next row Change color and with double yarn (K2tog) twice, K to last 4 sts, (K2tog) twice (26 sts).
Work in rev st st for 5 rows, beg with a K row.
Bind off.

Waistband
With no 5 needles and double yarn, cast on 14 sts.
Work in g st for 8 rows in each color, match sequence of colors in main piece.
Bind off.

Front band
Join sleeve seams and sew on waistband. With right side facing, using no 5 circular needle and double yarn pick up 14 sts from band, 99 sts from one front, 20 sts along back neck, 99 sts along second front and 14 sts from band.
1st–3rd row K.
4th row *K2, bind off 2 sts; rep from * twice, K to end.
5th row K to top buttonhole, *cast on 2 sts, K2; rep from * twice.

6th–7th row K.
Bind off.

Finishing

1 Darn in all ends neatly and lightly press on wrong side.
2 Sew three buttons on bottom of left band.
3 Make two braided cords and two pompons as shown on pp36–7.
4 Stitch a pompon to one end of each cord and sew the other ends to front bands.

part of sleeve after it is made up

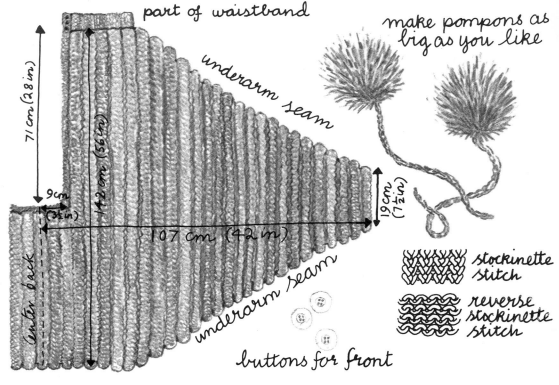

part of waistband

underarm seam

make pompons as big as you like

71 cm (28 in)

142 cm (56 in)

9 cm (3½ in)

107 cm (42 in)

19 cm (7½ in)

center back

underarm seam

buttons for front

stockinette stitch

reverse stockinette stitch

Winter warmers

Beat the blizzard with a colorful set of winter warmers. Combine color and texture to make a festive sweater with plenty of insulation. Then match it with hat, scarf and gloves scattered with vibrant flashes and stripes. The plain background is knitted in moss stitch with stockinette stitch highlights in carnival colors. They are worked in double knitting yarn with minimal shaping, which makes for speed and simplicity. See suggestions here for colors and shapes, but anything is possible and you will probably want to choose your own. All items will fit small to medium sizes and see pp34–5 for how to make bobbins for working with several colors within a row.

Materials
Sweater 450g (18oz) DK in main color (M)
25g (1oz) DK in each of 8 contrast colors (C=change contrast color)
1 pair no 6 (4½mm) needles
1 pair no 9 (6mm) needles
Hat 25g (1oz) DK in main color (M)
25g (1oz) DK in each of 8 contrast colors or remnants from sweater (C=change contrast color)
1 pair no 6 (4½mm) needles
1 pair no 9 (6mm) needles
Scarf 125g (5oz) DK in main color (M)
25g (1oz) DK in each of 8 contrast colors or remnants from sweater (C=change contrast color)
1 pair no 9 (6mm) needles
Gloves 75g (3oz) DK in main color (M)
25g (1oz) DK in each of 8 contrast colors or remnants from sweater (C=change contrast color)
1 pair no 3 (3¼mm) needles

Tension
16 sts and 27 rows to 10cm (4in) over moss st on no 9 needles.

Back
With no 6 needles and M, cast on 70 sts.
1st–19th row Work in K1, P1 rib.
20th row Work in rib, inc 1 in 3rd and every foll alt st to end 104 sts.
Change to no 9 needles.
21st–30th row Work in moss st as shown on p128.

31st row Moss st 14M, K8C, K8C, moss st 14M, K8C, K8C, moss st 14M, K8C, K8C, moss st 14M.
32nd row Moss st 14M, P8C, P8C, moss st 14M, P8C, P8C, moss st 14M, P8C, P8C, moss st 14M.
33rd–38th row Rep 31st–32nd row 3 times.
39th–46th row Change blocks of contrast colors and rep 31st–32nd row 4 more times.
47th row With M, moss st 14, (K16, moss st 14) 3 times.
48th–56th row Work in moss st.
57th row Moss st 29M, K8C, K8C, moss st 14M, K8C, K8C, moss st 29M.
58th row Moss st 29M, P8C, P8C, moss st 14M, P8C, P8C, moss st 29M.
59th–64th row Rep 57th–58th row 3 times.
65th–72nd row Change blocks of contrast colors and rep 47th–58th row 4 more times.
73rd row With M, moss st 29, K16, moss st 14, K16, moss st 29.
74th–82nd row Work in moss st.
83rd–98th row As 31st–46th row.
99th row As 47th row.
100th–138th row Work in moss st.
To shape neck
139th row Moss st 37, bind off 30, moss st 37.
140th–141st row Work in moss st, knitting each side separately.
To shape shoulders
142nd row Bind off 9 sts, work in moss st to end.
143rd row Work in moss st.
144th–147th row Rep 142nd–143rd row twice.
Bind off rem 10 sts.
Rejoin yarn at neck edge and rep shaping in reverse for the second shoulder.

Front
With no 6 needles and M, cast on 70 sts.
1st–99th row Work as for back.
100th–118th row Work in moss st.
To shape neck
119th row Moss st 37, bind off 30, moss st 37.
120th–141st row Work in moss st, knitting each side separately.
To shape shoulders
Work as for back from 142nd row to end.

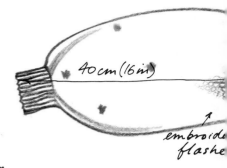

40cm (16in)

embroide flashe

Collar
With no 9 needles and M, cast on 30 sts.
1st–32nd row Work in moss st.
33rd row Work in moss st to last 4 sts, turn.
34th–36th row Work in moss st.
37th–48th row Rep 33rd–36th row 3 times.
49th–94th row Work in moss st.
95th–110th row Rep 33rd–36th row 4 times.
111th–142nd row Work in moss st. Bind off.

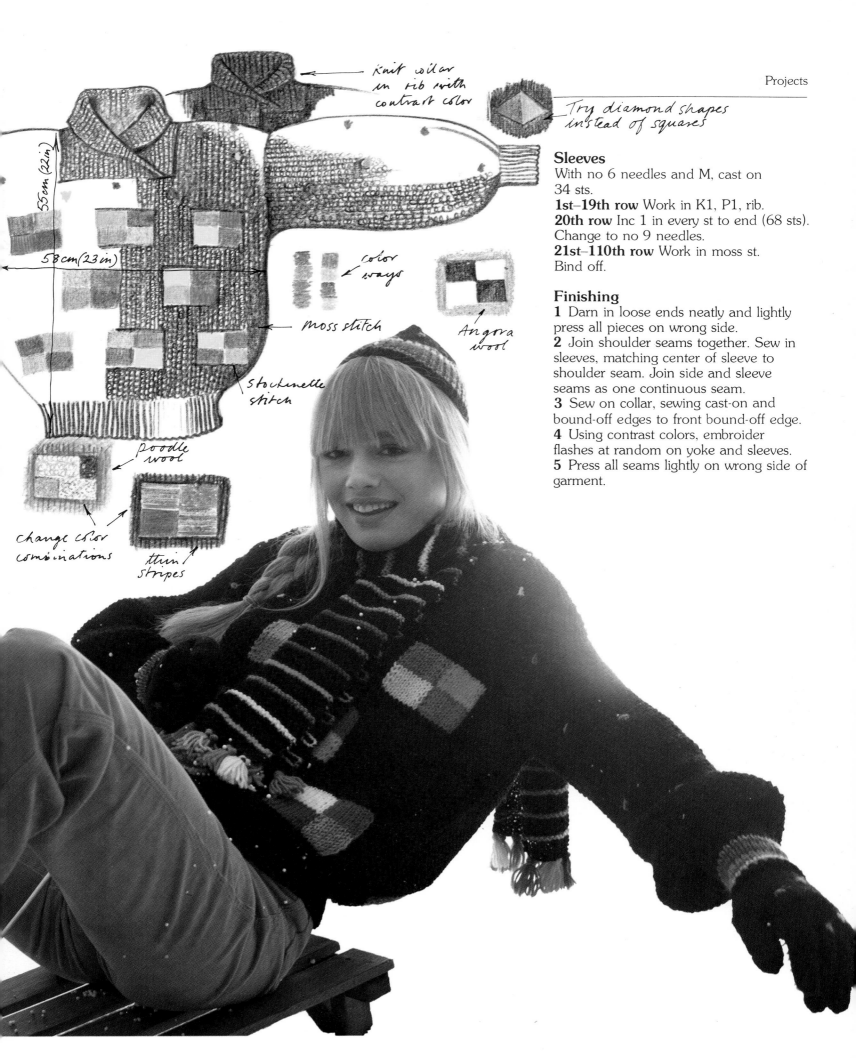

knit collar in rib with contrast color

Try diamond shapes instead of squares

55 cm (22 in)

58 cm (23 in)

color ways

moss stitch

Angora wool

stockinette stitch

poodle wool

change color combinations

thin stripes

Sleeves

With no 6 needles and M, cast on 34 sts.
1st–19th row Work in K1, P1, rib.
20th row Inc 1 in every st to end (68 sts).
Change to no 9 needles.
21st–110th row Work in moss st.
Bind off.

Finishing

1 Darn in loose ends neatly and lightly press all pieces on wrong side.
2 Join shoulder seams together. Sew in sleeves, matching center of sleeve to shoulder seam. Join side and sleeve seams as one continuous seam.
3 Sew on collar, sewing cast-on and bound-off edges to front bound-off edge.
4 Using contrast colors, embroider flashes at random on yoke and sleeves.
5 Press all seams lightly on wrong side of garment.

Gloves
Right glove
With no 3 needles and M, cast on
48 sts.
1st–2nd row Work in K1, P1 rib.
3rd–22nd row Continue in rib, working 2
rows in each of the contrast colors in
same sequence as on scarf, then 4 rows
in M.
Continue in M throughout.
23rd–26th row Work in st st.
27th row K24, inc 1, K1, inc 1, K21.
28th–30th row Work in st st.
31st row K24, inc 1, K3, inc 1, K21.
32nd–43rd row Continue to shape
thumb, inc 1 at each side of gusset
every 4th row, until there are 58 sts.
44th–46th row Work in st st.
Thumb
47th row K38, turn leaving rem sts on
stitch holder, cast on 2 sts.
48th row P16, turn leaving rem sts on
stitch holder, cast on 2 sts (18 sts).
49th–70th row Work in st st.
71st row *K2tog, K2 ; rep from * to last
2 sts, K2.

72nd row P.
73rd row K2tog to last st, K1.
Break off wool and thread through rem
sts. Draw up and fasten off.
With right-hand needle knit up 4 sts at
base of thumb. Pick up the sts from the
first stitch holder with the left-hand
needle, K to end.
Next row P across these sts and the sts
from the second stitch holder (48 sts).
Work in st st for 16 rows.
1st finger
Next row K31, turn, leaving rem sts on
stitch holder, cast on 1 st.
Next row P15, turn, leaving rem sts on
stitch holder, cast on 1 st. Work in st st
for 20 rows on these 16 sts.
****Next row** *K2tog, K2; rep from * to end.
Next row P.
Next row K2tog to end.
Break off yarn and finish as for thumb **
2nd finger
With right-hand needle knit up 2 sts at
base of 1st finger and knit across 6 sts
from first stitch holder, turn and cast on
1 st.

Next row P across these 9 sts and 6 sts
from the second stitch holder, turn and
cast on 1 st. Work in st st for 24 rows on
these 16 sts.
Rep from ** to ** and finish as for 1st
finger.
3rd finger
Work as for 2nd finger but work 20 rows
instead of 24.
4th finger
With right-hand needle knit up 2 sts at
base of 3rd finger and across rem 5 sts
from first stitch holder.
Next row Purl across these 7 sts and rem
5 sts from second stitch holder.
Work in st st for 16 rows on these 12 sts.
Next row *K2, K2tog; rep from * to end.
Next row P.
Next row K2tog to last st, K1.
Finish as for thumb.

Left glove
1st–26th row Work as for right glove.
27th row K21, inc 1, K1, inc 1, K24.
28th–30th row Work in st st.
31st row K21, inc 1, K3, inc 1, K24.

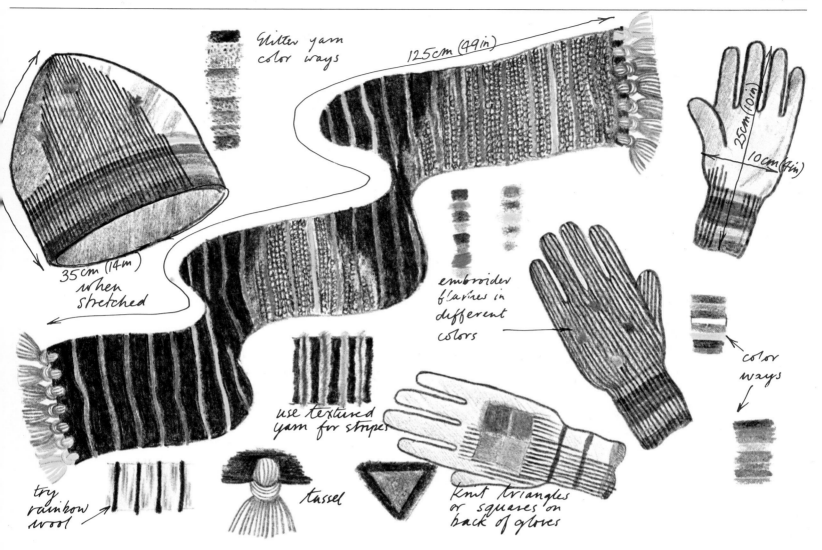

Glitter yarn color ways

125cm (49in)

35cm (14in) when stretched

embroider flashes in different colors

color ways

use textured yarn for stripes

try rainbow wool

tassel

knit triangles or squares on back of gloves

32nd–46th row Work as for right glove.
47th row K34, turn leaving rem sts on stitch holder, cast on 2 sts.
Finish thumb and fingers as for right glove.

Finishing

1 Darn all ends in neatly and lightly press on wrong side, omitting ribbing.
2 Using contrast colors, embroider flashes on back of each glove.
3 Join side seams and, avoiding ribbing, press seams.

Hat

With no 6 needles and M, cast on 91 sts.
1st–3rd row With M, work in K1, P1 rib, beg 2nd and every alt row with P1.
4th–20th row Continue in K1, P1 rib, working 2 rows in each of the contrast colors in same sequence as on scarf, and then 1 row in M.
Change to no 9 needles.
21st row *K8, K2tog; rep from * to last st, K1.

22nd row P.
23rd row *K7, K2tog; rep from * to last st, K1.
24th row P.
25th row *K6, K2tog; rep from * to last st, K1.
Continue in this way, working 1 st less between the dec sts on every alt row until 19 sts rem, end with a P row.
Next row K2tog to last st, K1.
Next row P.
Next row K2tog to end.
Next row P.
Next row K1, K3tog, K1.
Next row P3tog.
Fasten off.

Finishing

1 Darn in all loose ends neatly and lightly press on wrong side, omitting ribbing.
2 Join seam and, using contrast colors, embroider flashes or decorative motifs at random.
3 Press seam lightly on wrong wide, avoiding ribbing.

Scarf

With no 9 needles and M, cast on 41 sts.
1st–6th row Work in moss st.
7th–8th row With C, K.
9th row With M, K.
10th–14th row With M, work in moss st.
15th–16th row With C, K.
Rep 9th–16th row 6 times using a different contrast color each time.
Rep 7th–16th row 4 times keeping the same rotation of colors.
With M, work in moss st for 6 rows.
Bind off.

Finishing

1 Darn in all loose ends neatly and lightly press on wrong side.
2 With contrast colors, make tassels as shown on pp36–7 and attach to ends of scarf.

Nightline

After dark the mood changes from work to play and so do the clothes. Knit basic shapes in stunning materials to shine and shimmer through the night. These clothes, a waistcoat striped with metallic yarn, an evening dress or a glittering evening top, show how simple knitting can be put to dazzling effect. Choose sparkling metallic yarns for greatest impact or plain black for wicked good taste, and decorate with sequins. beads, feathers and anything else you can think of. Or you could work any number of variations to produce a sophisticated cotton sundress or a warm woollen waistcoat. You can also knit all your own accessories – see pp126–7 for knitted lipsticks, cigarettes and other ideas.

Top and armbands

Knitted in stockinette stitch with crochet cotton, this plain evening top and matching armbands may be decorated to devastating effect. If using sequins, thread about 200 on to three balls of yarn as shown on p40. Both top and bands will stretch to fit most sizes.

Materials

100g (4oz) crochet cotton, 3 ply equivalent
1 pair no 00 (2mm) needles
1.5m (1½yd) narrow elastic
About 600 sequins
A quantity of feathers and ribbon

Tension

40 sts and 56 rows to 10cm (4in) over st st on no 00 needles.

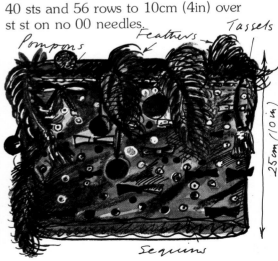

Pompons Feathers Tassels

25cm (10in)

Sequins

38 cm (15in)

Thread picot edge at the top and bottom with elastic

Knit in sequins and beads
or sew on afterwards

Top
Cast on 293 sts.
1st–5th row Work in st st, beg with a P row.
6th row K1, *yf, K2tog; rep from * to end.
Continue in st st until work measures 25cm (10in), end with a P row.
Rep 6th row.
Rep 1st–5th row.
Bind off.

Armbands (make 2)
Cast on 95 sts.
1st–3rd row Work in st st, beg with a P row.
4th row K1, *yf, K2tog; rep from * to end.
5th–11th row Work in st st, beg with a P row.
12th row As 4th row.
13th–15th row As 1st–3rd row.
Bind off.

Finishing
1 Fold in half and join center back seam. Fold upper and lower edges along pattern rows and slip stitch hems in place, leaving an opening for elastic.
2 Thread elastic through, join ends and sew up opening.
3 Following instructions on p37, make ribbon bows, tassels and pompons and sew them on as required.
4 Fold armbands along pattern rows and slip stitch hems. Join seams, leaving opening for elastic.
5 Thread elastic through, join ends together and sew up opening.
6 Sew on decorations as required.

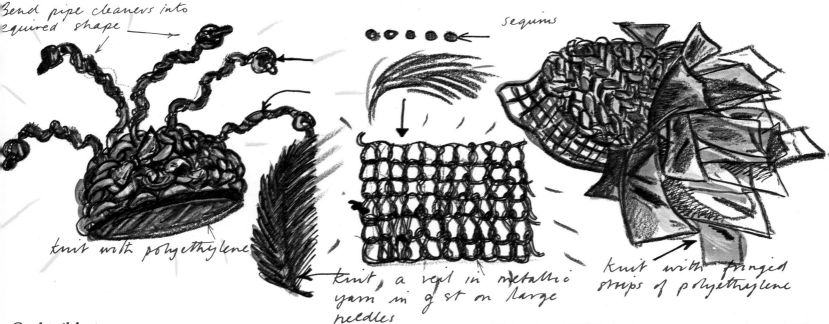

Bend pipe cleaners into required shape

knit with polyethylene

sequins

knit a veil in metallic yarn in g st on large needles

knit with fringed strips of polyethylene

Cocktail hats

Cocktail hats offer much scope for design. This spider hat is knitted from a black polyethylene bag cut into strips and decorated with black pipe cleaners twisted to form legs. Using the same material you could knit a band with fringed strips of polyethylene and then wire it to fit. Add a veil knitted from metallic yarn or silk cord. To make hats with extra sparkle, twist silver or gold thread in with the strips of polyethylene and knit them together as you go. Then adorn them with beads, sequins, feathers and anything else you can think of.

Materials

Black polyethylene (cut into 5cm (2in) wide strips)
1 pair no 11 (7½mm) needles
Wire
5 black chenille pipe cleaners
5 beads

With polyethylene, cast on 6 sts.
Work in g st until work measures 18cm (7in).
Bind off.

Finishing

1 Join cast-on and bound-off edges. Gather up one long side and stitch to form a flattened cone.
2 Thread wire round base of cone and oversew to neaten edges.
3 Sew a bead on to one end of each pipe cleaner.
4 Sew them down the seam of the hat and bend into shape.

Waistcoat

This tailored waistcoat has a knitted front and a satin back; it is lined with cotton. Embroider stripes in metallic thread for a pin-stripe effect and knit a lace handkerchief to tuck in the pocket. Alternatively the waistcoat could be knitted in fine bouclé and backed with tweed for a warmer, more countrified version. It will fit small to medium sizes.

Materials

75g (3oz) 2 ply wool
Small quantity silver metallic thread
1 pair no 00 (2mm) needles
1m × 90cm (1yd × 36in) cotton lining fabric
0.5m × 90cm ($\frac{1}{2}$yd × 36in) satin
0.5m ($\frac{1}{2}$yd) interfacing
5 buttons

Tension

44 sts and 64 rows to 10cm (4in) over st st on no 00 needles.

Pocket backs (make 3)
Cast on 36 sts.
Work in st st for 6cm (2$\frac{1}{2}$in), beg and end with a P row.
Leave sts on spare needle.

Left front
Cast on 2 sts.
1st row K1, m1, K1.
2nd row P1, m1, P2.
3rd row K1, m1, K2, m1, K1.
4th row P.
5th row K1, m1, K to last st, m1, K1.
Rep 4th–5th row until there are 24 sts.
Next row P.
Next row Cast on 10 sts, K to last st, m1, K1.
Rep 4th–5th row until there are 39 sts.
Next row P.
Next row Cast on 10 sts, K to last st, m1, K1.
Rep 4th–5th row once.
Next row P1, m1, P to end.
Next row K1, m1, K to last st, m1, K1.

Rep last 2 rows until there are 73 sts.
Next row P.
Next row Cast on 10 sts, K to last st, m1, K1.
Next row P1, m1, P to end.
Next row K1, m1, K to last st, m1, K1.
Rep last 2 rows until there are 90 sts.
Next row P.
Next row Cast on 10 sts, K to last st, m1, K1.
Next row P1, m1, P to end.
Next row K1, m1, K to last st, m1, K1.
Rep last 2 rows until there are 110 sts.
Continue in st st without shaping until work measures 8cm (3in) along straight edge, end with a P row.
To place lower pocket
Next row K38 sts, slip next 36 sts on to stitch holder, K across 36 sts of pocket back, K to end.
Continue in st st without shaping until work measures 23cm (9in) along straight edge, end with a P row.
To shape armholes and neck
Next row Bind off 8 sts, K to last 3 sts, K2tog, K1.
Next row P1, P2tog, P to last 3 sts, P2tog-tbl, P1.
Next row K1, sl 1, K1, psso, K to last 3 sts, K2tog, K1.
Rep last 2 rows until 75 sts rem, end with a P row.
To place top pocket
Next row K1, sl 1, K1, psso, K12, slip next 36 sts on stitch holder, K across 36 sts of pocket back, K to last 3 sts, K2tog, K1.
Next row P.
Next row K1, sl 1, K1, psso, K to last 3 sts, K2tog, K1.
Rep last 2 rows until 51 sts rem, end with a P row.
Next row K to last 3 sts, K2tog, K1.
Next row P.
Rep last 2 rows until 40 sts rem.
Dec 1 at neck edge on every 4th row until 32 sts rem, end with a P row.
Bind off.

Right front

Work as for left front, but reverse shaping and leave out top pocket.

Pocket edges (make 3)

Pick up 36 sts of pocket edge from stitch holder.
Work in st st for 18 rows.
Bind off.

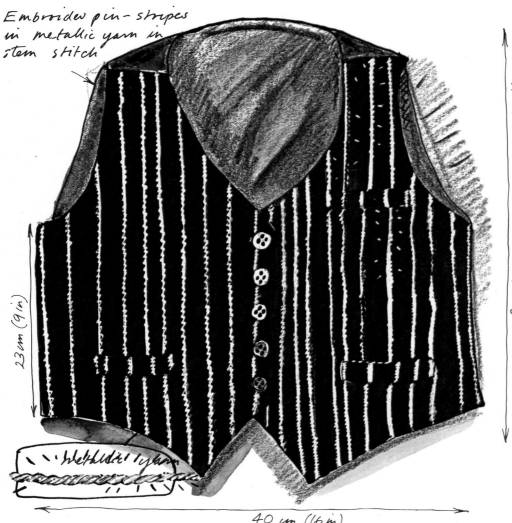

Embroider pin-stripes in metallic yarn in stem stitch

23 cm (9in)

Back measurement 40 cm (16in)

metallic yarn

40 cm (16in)

Finishing

1 Using metallic thread, sew vertical stripes in stem stitch as shown on p45.
2 Sew pocket backs in place. Fold pocket edges in half, hem and sew in place and press well.
3 Using the diagram cut out paper patterns for the fronts and back. Cut two fronts in interfacing, two fronts and one back in cotton lining fabric and one back in satin.
4 Tack the interfacing to the knitted fronts and stitch around the edges. Stitch the darts in the back and back lining and press well.
5 Join satin back to knitted fronts at side seams. Join lining back and fronts at side seams.
6 With right sides together, pin, tack and sew lining to waistcoat around the edges, leaving the shoulder seam and armholes open.
7 Turn right side out. Join shoulder seams and armhole edges.
8 Press well. Make buttonholes and sew buttons in place.

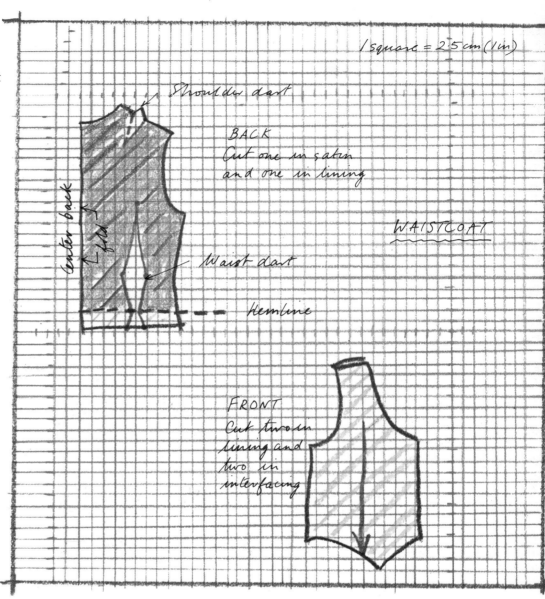

1 square = 2·5 cm (1 in)

Shoulder dart

BACK
Cut one in satin
and one in lining

WAISTCOAT

Waist dart

center back — fold

Hemline

FRONT
Cut two in
lining and
two in
interfacing

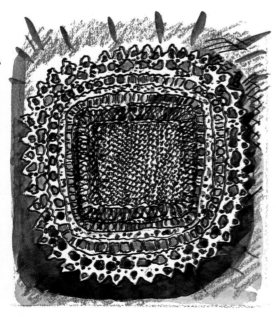

13 cm (5 in)

Handkerchief

This delicate white lace handkerchief is knitted in fine crochet cotton. The center is worked in moss stitch and the border in a simple lace stitch. It can be made larger with more rows and stitches.

Materials

25g (1oz) fine crochet cotton
1 pair no 00 (2mm) needles

Center

Cast on 24 sts.
Work in moss st for 6cm (2½in).
Bind off.

Edging

Cast on 11 sts.
1st row K.

2nd row K3, K2tog, yf, K1, K2tog, yf, K3.
3rd row K9, (yf, yrn, K1) twice (15 sts).
4th row (K2, K1 tbl) twice, (K1, K2tog, yf) twice, K3.
5th row K15.
6th row Bind off 4, K2, K2tog, yf, K1, K2tog, yf, K3 (11 sts).
Rep 3rd–6th rows until edging is long enough to fit round center, end with a 5th row.
Bind off.

Finishing

1 Block and press with a warm iron over a damp cloth.
2 Join cast-on and bound-off edges of edging, then sew round center. Press seams.

Dress

Nothing could be simpler to knit than this sinuous evening dress. Worked in ribbing it consists of a rectangle with ties down the long sides and will fit small to medium sizes. For a larger size, just cast on more stitches.

Materials

350g (14oz) metallic yarn 4 ply equivalent
1 pair no 4 (3¾mm) needles
1 no 1 crochet hook

Tension

46 sts and 32 rows to 10cm (4in).

Body

Cast on 200 sts.
Work in K1, P1 rib for 122cm (48in).
Bind off in rib.

Finishing

1 Using no 1 crochet hook join yarn to one corner of body. Work a chain 36cm (14in) long. Repeat at other three corners of body and at 15cm (6in) intervals along both side edges.
2 Darn in all loose ends neatly and fold body in half lengthwise.
3 Tie each pair of chains together, leaving one pair at top edge which can be tied on the shoulder or under the arm.
4 A double length of shirring elastic may be threaded through alternate knit stitches at top edge on wrong side of work for additional support.

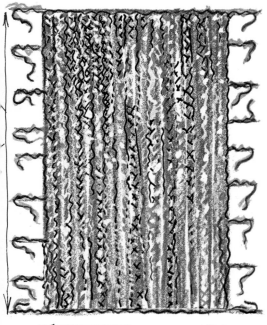

43 cm (17in)
(unstretched)

Fabrics for fashion

Experiment freely with knitting techniques to create exciting new fabrics. For example, combine different yarns and stitch patterns with ridges, tucks and tubes and stuff or interweave the resulting fabric with unusual materials such as vinyl strips, leather thongs or rovings (waste yarn from the mill). The samples shown here have been exploited to dramatic effect in the fashion drawings and were worked as follows.

Sample one With crochet cotton in first color (A), cast on a multiple of 4 sts, plus 2 extra. Work in st st for 6 rows then, join in second color (B) and work in pattern as follows.
1st row K1B, *K2togA, (yrn) twice in A, K2togB; rep from * to last st, K1A.
2nd row *P1A, P1B, P1A, K1A; rep from * to last 2 sts, P1A, P1B.
3rd row K1B, *K2togA, (yrn) twice in B, K2togB; rep from * to last st, K1A.
4th row *P1A, P2B, K1B; rep from * to last 2 sts, P1A, P1B.
Rep 1st–4th row until work is required length.
Work in st st for 6 rows.
Bind off.
Weave strips of vinyl through fabric.
Samples two, three and four These are worked in a variety of luxurious yarns using tubes on a striped or plain background. The tubes are worked on the same principle as the ridged edging described on p30. In sample two the ends of the yarn used in the tubes have been knotted at each side for a tufted effect. In sample three the tubes are stuffed with rovings. In sample four the ends of the yarn used in the tube have been carried across the front of the work to the next tube.
Sample five This consists of openwork tubes on a background of black mohair with tweedy stripes.
Cast on a multiple of 2 sts and work in st st to the position of the tube.
Next row With tweedy yarn, *K2tog, yrn; rep from * to end.
Work in st st for 3 rows, beg with a P row.
Next row *K1, yrn, drop 1 st; rep from * to end.
Next row P.
Next row Place rovings inside tube and close it as shown on p30.

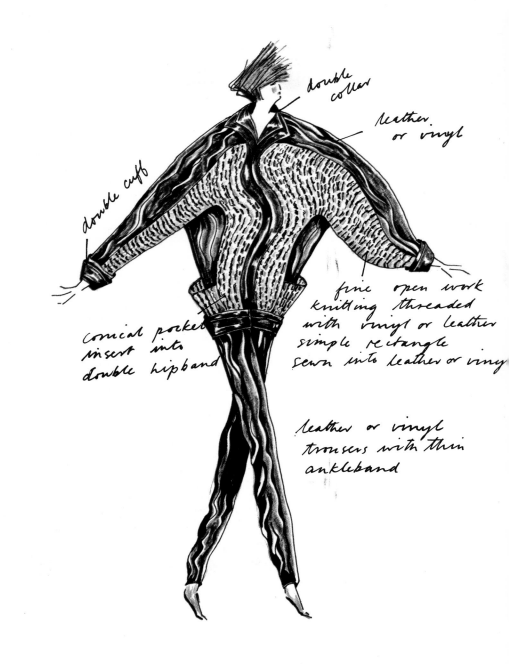

double collar

leather or vinyl

double cuff

fine open work knitting threaded with vinyl or leather simple rectangle sewn into leather or vinyl

conical pocket insert into double hipband

leather or vinyl trousers with thin ankleband

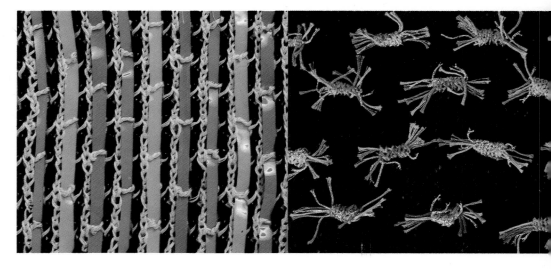

simple rectangle knitted in
with rovings on body of coat
vertically on body of coat
and horizontally on oblong
yoke and cuffs

knitted in rovings on
shoulders and edge

random stripes
of silver slub cotton
yarn on sleeves

shape
given to
simple
jacket
with
colored
cummerbund

bandeau
simple tube
and arm
tubes in soft
wool with
tied cotton and
metallic yarns

black white
and gold
striped woven
trousers

simple
rectangle
with
colored
cummerbund

simple footless
tights in wool
with random
knitted and
tied crochet
cotton and
metallic yarns

black soft yarn - fine
mohair with stripes and
ridges. Loose simple footless
tights with bandeau in
metallic yarn

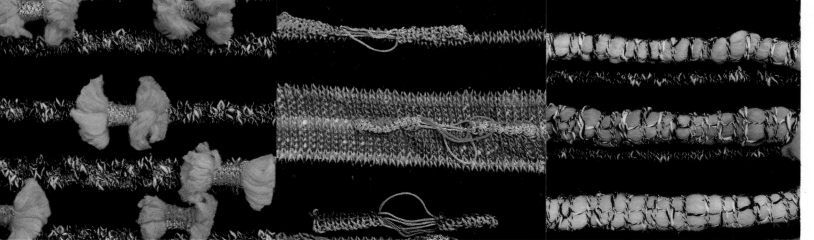

Dyes and dyeing

Yarns are usually bought ready-dyed but you can dye them yourself if a particular shade or color is unobtainable. Interesting effects can be achieved by space-dyeing or by dyeing yarn first in one color and then overlaying it with another by dyeing it a second time. You can also apply dyes freely by painting or spraying, or by a printing technique such as stenciling, on the surface of a knitted fabric for a variety of decorative and colored effects.

The dyeing of yarn is a process by which dyestuff and yarn are combined with each other; their chemical reaction results in the coloring of fibers. Several factors affect this process and need to be taken into consideration before you start work. These include the types of dyes, the nature of the yarn or fiber you want to dye and the various techniques at your disposal. There are basically two types of dyes: chemical and natural.

Chemical dyes
These are classified according to the way they act and the chemical they contain.

Substantive dyes These are suitable for dyeing wool, cotton, silk and various man-made fibers. Most household, hot-water dyes fall into this category. The addition of salt to the dye bath will encourage the fibers to accept the dye more readily. it will also help prevent fading and color loss as long as the fabric is not washed in too hot water.

Reactive dyes Use these for dyeing silk, linen, rayon and wool when a lighter shade of a color is required. Add salt or soda to make the color fast or, if dyeing wool, omit the soda and use malt or brown vinegar only.

Acid dyes These produce a strong brilliant color, especially on silk or wool. Known as fugitive dyes, they are often difficult to fix and are only obtainable from specialist dye suppliers and some good craft shops.

Natural dyes
These fall into two groups: those imported from abroad such as indigo (for blue), madder (for red) and saffron (for yellow), which can be purchased in a partially prepared form, and those that you can extract yourself from leaves, flowers, seeds, bark, lichens and roots. Both are sympathetic to natural fibers and the colors extracted tend to have a particular beauty and subtlety, in shade and hue, unequaled in chemical dyeing. However, they are not always fast and often require fixing by means of a mordant (from *mordre*, "to bite"). A range of mordants such as alum, tin, iron and chrome are available in powdered form. Different mordants added to the same dyestuff can result in wide variations of color and shade.

Equipment
A large galvanized bucket or a heavy enamel bowl is essential. The results will be poor if the vessel is too small for the amount of yarn being dyed. A small enamel saucepan is a good stand-by for experimenting with color and dyeing small samples. Other equipment includes a wooden spoon for stirring, a teaspoon and cup for mixing the dye to a paste, a measuring jug, scales for weighing the yarn, a pair of strong rubber gloves and a good quality liquid soap.

Using chemical dyes
These can be used on natural and synthetic yarns. All manufacturers specify the correct ratio of yarn to dye, and this will vary from make to make and sometimes even from color to color within the same brand.

1 Wind the yarn into bundles and tie them at regular intervals with figure-of-eight loops of thread to prevent the yarn tangling. It is not advisable to dye yarn in balls as the dye will be unable to penetrate evenly through to the center.

2 Weigh the yarn to estimate how much dye you will need and mix the correct amount with a little water to form a thick, creamy paste. Never add powdered dye directly to the dye-bath as uneven color could result.

3 Wash the yarn thoroughly in warm water and fill the dye-bath with enough water to cover the yarn completely and add the concentrated liquid dye together with salt if specified. Stir thoroughly to ensure an even distribution of the dye in the water, then add the yarn carefully to the dye-bath.

4 Leave the yarn to soak for about 40 minutes or the time specified by the manufacturer. The liquid remains colored even though the yarn absorbs dye. The longer the yarn is left in dye, the deeper the color. Remember,

Some unusual dyeing techniques

Apply special fabric paints directly on to wet and dry knitting. Fix with a hot iron over a dry cloth.

Accentuate eyelet holes with applied color

82

though, that it will dry a lighter shade.
5 Rinse the yarn through several changes of water to remove any excess dye and dry away from strong sunlight.

Using natural dyes

To extract dyes from natural sources, immerse the material you are using in water and soak or boil to break down the fibers and so release the color. The time this takes can vary from a few minutes for certain berries to several hours for leaves and woody substances. Apply mordants directly to the yarns before they are placed in the dye or add them to the liquid dye. Various specialist books of recipes are available and the chart gives some ideas. It is also interesting to experiment with various mordants and materials, keeping a record of the results of each one for future reference. The rest of the process is exactly the same as for chemical dyes.

Dyeing natural yarns

Natural yarns are usually delicate and should always be treated with great care. When dyeing fleece, you must first remove all the natural grease that would otherwise resist the dye. Lay the fleece in warm, soapy water, softened with sodium hexametaphosphate. This is sold under a number of trade names, so ask for advice at your local pharmacy. Ordinary household soap is unsuitable as it will only matt the fleece.
Leave the fleece to soak and then gently transfer it to another bath of clean water of the same temperature. Repeat until every trace of soap has disappeared. The fleece can then be dyed in the same way as any natural yarn, which is as follows.
1 Wet yarn before dyeing, preferably soaking it overnight.
2 Place the yarn in a dye-bath over a low heat and slowly bring to simmering point. Do not let it boil as the fibers will harden and shrink, and only stir a few times as wool reacts badly to agitation.
3 Leave the yarn to soak for as long as possible as lengthy dyeing gives by far the best results.
4 When the process is complete, remove the dye-bath from the heat and allow the yarn to cool. Then wash it in the same way as described for a fleece, squeezing out any surplus liquid before drying away from direct heat.

Some natural dyes and mordants

Dandelion heads + alum = pale yellow

Apple tree + alum = lemon yellow
+ chrome = rust
+ tin = bright yellow

Roots without mordant = purple

+ alum = brown
walnut shrub and husks

Grapes + alum = violet

Blackberry + alum and salt = blue-gray
+ alum = purple

Buttercups + alum = yellow

Dyeing man-made fibers

Man-made fibers are often a mixture of two or more fibers such as nylon and polyester and they may also include a natural fiber. Some fibers take color easily while others reject it and it is therefore sometimes difficult to achieve an even color. Man-made fibers are generally stronger than natural ones due to the construction of the fibers. Apart from this the actual process is the same as for natural yarns except that it is shorter as man-made fibers tend to react faster to dye.

Spray dye through a stencil for a defined outline

Stitches for texture

Embroidery works just as well on knitting as on woven fabrics and offers great potential for experiment. Knitted fabric has individual characteristics according to the yarn with which it is worked and the stitches which give it shape and texture; take these into consideration before beginning on embroidery. Knitted stitches and the patterns they create will stimulate ideas for surface stitching as will the lines and shape of the item you are knitting. Some basic embroidery stitches are given on pp44–5 and there are many variations on these, some of which are explored here and others elsewhere in the book. It is also possible to use smocking, appliqué, quilting and any other suitable needlecraft techniques you can think of on knitting. Follow the knitted stitches exactly, or work freely for a more random effect. Stitches should be applied fairly loosely as knitting is an elastic fabric. Stitches which are too tight may pucker knitting or break during wear. (For techniques see p45). Colors can be used to strong, even strident, effect; try working with bright primary colors on a plain knitted background or go to the other extreme and keep the shades subtle and subdued. These samples illustrate how knitted fabric in a variety of textures can be made highly individual by combining embroidery stitches with other decorative accessories.

Sample one This is knitted in mohair twisted with metallic yarn. Bands of stockinette stitch and reverse stockinette stitch produce a textured fabric which can be emphasized using metallic yarn and cotton. Ribbons and pearls can also be added. Starting at the top, work the following rows of stitches or substitute them with others of your own choice: fly stitch, cross stitch couched over ribbon, two rows of interlacing stitches divided by a row of pearls, chequered chain stitch, straight stitches couched double over ribbon, zigzag chain stitch, herringbone stitch couched over ribbon, and two rows of interlacing blanket stitches.

Sample two This is knitted in mercerized cotton yarn in stockinette stitch and quilted with machine and hand-stitched appliqué. Secure the pieces in place with small satin stitches or buttonhole stitch and emphasize the quilting by stuffing extra pieces of loose batting into the center of the design. Add French knots or other embroidery stitches as required for extra decoration. Appliqué can be worked with shaped pieces knitted to a preplanned design, or any woven fabric.

Sample three This is knitted in a random-dyed bouclé yarn in stockinette stitch to form a highly textured surface. It is embroidered with stranded cotton and tapestry wool. Embroider flowers with French knots or use small pearl buttons and stitch them in place with French knots worked into each hole. Join them to stems worked in straight or feather stitch and couch down lengths of wool with stranded cotton for branches. Work undulating lines of chain stitch and suggest vegetation by winding yarn around a pencil and securing it with a firm back stitch before going on to work the next loop.

Sample four This smocked sample is worked with 4 ply yarn in stockinette stitch. When smocking knitting, work twice the number of stitches required for the finished width and then gather it to the appropriate size. It can then be smocked in wave stitch by taking yarn or thread from the left side of one gather to the right side of the next and then moving up to the next position. Tie shells lengthwise with gold thread and use the thread ends to secure the shells firmly to the smocked knitting.

Sample five A braided cable with a four-stitch cable on either side on a background of reverse stockinette stitch form the basis of this sample. It is worked in double knitting yarn and embroidered with tapestry wool. Emphasize the spiral effect of the cables with chain stitch and embroider vertical lines of feather stitch in between. Extend the chain stitch on the four-stitch cables to form stems each bearing clusters of grapes which can be worked in satin stitch or French knots. There are numerous cable patterns with which to experiment in this way.

Pastoral pullover

Wrap up against the elements in a sweater that enables you to blend in with the landscape. The basic background shape is knitted first in stockinette stitch in two colors; the landscape itself is built up by knitting a number of different shapes in a variety of colored and textured yarns, which are then sewn on and padded to give an impression of rolling hills and valleys. The drawing shows how you can put together a landscape like this or one of your own design. Using some of the stitches described on pp44–5, embroider fences, lambs, paths and sheaves of wheat. The trees, bushes and sheep are made from pompons trimmed to shape. Strands of French knitting make up the fence along the hem, and the gate which opens and closes is stiffened with pipe cleaners. You can complete the picture with a matching hat with a sun pompon on the top. Using these techniques it is possible to create all sorts of different scenes to make a variety of different garments, rugs, wall hangings or even cushions. The sweater and hat will fit small to medium sizes.

Materials
350g (14oz) green 4 ply (A)
100g (4oz) blue 4 ply (B)
A selection of yarns in various colors and textures
1 pair no 1 (2¾mm) needles
1 pair no 3 (3¼mm) needles
French knitting reel
Dacron batting
Pipe cleaners

Tension
28 sts and 40 rows to 10cm (4in) over st st on no 3 needles.

Front
With no 3 needles and A, cast on 156 sts.
1st–22nd row Work in st st.
23rd row Fold work in half lengthwise wrong sides tog, *Ktog 1 st from needle and 1 st from cast-on edge; rep from *
24th–120th row Work in st st.
121st row K36A to position of motif then foll 1st row of shepherd and dog chart, K92A.
122nd–153rd Continue in st st, foll chart for shepherd and dog.
With A, continue in st st until work measures 53cm (21in) from hemline.
With B, continue in st st, until work measures 66cm (26in) from hemline.
To shape neck
Next row K65, bind off 26, K65.
Working each side separately, dec 1 at neck edge on next 15 rows (50 sts). Continue in st st without shaping until work measures 74cm (29in).
Bind off.

Back
Work as for front for 53cm (21in) but leave out shepherd and dog.
With B, continue in st st until work measures 71cm (28in).
To shape neck
Next row K55, bind off 46, K55.
Working each side separately, bind off 5 sts at neck edge on next row (50 sts). Continue in st st without shaping until work measures 74cm (29in).
Bind off.

Sleeves
With no 1 needles and A, cast on 70 sts.
Work in K2, P2 rib for 28 rows.
Change to no 3 needles.
Continue in st st, inc 1 at each end of 7th and every foll 8th row until there are 86 sts and then at each end of every foll 6th row until there are 106 sts.
Continue in st st without shaping until work measures 53cm (21in) from beg.
Bind off.

Neckband
Join left shoulder seam.
With no 1 needles and B, pick up 142 sts around neck edge.
Work in K2, P2 rib for 8 rows.
Bind off loosely in rib.

Finishing
1 Darn in all ends neatly and press. Join right shoulder seam and neckband.
2 Matching center of sleeve to shoulder seam, sew sleeves in flat.
3 Join side and sleeve seams.
4 Create landscape; some suggestions are given above.

Materials

100g (4oz) blue 4 ply (A)
25g (1oz) white mohair (B)
25g (1oz) yellow DK (C)
1 pair no 3 (3¼mm) needles
1 pair no 9 (6mm) needles
Dacron batting

With no 3 needles and A, cast on
126 sts.
Work in K2, P2 rib for 13cm (5in),
inc 1 at end of last row (127 sts).
Work in st st for 10cm (4in).
Next row K6, *sl 1, K2tog, psso, K11;
rep from * to last 9 sts, sl 1, K2tog, psso,
K6.
Work in st st for 3 rows.
Next row K5, *sl 1, K2tog, psso, K9; rep
from * to last 8 sts, sl 1, K2tog, psso, K5.
Work in st st for 3 rows.
Next row K4, *sl 1, K2tog, psso, K7; rep
from * to last 7 sts, sl 1, K2tog, psso, K4.
Work in st st for 3 rows.
Next row K3, *sl 1, K2tog, psso, K5; rep
from * to last 6 sts, sl 1, K2tog, psso, K3.
Work in st st for 3 rows.
Next row K2, *sl 1, K2tog, psso, K3; rep
from * to last 5 sts, sl 1, K2tog, psso, K2.
Work in st st for 3 rows.
Next row K1, *sl 1, K2tog, psso, K1; rep
from * to end.
Work in st st for 3 rows.
Thread yarn through rem sts, gather up
tightly and fasten off.

Clouds (make 4)

With no 9 needles and B, cast on
16 sts.
1st row P.
2nd row K.
3rd row P2tog, P14.
4th row K2tog, K9, (K2tog) twice.

5th row P8, (P2tog) twice.
6th row K8, K2tog.
7th row P2tog, P5, P2tog.
8th row (K2tog) twice, K3.
9th row P2tog, P1, P2tog.
10th row K3tog.
Thread yarn through the last st, gather
up tightly and fasten off.

Finishing

1 Join seam.
2 Pad clouds with a little batting and
sew to sides of hat.
3 Using C, make a pompon to a
diameter of about 10cm (4in) as shown
on p37 and sew to top of hat.

Cover-ups

This set of pretty lingerie is both luxurious and feminine to wear. All the patterns are easy to make with the minimum of shaping. The camisole top and knickers are knitted in lacy, openwork stitches in a soft cotton yarn that makes them comfortable to wear. The stockings and suspender belt can be made in a matching or contrasting color. The set will fit small to medium sizes.

Camisole top and knickers

Two rectangular strips knitted in vine lace zigzag stitch and quatrefoil eyelet stitch respectively form the basis of this top and knickers. They are decorated and tied with braided cords but you could also use French knitting. The top is gathered at both ends and the knickers at the waist.

Materials

300g (12oz) medium crochet cotton
1 pair no 4 (3¾mm) needles
6m (5½yd) lace
Narrow elastic

Tension

28 sts and 48 rows to 10cm (4in) over pattern on no 4 needles.

Knickers

Cast on 254 sts.
Work in quatrefoil eyelet stitch as shown on p136 for 25cm (10in).
Bind off.

Gusset

Cast on 40 sts.
Work in quatrefoil eyelet, dec 1 at each end of every 6th row of pattern until 20 sts rem.
Bind off.

Finishing

1 Darn in all ends neatly, block and press.
2 Join side seam. Find center front and back and match to front (bound-off edge) and back (cast-on edge) of gusset. Join with a flat seam.
3 Turn under a narrow hem at waist and thread elastic through. Turn under narrow hems around legs and trim with pleated lace.
4 Make braided cords and thread through pattern holes at each side.

Top

Cast on 81 sts.
1st–10th row Work in st st.
11th row K3, *sl 1, K1, psso, (yf, K1) twice, K5, K2tog, K1, rep from * to last 6 sts, K3, yf, K2tog, K1.
12th row and all other alt rows P.
13th row K3, *sl 1, K1, psso, K1, (yf, K1) twice, K4, K2tog, K1, rep from * to last 6 sts, K6.
15th row K3, *sl 1, K1, psso, K2, (yf, K1) twice, K3, K2tog, K1, rep from * to last 6 sts, K6.
17th row K3, *sl 1, K1, psso, K3, (yf, K1) twice, K2, K2tog, K1, rep from * to last 6 sts, K6.
19th row K3, *sl 1, K1, psso, K4, (yf, K1) twice, K1, K2tog, K1; rep from * to last 6 sts, K6.
21st row K3, *sl 1, K1, psso, K5, (yf, K1) twice, K1, K2tog, K1; rep from * to last 6 sts, K6.
23rd row K3, *sl 1, K1, psso, K6, yf, K1, yf, K2tog, K1; rep from * to last 6 sts, K3, yf, K2tog, K1.
25th row As 21st row.
27th row As 19th row.

29th row As 17th row.
31st row As 15th row.
33rd row As 13th row.
34th row P.
Rep 11th–34th row until work measures 80cm (32in), end on a 12th row.
Work in st st for 10 rows.
Bind off.

Finishing

1 Darn in all ends neatly, block and press.
2 Turn under each short side (cast-on and bound-off edges) and hem to a depth of five rows.
3 Pleat lace and sew it neatly to top and bottom edges.
4 Using six strands of yarn make a braided cord 120cm (48in) long as shown on p36 and thread through eyelet holes in wide border for bust.
5 Make a braided cord 90cm (36in) long and thread through second set of pattern rows from bottom for waist.
6 Make four braided cords 75cm (30in) long and attach to top edge for shoulder straps.
7 Make four braided cords 38cm (15in) long, thread through pattern holes in center front and tie in small bows.

Suspender belt and stockings

The stockings are knitted on two needles in a simple mesh stitch. Begin at the top and work straight until the shaping for the heel and instep, wjich is minimal and easy to master. Knit five strips in stockinette stitch for the suspender belt in a matching or contrasting yarn. Then frill them and sew over elastic which for a really coordinated effect can be dyed to match the yarn.

Materials

12 small balls fine mercerized cotton (A)
A small quantity crochet cotton in a contrasting colour (B)
1 pair no 00 (2mm) needles
1 pair no 2 (2¾mm) needles
2m × 1cm (2yd × ½in) elastic
4 suspenders

Belt

With no 00 needles and A, cast on 14 sts.
Work in st st for 95cm (38in).
Bind off.

Suspender strips (make 4)

With no 00 needles and A, cast on 14 sts.
Work in st st for 30cm (12in).
Bind off.

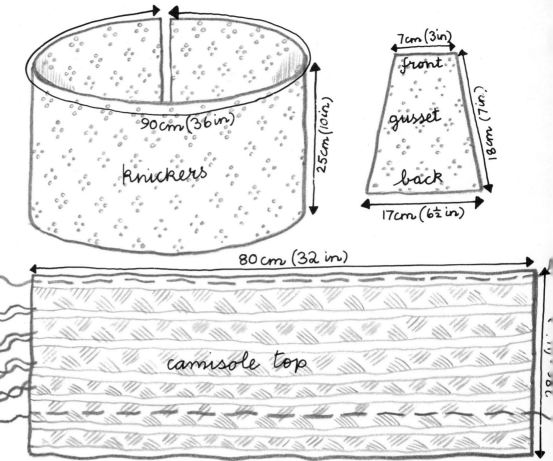

knickers — 90cm (36in), 25cm (10in)

gusset — front 7cm (3in), back 17cm (6½in), 18cm (7in)

camisole top — 80cm (32in)

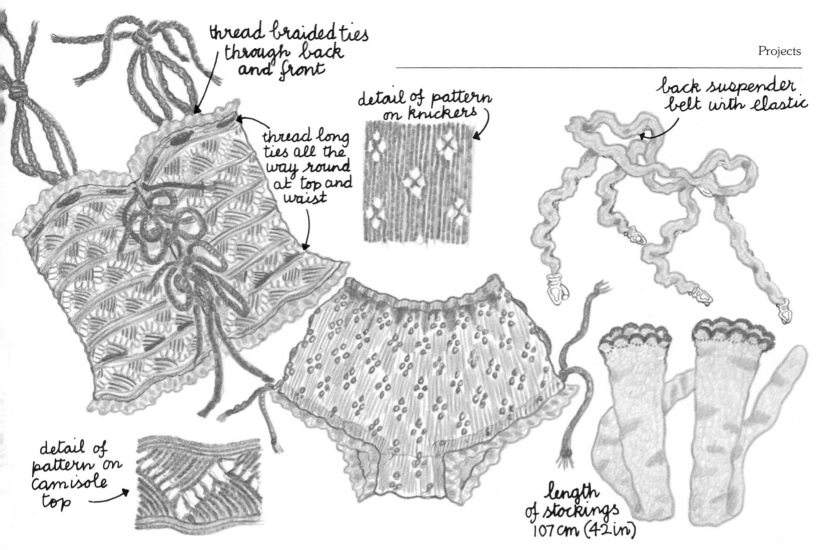

thread braided ties through back and front

thread long ties all the way round at top and waist

detail of pattern on knickers

back suspender belt with elastic

detail of pattern on camisole top

length of stockings 107 cm (42 in)

Finishing

1 Cut one piece of elastic 58cm (23in) long, and four pieces 23cm (9in) long.
2 Sew knitted belt to longer piece of elastic, pulling elastic as you sew to frill strip automatically.
3 Sew suspender strips to shorter pieces of elastic in the same way. Attach a suspender to each one.
4 Find center of waistband and attach a suspender strip 6cm (2½in) from center on each side.
5 Attach other two suspender strips 25cm (10in) from center on each side. Sew ends of waistband securely together.

Stockings

With no 2 needles and A doubled, cast on 99 sts.
Work in K1, P1 rib for 8 rows.
With B, work in K1, P1 rib for 2 rows.
With A doubled, work in K1, P1 rib for 8 rows.
Next row With B, work in K1, P1 rib.
Next row With A, used singly K2, *yf, K3, slip first of these 3 sts over other two from behind; rep from * to last st, K1.
Rep this row, which forms the pattern, until work measures 35cm (14in) from cast-on edge.

To shape leg

Continue in pattern, dec 1 at each end of next and every foll 4th row until 63 sts rem.
Continue without shaping until work measures 63cm (25in) from beg.

To divide for heel and instep

Next row Pattern 48 sts, turn.
Next row Pattern 33 sts, turn.
Leave rem sts on stitch holders and continue on these 33 sts for instep.
Continue in pattern for 15cm (6in).
Lengthen or shorten foot here.
Change to no 00 needles.

To shape toe

*Next row K1, K2tog, K to last 3 sts, K2tog, K1.
Next row K1, P to last st, K1.*
Rep from * to * until 11 sts rem.
Leave sts on stitch holder.
Return to heel sts and slip both sets of sts onto a needle with sides toward center to form back seam.
Next row (K2, inc 1) 10 times (40sts).
Work in st st for 33 rows, beg with a P row.

To turn heel

Next row K26, K2tog, turn.
Next row P13, P2tog, turn.
Next row K14, K2tog, turn.

Next row P15, P2tog, turn.
Continue dec in this manner until all side sts are worked off and 26 sts rem, end with a P row.
Break off yarn.
With right side facing pick up and knit 17 sts along one side of heel flap, K the 26 sts, then pick up 17 sts along other side of heel flap (60 sts).
Next row P.

To shape instep

*Next row K2, K2tog, K to last 4 sts, sl 1, K1, psso, K2.
Next row K1, P to last st, K1.*
Rep from * to * until 40 sts rem.
Continue in st st for 15cm (6in), end with a K row.
Lengthen or shorten foot here.
Next row (P3, P2tog) 7 times, P5 (33 sts).
Shape toe as given for top of foot until 11 sts rem.
Graft the two sets of sts together as shown on p27.
Make second stocking to match in exactly the same way.

Finishing

1 Press carefully over a damp cloth.
2 Join foot and leg seams neatly.

91

Sweet-bag raincoat

It is possible to knit with anything, not least polyethylene. This plastic hooded raincoat shows that the most unlikely materials can work extraordinarily well in knitting. Simply cut polyethylene sheeting into strips and knot them together as you knit. The knots can be pushed through to the wrong side afterward. The resulting fabric is surprisingly soft and comfortable to wear as well as fairly waterproof. Its shiny almost silvery surface can be well set off, as it is here, with a

Materials
4 clear polyethylene sheets each measuring 2.7 × 1.8m (3 × 2yd), cut into strips 5cm (2in) wide
1 pair no 11 (7½mm) needles
35cm (14in) zipper
Colored beads and pipe cleaners

scattering of brightly colored beads and rainbow twists of silky chenille pipe cleaners with the ends bound so that they do not catch or snag. As an alternative you could knit the same pattern in a bulky yarn for a warm winter coat and decorate it with some of the ideas suggested on pp44–5, but remember to knit a tension square before you start. The raincoat will fit a two-to-three-year-old and as the shaping is minimal it can easily be made larger by working more rows on more stitches.

Tension
12 sts and 16 rows to 10cm (4in) over st st on no 11 needles.

Back
Cast on 48 sts.
Work in st st for 41cm (16in).

To shape shoulders
Bind off 8 sts at beg of next 4 rows.
Bind off rem 16 sts.

Right front
Cast on 24 sts.
Work in st st for 35cm (14in), end with a P row.
To shape neck
Bind off 2 sts at beg of next and foll 3 alt rows, end with a K row.
To shape shoulders
Bind off 8 sts at beg of next and foll alt row.

Left front
Work as for right front but reverse all shaping.

Sleeves
Cast on 32 sts.
Work in st st for 18cm (7in).
Bind off.

Hood
Cast on 20 sts.
Work in st st for 4 rows.
Inc 1 at beg of next and every foll 4th row until there are 28 sts.
Work in st st for 5 rows without shaping.
Dec 1 at beg of next and every foll 4th row until 20 sts rem.
Work in st st for 4 rows.
Bind off.

Finishing
1 Join shoulder seams and, matching center of sleeve to shoulder seam, sew in sleeves.
2 Sew zipper to front edges as shown on p29.
3 Sew beads onto garment, scattering them at random over back, front, sleeves and hood.
4 Intersperse chenille pipe cleaners between beads by inserting one end through the base of one stitch from back to front. Then thread pipe cleaner from right to left through two loops of same stitch, one row above, then back down through the back of the stitch. Twist two ends together at back of fabric to secure them, snip off any excess length and bind any rough edges.
5 Join side and sleeve seams in one continuous seam.
6 Fold hood in half, join shaped sides together and sew to neck edge.

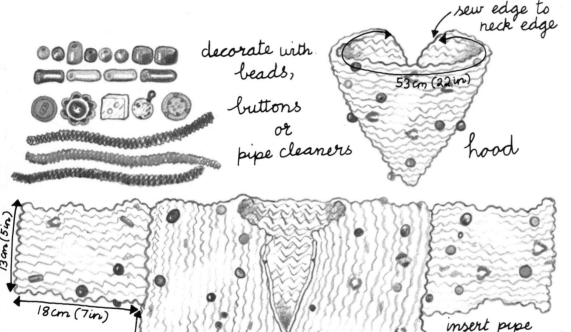

decorate with beads, buttons or pipe cleaners

sew edge to neck edge

53cm (22in)

hood

13cm (5in)

18cm (7in)

28cm (11in)

40cm (16in)

insert pipe cleaner through stitches

twist ends together at back of fabric

Armadillo wrap

Be beautiful without being cruel and knit yourself a wonderful animal wrap to drape around your shoulders for a glamorous effect. Animal skins are a superb source of texture and pattern for knitting. Experiment with different stitches, yarns and colors until you capture the right quality. An armadillo has been chosen here and it is knitted in honeycomb stitch with crewel wool which brings out the tactile scaliness of the animal to perfection. Animals with exotic furs may also offer inspiration as may many members of the cat family such as lions, tigers and leopards.

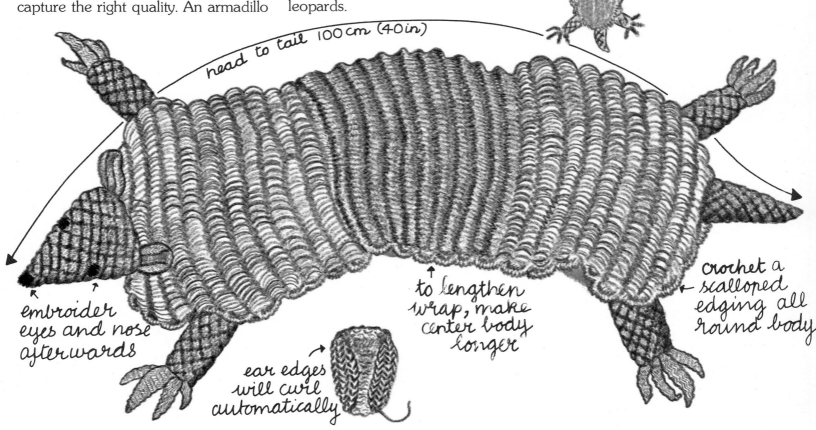

crochet cotton for lining width of body 30cm (12in)

head to tail 100cm (40in)

embroider eyes and nose afterwards

ear edges will curl automatically

to lengthen wrap, make center body longer

crochet a scalloped edging all round body

Materials
75g (3oz) rust DK (A)
25g (1oz) dark brown crewel wool (B)
25g (1oz) light brown crewel wool (C)
100g (4oz) rayon yarn (D)
1 pair no 3 (3¼mm) needles
1 pair no 6 (4½mm) needles
Stuffing

Tension
23 sts and 27 rows to 10cm (4in) over st st on no 6 needles using A.

Center Body
With no 6 needles and A, cast on 70 sts.
*Work in st st for 8 rows.
With C, work 2 rows.*
Rep from * to * 10 times or until work measures required length.
With A, work 8 rows.
Bind off.

Body Ends (make 2)
With no 6 needles and A, cast on 52 sts.
Work in st st until work measures 28cm (11in).
Next Row *sl 2, drop 3 sts off needle; rep from * to end.
Allow dropped sts to run through to cast-on edge.
Break off yarn leaving end about 50cm (20in) long. Thread yarn on tapestry needle and thread through rem sts, back stitching into each pair of sl sts and taking care not to pull edge up tight.

Tail
With no 6 needles and B, cast on 32 sts.
Work in honeycomb pattern as follows.
1st–2nd row Work in st st.
3rd row With A, *sl 1, K3; rep from * to end.

4th row With A, * P3, sl 1; rep from * to end.
5th row With B, K to end.
6th row With B, P to end.
7th row With A, *K2, sl 1, K1; rep from * to end.
8th row With A, *P1, sl 1, P2; rep from * to end.
9th row With B, K.
10th row With B, P.
Rep 1st–10th row twice.
Continue in pattern dec 1 at each end of every 4th row until 6 sts rem.
Bind off.

Head top
With no 6 needles and B, cast on 40 sts.
Work in honeycomb pattern for 26 rows.
Dec 1 at each end of next and every 4th row until 8 sts rem.
Bind off.

Head underpiece
With no 6 needles and A, cast on
30 sts.
Work in st st for 24 rows.
Dec 1 at each end of next and every 4th
row until 12 sts rem.
Dec 1 at each end of next and every alt
row until 6 sts rem.
Bind off.

Ears (make 2)
With no 6 needles and A, cast on 20 sts.
Work in st st for 8 rows.
Dec 1 at each end of every row until
4 sts rem.
Bind off.

Legs (make 4)
With no 6 needles and B, cast on 28 sts.
Work in honeycomb pattern for 10cm
(4in).
Bind off.

Small claws (make 8)
With no 3 needles and C doubled, cast
on 10 sts.
1st row K to last 2 sts, turn.
2nd row P.
3rd row K to last 4 sts, turn.
4th row P.
Continue to work 2 sts less on every K
row until 2 sts rem, end with a P row.
Next row K.
Bind off.

Large claws (make 8)
With no 3 needles and C doubled, cast
on 14 sts.
Complete as for small claws.

Lining
With no 3 needles and D, cast on
90 sts.
Work in st st for required length.
Bind off.

Finishing
1 Oversew side edge of one body end to
each end of center body.
2 If desired, crochet a scalloped edge on
long sides of body.
3 Join two long sides of tail to make a
cone shape and stuff lightly.
4 Gather end of body and sew on tail.
5 Join two head pieces and stuff.
6 Gather other end of body and sew on
head.
7 Sew on ears allowing edges to curl
inward and embroider nose and eyes.
8 Sew legs into tubes. Gather one end
and stuff.
9 Join cast-on and bound-off edges of
claws. Sew two large and two small claws
to each leg. Sew legs on body.
10 Pin lining to underside of body inside
crochet edging if worked. Oversew long
edges. Gather up short edges to fit under
head and tail and sew in place.

Amazing ties

Quite ordinary objects can be the inspiration for extraordinary garments, for example knitted ties using exciting yarns and simple stitches. A cactus, fountain pen, cocktail glass and can of sardines have been chosen here and they are all easy to knit.

Materials
Cocktail glass tie 50g (2oz) metallic yarn 4 ply equivalent in main color (A)
Scraps of metallic yarn 4 ply equivalent in 4 contrast colors (B,C,D,E)
1 pair no 3 (3¼mm) needles
1 styrofoam ball 2.5cm (1in) in diameter
2 2.5cm (1in) styrofoam cubes
Elastic
Wire
Pen point tie 75g (3oz) metallic yarn 4 ply equivalent in main color (A)
25g (1oz) metallic yarn 4 ply equivalent in contrast color (B)
25g (1oz) metallic yarn 4 ply equivalent in contrast color (C)
1 pair no 3 (3¼mm) needles
Sardine can tie 125g (3oz) metallic yarn 4 ply equivalent in main color (A)
25g (1oz) metallic yarn in contrast color (B)
Scraps of metallic yarn in 5 colors (C)
1 pair no 3 (3¼mm) needles
1 pair no 6 (4½mm) needles
Cactus tie 50g (2oz) green DK
Scraps of metallic yarn in contrast color
1 pair no 4 (3¾mm) needles
1m (1yd) lining fabric

Cocktail glass tie
Front
With A, cast on 8 sts.
Work in st st for 2 rows.
Next row K to last 2 sts, (inc 1) twice.
Next row P.
Rep last 2 rows until there are 28 sts.
Next row P.
Work in st st for 26 rows, dec 1 at end of next and every 12th row.
Begin motif as follows still dec 1 at end of every 12th row.
Next row K11A, K3B, K11A.
Next row P11A, P3B, P11A.
Rep last 2 rows once.
Next row K10A, K5B, K10A.
Next row P9A, P7B, P9A.
Continue in this way inc B sts and dec A sts on every row until all sts are B.
With B, continue in st st for 24 rows still dec 1 on every 12th row.

With A, work in st st and dec 1 as before until 14 sts rem.
Work in st st until work measures 43cm (17in).
Bind off.

Back
With A, cast on 28 sts.
Work in st st for 2 rows.
Dec 1 at beg of next and every 12th row until 14 sts rem.
Continue in st st until work measures 38cm (15in).
Bind off.

Knot
With A, cast on 24 sts.
Work in st st for 9cm (3½in).
Bind off.

Cherry
With C, cast on 12 sts.
Work in st st for 4cm (1½in).
Bind off.

Ice cubes (make 2)
With D, cast on 12 sts.
Work in st st for 4cm (1½in).
Bind off.

Finishing
1 Sew front to back of tie at side seams.
2 Fold knot in half lengthwise and join.
3 Fold over 2.5cm (1in) on top of tie, sew in position and thread with elastic.
4 Wrap knot around top of tie and sew ends to back.
5 Bend wire into shape of cocktail glass. Glue and bind with metallic yarn.
6 Sew glass in position around motif.
7 Embroider "bubbles" in E on motif.
8 Sew ice cube pieces around styrofoam cubes and sew to motif.
9 Sew cherry piece around styrofoam ball. Pierce with wire bound with metallic yarn and place in glass.

Pen point tie
Point and pen
*With B, cast on 2 sts.
Work in st st for 4 rows.
Next row K1, inc 1.
Work in st st for 3 rows.
Next row K1, inc 1, K1.
Work in st st for 3 rows.
Next row K2, inc 1, K1.
Work in st st for 3 rows.
Next row K2, inc 1, K2.

Next row P.
Inc 1 at each end of next and every 4th row until there are 12 sts.
Next row P.
Inc 1 at each end of next and every alt row until there are 16 sts.
Inc 1 at each end of next 4 rows (24 sts).
Dec 1 at each end of next and every alt row until 18 sts rem.
Work 7 rows.
Dec 1 at each end of next and foll 10th row.
Work 9 rows.*
With A, cast on 8 sts at beg of next 2 rows (30 sts).
Mark last row with contrast thread.
Work in st st for 8 rows.
Mark last row with contrast thread.
Cast on 1 st at each end of next row.
Next row P.
Continue in st st for 324 rows, dec 1 at each end of every 44th row until 20 sts rem, then continue straight until work measures 82cm (32in) from beg of A.
Mark last row with contrast thread.
Cast on 2 sts at beg of next 2 rows.
Work in st st for 6 rows.
Mark last row with contrast thread.
Work in st st for 24cm (9in).
Dec 1 at beg of next 12 rows (12 sts).
Bind off.

Point liner
With C, work as for point from * to *.
Bind off.

Finishing
1 Take in a tuck on right side of work between each pair of marking threads.
2 Fold long sides of tie to middle and

seam together down center back.

3 Using back stitch, embroider a line from end of point to last increase row and work a circle in satin stitch on last stitch.

4 Oversew point liner to point.

Sardine can tie
Main piece
With no 3 needles and A, cast on 16 sts. Work in st st, inc 1 at each end of next and every alt row until there are 32 sts. Continue straight until work measures 120cm (47in) from beg, end with a P row. Dec 1 at each end of next and every alt row until 16 sts rem. Bind off.

Lining
With no 3 needles and B, cast on 8 sts. Work in st st, inc 1 at each end of next and every alt row until there are 16 sts. Continue without shaping for 13cm (5in). Bind off.

Sardines (make 3)
With no 6 needles and one strand of each of C worked together cast on 2 sts. Work in st st for 2 rows. Continue in st st, inc 1 at each end of next and every alt row until there are 8 sts. Work 3 rows. Dec 1 at each end of next and every alt row until 4 sts rem, end with a P row.
Next row K1, K2tog, K1.
Next row K.
Next row Inc 1, K1, inc 1.
Next row Inc 1, K3, inc 1.
Next row Inc 1, K5, inc 1.
Bind off.

Finishing
1 Fold each fish in half lengthwise and seam from top to tail. Embroider large French knots for eyes.
2 Cut 23cm (9in) length of wire. Glue along length and bind with metallic yarn. Bend into shape of a can opener.
3 Sew center back seam of main piece and oversew lining to back of one end.
4 Wrap lined end of tie once round can opener and sew in place.
5 Wind up opener until tie has been wrapped round three times and sew in place.
6 Sew sardines across tie above opener.

Cactus tie
Main piece
Cast on 12 sts.
Work in st st until work measures 70cm (28in).
Bind off.

Cactus section – size 1 (make 2)
Cast on 6 sts.
Work in st st for 4 rows.
Inc 1 at each end of next and every foll 4th row until there are 20 sts.
Work 3 rows.
Dec 1 at each end of next and foll 4th row, then every alt row until 6 sts rem.
Bind off.

Cactus section – size 2 (make 2)
Cast on 6 sts.
Work in st st for 4 rows.
Inc 1 at each end of next and every foll 4th row until there are 16 sts.
Work 3 rows.
Dec 1 at each end of next and every foll

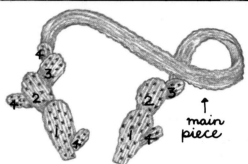

4th row until 8 sts rem.
Work 3 rows.
Bind off.

Cactus section – size 3 (make 2)
Cast on 6 sts.
Work in st st for 4 rows.
Inc 1 at each end of next and every alt row until there are 14 sts.
Work 3 rows.
Dec 1 at each end of next and every alt row until 4 sts rem.
Bind off.

Cactus section – size 4 (make 4)
Cast on 4 sts.
Work in st st for 4 rows.
Inc 1 at each end of next and foll 2 alt rows (10 sts).
Work 3 rows.
Dec 1 at each end of next and foll 2 alt rows (4 sts).
Bind off.

Finishing
1 Embroider all cactus sections with small cross stitches as shown on p45.
2 Line all pieces with lining fabric.
3 Assemble pieces and sew together as shown.

Beastly hats

Animal heads are a wonderful source of inspiration for children's hats. They will keep them warm and also present plenty of opportunities for ferocious noises and funny faces. Experiment with different colored yarns, patterns and stitches to capture lifelike shapes.

Duck hat
A garter-stitch scarf folded in half across the head forms the basis of this hat. It is shaped at the ends to form webbed feet and seamed a little way down the back to fit snugly like a hood.

Materials
125g (5oz) yellow DK (A)
50g (2oz) orange DK (B)
25g (1oz) blue DK (C)
25g (1oz) red DK (D)
1 pair no 4 (3¾mm) needles
1 pair no 5 (4mm) needles
Foam

Tension
16 sts and 36 rows to 10cm (4in) over g st on no 5 needles.

Scarf
With no 5 needles and A, cast on 30 sts.
Work in g st for 30cm (12in).

Next row Inc 1, K to end.
Next row K.
Rep last 2 rows 4 times (35 sts).
Continue in g st without shaping for 27cm (10½in).
Next row K2tog, K to end.
Next row K.
Rep last 2 rows 4 times (30 sts).
Continue in g st without shaping for 30cm (12in).

Legs and feet
Change to no 4 needles and B.
Next row K2tog to end (15 sts).
Work in g st for 4 rows.
Next row K2tog, K to last 2 sts, K2tog.
Rep last row once (11 sts).
Work in g st for 4 rows.
Next row Inc 1, K to end.
Rep last row 11 times (23 sts).
Work in g st for 4 rows.
Next row Inc 1, K to end.
Rep last row 6 times (30 sts).
Next row K.
Next row Cast off 8, K to end (22 sts).
Work in g st for 11 rows.
Next row Cast off 10, K to end (12 sts).
Work in g st for 8 rows, dec 1 at beg of next row, then at same edge on foll 7 rows (4 sts).
Bind off.
With no 4 needles and B, pick up and K 30 sts along cast-on edge and work to match first leg and foot, reversing shaping.

Beak
With no 4 needles and B, pick up 30 sts from center front of scarf.
1st–4th row Work in g st.
5th–10th row K2tog, K to end (24 sts).
11th–20th row Work in g st.
21st–26th row As 5th–10th row (18 sts).
27th–30th row Work in g st, dec 1 at each end of every row (10 sts).
31st–34th row Work in g st, inc 1 at each end of every row (18 sts).
35th–40th row Inc 1, K to end (24 sts).
41st–50th row Work in g st.
51st–56th row As 35th–40th row (30 sts).
Work in g st for 4 rows.
Bind off.

Duck's bonnet
With no 4 needles and C, cast on 14 sts.
Work in g st for 51cm (20in).
Bind off.

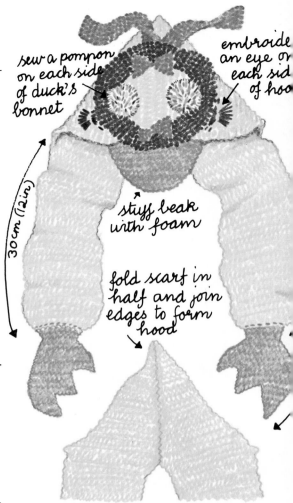

sew a pompon on each side of duck's bonnet

embroider an eye on each side of hood

stuff beak with foam

fold scarf in half and join edges to form hood

30cm (12in)

Bows (make 2)
With no 4 needles and D, cast on 6 sts.
1st–4th row Work in g st.
5th row K2tog, K to last 2 sts, K2tog.
6th row K.
7th–8th row As 5th–6th row.
9th row Inc 1, K to last st, inc 1.
10th row K.
11th–12th row As 9th–10th row.
13th–16th row Work in g st.
Bind off.

Ribbon
With no 4 needles and D, cast on 6 sts.
Work in g st for 30cm (12in).
Bind off.

Finishing
1 Fold scarf in half and sew two sides together 19cm (7½in) down from center back to form hood.
2 Join beak together at sides, stuff with foam and sew edges to hood.
3 Fold duck's bonnet in half lengthwise, sew ends together and stitch outer edges to crown of hood to form a circle.
4 Sew bows on front and back of duck's bonnet and ribbons under back brim.
5 Using each of the four colors, make two pompons as shown on p36 and sew one on to either side of duck's bonnet.
6 Embroider eyes on hood.

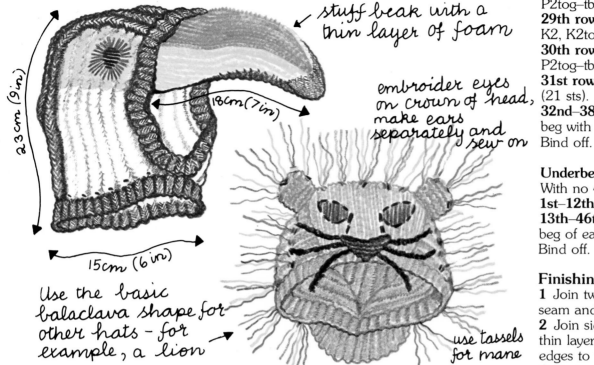

stuff beak with a thin layer of foam

embroider eyes on crown of head, make ears separately and sew on

use tassels for mane

23cm (9in)

18cm (7in)

15cm (6in)

Use the basic balaclava shape for other hats – for example, a lion →

P2tog–tbl, P10C.
29th row K10C, with D, sl 1, K1, psso, K2, K2tog, K10C.
30th row P10C, with D, P2tog, P2tog–tbl, P10C.
31st row With C, K10, K2tog, ·K10 (21 sts).
32nd–38th row With A, work in st st, beg with a P row.
Bind off.

Underbeak
With no 4 needles and A, cast on 40 sts.
1st–12th row Work in g st.
13th–46th row Work in g st, dec 1 at beg of each row (6 sts).
Bind off.

Finishing
1 Join two crown seams, join center front seam and face band.
2 Join side seams of beak, stuff with a thin layer of foam and attach cast-on edges to top of face under face band.
3 Embroider eyes on head.

Toucan hat
This basic balaclava is worked in a decorative rib pattern with plain ribbed welts. The top of the beak is worked in stockinette stitch, the underside in garter stitch and the whole beak is padded. The eyes are embroidered afterward. The pattern is simple and is a good starting-off point for any bird or animal head you can think of, such as the lion's head above.

Materials
100g (4oz) navy DK (A)
50g (2oz) white DK (B)
25g (1oz) yellow DK (C)
25g (1oz) orange DK (D)
25g (1oz) pale blue DK (E)
1 pair no 2 (3mm) needles
1 pair no 4 (3¾mm) needles
Foam padding

Tension
20 sts and 33 rows to 10cm (4in) over pattern on no 4 needles.

Head
With no 2 needles and A, cast on 83 sts.
Work in K1, P1 rib for 2.5cm (1in).
Change to no 4 needles.
Next row K28B, K27A, K28B.

Next row Keeping the same sequence of colors, *K2, P2; rep from *, end K2, P1.
Rep last row for 13cm (5in).
Change the sequence of colors to 28C, 27A, 28C and work in pattern for a further 7cm (2½in).
Bind off 28 sts at beg of next 3 rows (27 sts).
With A, work in pattern for 11cm (4½in).
Break off yarn and leave sts on stitch holder.
With no 2 needles and A, and with right side facing, pick up and K 42 sts up the side, K 27 sts from stitch holder, then pick up and K 42 sts down the other side, finishing at other end of 1st pattern row.
Work in K1, P1 rib for 7 rows.
Bind off.

Beak top
With no 4 needles and C, cast on 40 sts.
1st row K15C, K10D, K15C.
2nd row P15C, P10D, P15C.
3rd–12th row Rep 1st–2nd row 5 times.
13th–22nd row Keeping colors as set, work in st st, dec 1 at each end of every K row (30 sts).
23rd–26th row Work in st st.
27th row K10C, with D, sl 1, K1, psso, K6, K2tog, K10C.
28th row P10C, with D, P2tog, P4,

Jungle jewelry

Wire can be used for French knitting to make exotic necklaces and bracelets. You need soft, pliable wire; the best place to obtain it is in an electrical wholesale supply shop. Gold and silver wire are the most suitable but naturally they are expensive. Tinned copper is preferable to plain copper wire, which tends to tarnish and is difficult to clean once knitted. If you decide to use an uncoated base metal you can prevent it tarnishing by coating it with a thin layer of clear lacquer. Always test lacquer first on a piece of scrap metal to make sure it takes evenly. You can also use a plastic-coated wire which comes in a variety of colors, but it tends to be rather on the thick side. When you have chosen your wire work with an ordinary French knitting reel or, if you want more than four stitches,

make one for yourself from a block of wood. The number of prongs you use and the size of the hole in the middle depend on how wide you want the tube. Wire can be French knitted as shown on p38, but work the stitches with a pointed, blunt-edged tool such as a cable needle so as not to damage the wire. When you have knitted the required length bind off in the usual way and join the two ends together by ties or a clasp. If using the latter, remember that unless you are working with silver or gold wire, it is not advisable to heat wire and therefore a strong glue is better than soldering. French-knitted jewelry can also be made with other materials such as wool or metallic yarns which could be braided, coiled and twisted together to make bracelets and necklaces.

Materials
Tinned copper wire between 25 and 35 gauge
3 pairs necklace clasps
1 French knitting reel with 16 prongs
1 French knitting reel with 8 prongs
Strong glue

Thick necklace
With 16-prong French knitting reel make a tube 46cm (18in) long.
Thread wire through sts on prongs and pull up tight.

Thin necklace
With 8-prong French knitting reel make a tube 62cm (24in) long.
Thread wire through sts on prongs and pull up tight.

Bracelet
With 16-prong French knitting reel make a tube 25cm (10in) long.
Thread wire through sts on prongs and pull up tight.

Finishing
1 Squeeze ends of tubes gently to taper.
2 Glue ends into clasps.
3 Link clasps.

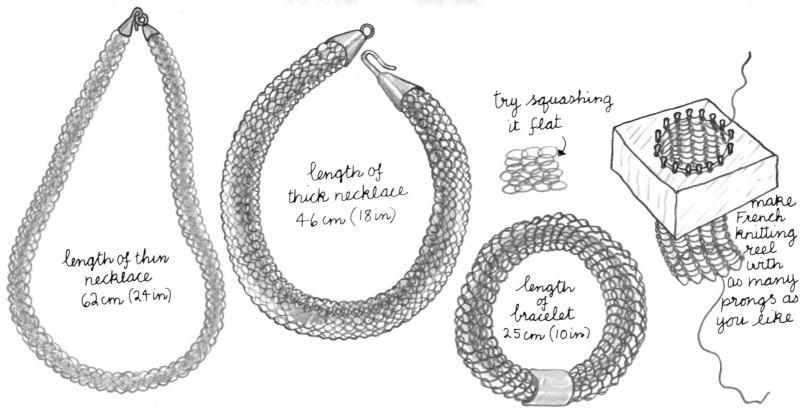

length of thin necklace 62cm (24in)

length of thick necklace 46cm (18in)

try squashing it flat

length of bracelet 25cm (10in)

make French knitting reel with as many prongs as you like

Silly socks

Knit colorful socks and sole them with thin leather or suede so that you can wear them around the house. All the socks shown here except for the webbed feet are variations of a single basic design and can be knitted on two needles. Shaping is minimal, there is no turn at the heel and both feet can be knitted to the same pattern. They will fit a medium-sized adult foot and can easily be made longer or shorter.

Materials
Spotted socks 100g (4oz) mohair
Scraps of mohair in various colors
1 pair no 6 (4½mm) needles
1 pair no 8 (5½mm) needles
Stripy socks 100g (4oz) random-dyed DK
1 pair no 6 (4½mm) needles
1 pair no 8 (5½mm) needles
Loopy socks 250g (10oz) random-dyed slub yarn (A)
150g (6oz) mohair (B)
1 pair no 6 (4½mm) needles
1 pair no 8 (5½mm) needles
Leopard's paws 100g (4oz) yellow mohair Acrylic mixture (A)
Scraps of brown mohair (B)
Scraps of black DK (C)
1 pair no 6 (4½mm) needles
1 pair no 8 (5½mm) needles
Scraps of glove leather
Ballet shoes 75g (3oz) red mohair Acrylic mixture (A)
25g (1oz) white DK (B)
25g (1oz) pink DK (C)
1 pair no 6 (4½mm) needles
1 pair no 8 (5½mm) needles
French knitting reel
Webbed feet 100g (4oz) orange mohair Acrylic mixture (A)
25g (1oz) yellow DK (B)
1 pair no 3 (3¼mm) needles
1 pair no 6 (4½mm) needles
Stuffing

Spotted socks
With no 6 needles cast on 40 sts.
Work in K2, P2 rib for 10 rows.
With no 8 needles, work in st st until work measures 50cm (20in), end with a P row.
To shape toe
Next row (K1, K2tog, K14, sl 1, K1, psso, K1) twice.

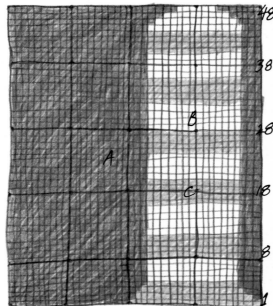

Chart for ballet shoe socks

Next row P.
Next row (K1, K2tog, K12, sl 1, K1, psso, K1) twice.
Next row P.
Next row (K1, K2tog, K10, sl 1, K1, psso, K1) twice.
Next row (P1, P2tog-tbl, P8, P2tog, P1) twice.
Next row (K1, K2tog, K6, sl 1, K1, psso, K1) twice.
Next row (P1, P2tog-tbl, P4, P2tog, P1) twice.
Next row (K1, K2tog, K2, sl 1, K1, psso, K1) twice.
Bind off.

Finishing
1 Press with damp cloth.
2 Fold socks lengthwise and join leg and toe seams.
3 Make pompons from wool scraps and sew on socks. Alternatively Swiss darn spots on socks as shown on p45.

Stripy socks
Work as for spotted socks for 10 rows. Continue in K2, P2 rib spiraly by moving the rib 1 st to the left on each row until work measures 50cm (20in). Alternatively you can continue in straight K2, P2 rib for looser-fitting socks.
To shape toe
Work as for spotted socks.

Finishing
Fold socks lengthwise and join leg and toe seams.

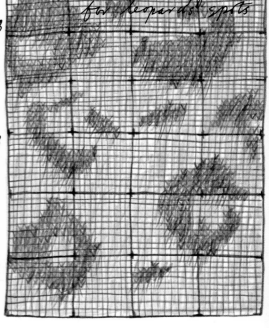

Swiss darning chart for leopards' spots

Leopard's paws
With A, work as for spotted socks but omit toe shaping and add about 5cm (2in) to the overall length.

Finishing
1 Join side and toe seams and seam top and bottom of socks together for about 2.5cm (1in) in two places for toes.
2 Following the chart, Swiss darn leopard's skin markings on each sock with B as shown on p45.
3 Brush with a wire brush to achieve furry effect.
4 With C, embroider claws on each toe.
5 Make pads from leather and sew under toes and heel.

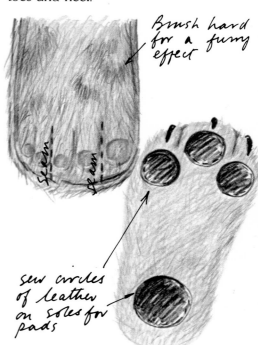

Brush hard for a furry effect

seam

sew circles of leather on soles for pads

Ballet shoes

Work as for spotted socks until work measures 25cm (10in), working the rib in B and the st st in 4 row stripes in B and C alternately.

With A doubled and B and C, follow chart for next 48 rows.

To shape toe

With A doubled, work as for spotted socks.

Finishing

1 Join leg and side seams.
2 With A, work four lengths of French knitting 45cm (18in) long. Attach one to either side of each sock and tie.

Loopy socks

With A and B together, work as for spotted socks, making a loop st (p141) in every alt st of the 1st and every 6th row of st st until work measures 38cm (15in). Bind off.

With B, pick up 40 sts from cast-on edge and work in K2, P2 rib for 23cm (9in).

To shape toe

Work as for spotted socks.

Finishing

Join seams.

Webbed feet

With no 3 needles and A, cast on 56 sts.

Work in K2, P2 rib for 12 rows. Continue in st st until work measures 25cm (10in), end with a P row.

To shape underside

1st row K1, m1, K6, m1, K7, m1, K7, m1, K6, m1, K1, turn and slip first 28 sts onto stitch holder (33 sts).
2nd row P.
3rd row K1, m1, K8, m1, K7, m1, K8, m1, K8, m1, K1 (38 sts).
4th row P.

Inc 1 at each end of every foll 4th row until there are 58 sts.

To shape toe

Dec 1 at each end of every row until 30 sts rem.
Bind off.
Slip first 9 sts off stitch holder onto needle.
*Inc 2 sts at each end of next row and work in st st until work measures 15cm (6in) (13 sts).
Next row K2tog to last st, K1 (7 sts).
Next row (P2tog) 3 times, P1 (4 sts).
Bind off.*
Slip next 10 sts off stitch holder onto needle.

Inc 2 at each end of next row and work in st st until work measures 19cm (7½in).
Next row K2tog to end (7 sts).
Next row (P2tog) 3 times, P1 (4 sts).
Bind off.
Slip last 9 sts off stitch holder onto needle.
Rep from * to *.

Web

With no 6 needles and B, cast on 36 sts.
1st–3rd row K.
4th row P.
Rep 1st–4th rows, inc 1 at end of next and every foll 4th row until there are 58 sts.
Work 3 rows.

To shape toe

Dec 1 at each end of every row until 2 sts rem.
Bind off.

Finishing

1 Press all parts with a damp cloth.
2 Join three toe sections to form tubes and stuff lightly.
3 Sew web section to underside round sides and toe to form a bag.
4 Sew toes to web and join leg seam.

Crown jewels

Rubies, sapphires, diamonds and emeralds are displayed to outrageous effect in knitted metallic yarn settings. Imitate full regalia complete with sash and tiara for a truly devastating effect, using simple stitches to construct intricate designs. Twisted cords and fringes add an extra decorative touch. The jewels themselves are made of large and small bobbles in a variety of colors which you can change as required. Make large bobbles (LB) following the instructions on p39 and small bobbles (SB) in the same way but with three rather than five stitches.

Materials
50g (2oz) blue metallic yarn (A)
25g (1oz) gold metallic yarn (B)
25g (1oz) silver metallic yarn (C)
Scraps of metallic yarn in a variety of colors
1 pair no 3 (3¾mm) needles
1 pair earring clips
Wire

Tiara
Begin with a simple band of garter stitch, then work separate shapes in stockinette stitch, decorated with jewel bobbles, and sew them in place. Wire the band and wrap a gold twisted cord round for a crisscross effect.

Center piece
With C doubled, cast on 25 sts.
1st–2nd row Work in st st.
3rd row K11, sl 2, K1, p2sso, K11.
4th row and every alt row P.
5th row K10, sl 2, K1, p2sso, sl last st back on left-hand needle, make SB, K10.
7th row K5, make SB, K3, sl 2, K1, p2sso, sl last st back on left-hand needle, make LB, K3, make SB, K5.
9th row K3, make SB, K4, sl 2, K1, p2sso, K4, make SB, K3.
11th row K5, make SB, K1, sl 2, K1, p2sso, K1, make SB, K5.
13th row K6, sl 2, K1, p2sso, sl last st back on left-hand needle, make SB, K6.
14th–18th row Work in st st.
Bind off.

Large side piece (make 2)
With C doubled, cast on 19 sts.
1st–2nd row Work in st st.
3rd row K8, sl 2, K1, p2sso, K8.

4th row and every alt row P.
5th row K7, sl 2, K1, p2sso, sl last st back on left-hand needle, make SB, K7.
7th row K4, make SB, K1, sl 2, p2sso, K1, make SB, K4.
9th row K2, make SB, K2, sl 2, K1, p2sso, K2, make SB, K2.
11th row K5, make LB, K5.
13th row K4, sl 2, K1, p2sso, K4.
14th–15th row Work in st st.
Bind off.

Small side piece (make 2)
With C doubled, cast on 13 sts.
1st–2nd row Work in st st.
3rd row K5, sl 2, K1, p2sso, K5.
4th row and every alt row P.
5th row K4, sl 2, K1, p2sso, sl last st back on left-hand needle, make SB, K4.
7th row K3, sl 2, K1, p2sso, K3.
9th row K2, sl 2, K1, p2sso, K2.
10th row P.
Bind off.

Band
With C doubled, cast on 6 sts.
Work in g st for 36cm (14in).
Bind off.

Finishing
1 Press all pieces with a warm iron.
2 Sew center piece in middle of band.
3 Sew one large side piece and one small side piece on either side of the center piece.
4 Make twisted cords as shown on p36 and wind them round the tiara between upright pieces.
5 Stiffen band with wire.

Sash
Work a long strip of stockinette stitch and fringe at both ends. Then knit a star, a rosette and a bow, decorate them with jewels and attach them to the sash.

Ribbon
With A, cast on 26 sts.
Work in st st for 2 rows.
Next row K2A, K3B, K16A, K3B, K2A.
Next row P2A, P3B, P16A, P3B, P2A.
Rep last 2 rows until work measures 128cm (51in).
With A, work in st st for 2 rows.
Bind off.

Rosette
With A, cast on 18 sts.
*Work in st st for 10 rows.
With B, work in st st for 10 rows.
Join in A.*
Rep from * to * 5 more times.
Bind off.

Rosette bow
With A, cast on 7 sts.
1st row K2A, K3B, K2A.
2nd row P2A, P3B, P2A.
Rep 1st–2nd row until work measures 10cm (4in).
Bind off.

Star points (make 6)
With B doubled, cast on 20 sts.
Work in st st for 2 rows.
Next row K9, sl 1, K2tog, psso, K8.
Next row P.
Next row K8, sl 1, K2tog, psso, K7.
Next row P.
Next row K7, sl 1, K2tog, psso, K6.
Next row P.
Next row K7, make LB, K6.

Next row P.
Continue to dec in center of every row until 2 sts rem.
Bind off.

Star center
*With C doubled, cast on 10 sts.
Work in g st for 4 rows.
Next row K4, sl 1, K2tog, psso, K3.
Next row K.
Next row K4, make LB, K3.
Next row K.
Next row K3, sl 1, K2tog, psso, K2.
Work in g st for 3 rows.
Next row K2, sl 1, K2tog, psso, K1.
Work in g st for 5 rows.
Bind off.*
Rep from * to * 3 times.
Pick up 4 sts from bound-off edge of each piece (16 sts).
Next row K.
Next row K7, make LB, K8.
Pull yarn through sts and secure.

Shoulder bow
With C doubled, cast on 19 sts.
1st–2nd row K.
3rd row K8, sl 2, K1, p2sso, K8.
4th row K.
5th row K7, sl 2, K1, p2sso, K7.
6th–8th row K.
9th row K6, sl 2, K1, p2sso, K6.
10th row K.
11th row K5, sl 2, K1, p2sso, K5.
12th–14th row K.
15th row K4, sl 2, K1, p2sso, K4.
16th row K.
17th row K3, sl 2, K1, p2sso, K3.
18th row K.
19th row (K1, make SB) 3 times, K1.
20th row K.
21st row K2, make SB, K1, make SB, K2.

22nd–25th row As 18th–21st row.
26th–27th row As 18th–19th row.
28th row K.
29th row K3, (inc 1) twice, K2.
30th row K.
31st row K4, (inc 1) twice, K3.
32nd–34th row K.
35th row K5, (inc 1) twice, K4.
36th–38th row K.
39th row K6, (inc 1) twice, K5.
40th row K.
41st row K7, (inc 1) twice, K6.
42nd row K.
43rd row K8, (inc 1) twice, K7.
44th row K.
Bind off.

Bow ribbons (make 2)
With C doubled, cast on 6 sts.
Work in g st for 28 rows.
29th row K2tog, K to end.
30th row K.
31st–36th row Rep 29th–30th row 3 times (2 sts).
Bind off.

Finishing
1 Knot fringes onto ends of ribbon.
2 Join cast-on and bound-off ends of rosette. Run thread along one edge. Pull up and secure center.
3 Shape rosette bow and sew in position over center of rosette.
4 Arrange star points in star shape with corners overlapping and secure.
5 Sew star center in place, bow ribbons onto back of bow and bow to front of sash just below shoulder.
6 Sew star 33cm (13in) below bow.
7 Sew on rosette at hip.
8 Sew sash together at one corner of each end just above the hip.

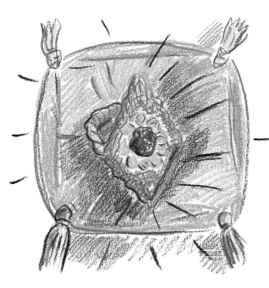

Ring

Work a narrow band of stockinette stitch, then make a separate diamond in garter stitch decorated with bobbles and sew neatly in place.

Center

With C doubled, cast on 2 sts.
1st–7th row Work in g st, inc 1 at beg of each row.
8th row K4, make SB, K4.
9th row Inc 1, K to end.
10th row Inc 1, K1, make SB, K3, make SB, K3.
11th row K.
12th row K2, make SB, K2, make LB, K2, make SB, K2.
13th row K.
14th row K2tog, K1, make SB, K3, make SB, K3.
15th row K2tog, K to end.
16th row K4, make SB, K4.
17th–23rd row Work in g st, K2tog at beg of each row.
Bind off.

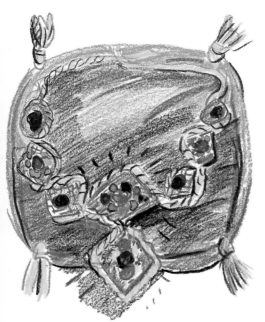

Band

With C doubled, cast on 4 sts.
Work in st st for 22 rows.
Bind off.

Finishing

1 Sew band into a ring.
2 Sew center to seam of band.

Necklace

Knit a line of diamond shapes decorated with jewels and hang one from the middle for a pendant. Make a cord and weave it in and out leaving ends to tie.

With C doubled, cast on 2 sts.
Work in g st for 10 rows.
*Inc 1 at beg of next 6 rows.
Next row K4, make LB, K3.
Work in g st for 2 rows.
K2tog at beg of next 6 rows.
Work in g st for 4 rows.*
** Inc 1 at beg of next 4 rows.
Next row Inc 1, K1, make SB, K3.
Next row Inc 1, K to end.
Next row Inc 1, make SB, K3, make SB, K2.
Next row Inc 1, K to end.
Next row Inc 1, K3, make LB, K5.
Next row K2tog, K to end.
Next row K2tog, K1, make SB, K3, make SB, K2.
Next row K2tog, K to end.
Next row K2tog, K2, make SB, K3.
Next row K2tog, K to end.
K2tog at beg of next 4 rows.
Work in g st for 4 rows.**
Rep from * to *.
***Inc 1 at beg of next 4 rows.
Next row Inc 1, K1, make SB, K3.
Next row Inc 1, K to end.
Next row Inc 1, make SB, K3, make SB, K2.
Next row Inc 1, K to end.
Next row Inc 1, make SB, K2, make LB, K2, make SB, K2.
Next row K2tog, K to end.
Next row K2tog, K1, make SB, K3, make SB, K2.
Next row K2tog, K to end.
Next row K2tog, K2, make SB, K3.
K2tog at beg of next 5 rows. ***
Work in g st for 4 rows.
Rep from * to *.
Rep from ** to **.
Rep from * to * once more.
Work in g st for 6 rows.
Bind off.

Pendant

With C doubled, cast on 2 sts.
Work as for necklace from *** to ***, changing colors as required.
Bind off.
Pick up 8 sts on two sides of the diamond shape (16 sts).
Work in g st for 2 rows.
Bind off.
Pick up 8 sts on other two sides of the diamond shape and rep last 2 rows.
Bind off.

Finishing

1 Join pendant to center piece.
2 Make a twisted cord as shown on p36 and wind it round the necklace, catching it to the jewels at intervals with a few stitches and leaving a length at either side for ties.

Earrings (make 2)

Knit two diamond shapes, one above the other and decorate with bobble jewels and attach clasps on the backs.

With C doubled, cast on 2 sts.
1st–16th row Work as given for ring, changing colors as required.
17th–22nd row K2tog, K to end. (3 sts).
23rd row K.
24th–26th row Inc 1, K to end.
27th–29th row K.
30th–32nd row K2tog, K to end.
Bind off.

Finishing

1 Press lightly with warm iron over a damp cloth.
2 Glue earring clips to back of smaller diamond shapes.

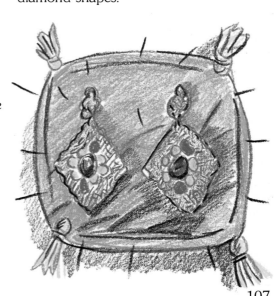

Flora and fauna

Combine simple stitches, thin wire and a little ingenuity and knit glittering creatures to sparkle after dark, stunning flowers with sinuous stems and glowing insects with gossamer-fine wings. The basic principles are easy to follow and to adapt for a whole host of glamorous accessories. Remember when making your own designs to stick to strong, simple shapes for maximum impact and minimum effort.

Fly

This pattern for a fly can be adapted to any species of insect you like; simply choose two colors and start to knit. The body is made with chenille and 4 ply and the wings with fine metallic yarn. Both are wired so that they can be bent into shape. The legs and antennae are made from wire twisted with metallic yarn and are sewn on afterward.

Materials

Scraps of chenille in main color (A)
Scraps of 4 ply in contrast color (B)
Scraps of fine metallic yarn in a variety of colors (C)
1 pair no 0 ($2\frac{1}{4}$mm) needles
Stuffing and wire

Body

With A, cast on 10 sts.
Work in st st for 4 rows.
With B, work 4 rows.
With A, inc 1 at each end of next and every foll row until there are 16 sts.
With B, work 4 rows.

twist wire with metallic yarn for legs and antennae, and sew on body

Finishing

1 Fold body lengthwise right sides together and seam.
2 Gather up tail end (cast-on edge) to a point and sew.
3 Turn right side out and stuff.
4 Insert length of wire into body and sew up open end.
5 With C, embroider large knots for eyes.
6 Make legs and antennae from lengths of wire twisted with C and sew in position on body.
7 Thread wire round edges of wings and neaten with oversewing.
8 Sew wings to body on either side of head just behind the eyes.

With A, dec 1 at each end of next and every foll alt row until 10 sts rem.
Work 3 rows.
With B, work 16 rows.
Bind off.

Wings (make 2)
With C, cast on 4 sts.
Work in st st for 4 rows.
Inc 1 at each end of next and every foll alt row until there are 16 sts.
Work 5 rows.
Dec 1 at each end of next and every foll alt row until 4 sts rem.
Bind off.

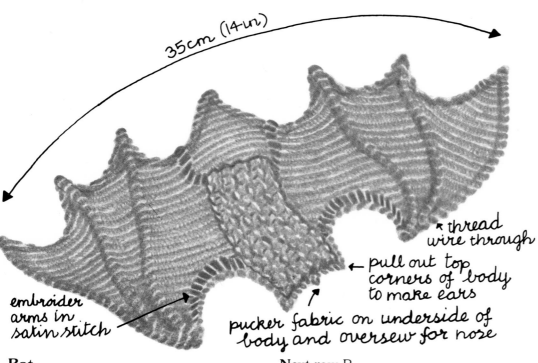

35cm (14in)

embroider
arms in
satin stitch

*pucker fabric on underside of body and oversew for nose

*pull out top corners of body to make ears

*thread wire through

Bat

Wear this bat on the shoulder or on the head as a simply sensational hat. The wide-spreading wings are made in one piece and the upper and under body are sewn on afterward. The whole bat is wired so that it can be molded to the required shape.

Materials

25g (1oz) metallic yarn 4 ply equivalent (A)
Scraps of chenille (B)
Scraps of mohair (C)
1 pair no 3 (3¼mm) needles
1 pair no 7 (5mm) needles
Wire

Wings (make 2)

With no 3 needles and A, cast on 28 sts.
Work in st st for 6 rows.
*Next row K2tog, K to last 2 sts, turn.
Next row P.
Next row K2tog, K to end.
Next row P.
Rep last 4 rows twice (22 sts).
Next row Inc 1, K to last 2 sts, turn.
Next row P.
Next row Inc 1, K to end.
Next row P.
Rep last 4 rows twice (28 sts).
Work in st st for 6 rows.*
Rep from * to *.
**Next row K2tog, K to last 2 sts, K2tog.
Next row P.
Rep last 2 rows until 18 sts rem.
Next row Inc 1, K to last st, inc 1.
Next row P.
Rep last 2 rows until there are 28 sts.**
Next row Inc 1, K to end.
Next row P.
Rep last 2 rows until there are 33 sts.
Next row K2tog, K to end.

Next row P.
Rep last 2 rows until 28 sts rem.
Rep from ** to **.
Work in st st for 6 rows.
Rep from * to * twice more.
Bind off.

Upper body

With no 7 needles and B and C together, cast on 8 sts.
Work in st st for 32 rows.
Bind off.

Under body

With no 7 needles and B and C together, cast on 8 sts.
Work in st st for 16 rows.
Bind off.

Finishing

1 The six-row sections of straight knitting provide the ribs of the batwings. Fold each one wrong sides together lengthwise and sew in place to a depth of three rows, making six tucks.
2 Take six lengths of wire 15cm (6in) long and thread one into each of the tucks. Thread wire along outside of wings and oversew in place.
3 Press, stretching the fabric until it is taut and in required shape.
4 Fold upper body in half and place it on top of batwings opposite tail.
5 Place under body in same position on underside and sew together securely through wings.
6 Pull out top corners to form ears and oversew head all round with A.
7 Pucker a small piece of fabric on underside and oversew to form a nose.
8 With C doubled, embroider legs and arms on upper surface of wings in satin stitch.

Poppy

Four petals on a stem of French knitting form the basis of this poppy. The pattern can easily be adapted to make a variety of flowers.

Materials

Scraps of Acrylic mohair in main color (A)
Scraps of Acrylic mohair in contrast color (B)
Scraps of crochet cotton (C)
1 pair no 3 (3¼mm) needles
Wire
French knitting reel

Petals (make 4)

With A, cast on 6 sts.
Work in st st for 2 rows.
Inc 1 at each end of next and every alt row until there are 16 sts.
Work 6 rows.
Dec 1 at each end of next and every alt row until 10 sts rem.
Bind off.

Stem

With B, French knit a tube to desired length but do not bind it off. Pick up sts from French knitting reel with a knitting needle.

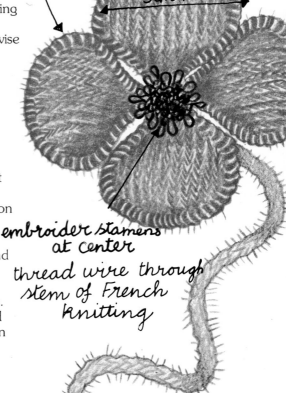

oversew wire round petal edge

5cm (2in)

embroider stamens at center

thread wire through stem of French knitting

110

15 cm (6½)

attach small knots for legs

Work in st st for 6 rows, inc 1 at each end of next and every alt row.
Bind off.

Finishing
1 Oversew wire round edge of each petal leaving about 10cm (4in) wire hanging at each side of base.
2 Arrange petals together and twist free lengths of wire round each other firmly.
3 Run a length of wire through stem and attach to wire hanging from petals.
4 Sew shaped piece of knitting at top of stem around twisted wire and join it to bottom of petals.
5 With C, embroider stamens in center.

Bee
The striped body of this bee is knitted in stockinette stitch with chenille in three contrasting colors. The wings are made from fine metallic yarn.

Materials
Scraps of chenille in 3 different colors (A, B, C)
Scraps of fine metallic yarn in a variety of colors (D)
1 pair no 0 (2¼mm) needles
Stuffing
Wire

Body
With A, cast on 10 sts.
Work in st st for 4 rows.
Next row Inc 1, K to last st, inc 1.
Next row P.
With B, work 2 rows.
With A, inc 1 at each end of next and foll alt row, end with a P row.
Next row K6B, K4A, K6B.
Next row P6B, P4A, P6B.
Next row K7B, K2A, K7B.
Next row P7B, P2A, P7B.
With A, dec 1 at each end of next and every alt row until 10 sts rem.
With C, work in st st for 2 rows.
Inc 1 at each end of next and every alt row until there are 16 sts.
Dec 1 at each end of next and every alt row until 10 sts rem.
Bind off.

Wings (make 2)
With D, work as for wings for fly.

Finishing
Make up as for fly.

Caterpillar
Combine metallic yarn with chenille and crochet cotton to knit this caterpillar. Embroider spots on the back of the body.

Materials
Scraps of metallic yarn in main color (A)
Scraps of chenille in contrast color (B)
Scraps of crochet cotton in 2nd contrast color (C)
1 pair no 0 (2¼mm) needles
Stuffing
Wire

Body
With A, cast on 14 sts.
Work in st st for 4 rows.
*Next row K5A, K1C, K2B, K1C, K5A.
Next row P5A, P1C, P2B, P1C, P5A.
Rep last 2 rows once.*
With A, work 2 rows.
Rep from * to *.
Next row With A, inc 1, K to last st, inc 1.
Next row P.
Next row K5A, K1C, K4B, K1C, K5A.
Next row P5A, P1C, P4B, P1C, P5A.
Rep last 2 rows twice.**
With A work 2 rows.
Next row K3A, K1C, K8B, K1C, K3A.
Next row P3A, P1C, P8B, P1C, P3A.
Rep last 2 rows twice.
With A, work 2 rows.
Rep from ** to **.
Next row With A, K2tog, K to last 2 sts, K2tog.
Next row P.
Rep from * to *.
With A, work 2 rows.
Rep from * to *.
With A, work 4 rows.
Bind off.

Finishing
1 Seam body into a tube.
2 Gather one end into point.
3 Stuff, inserting a length of wire in body.
4 Sew up open end.
5 With B, embroider spots on back.
6 With A, make small knots and attach in pairs to underbody for legs.

thread wire through edges of wings and oversew

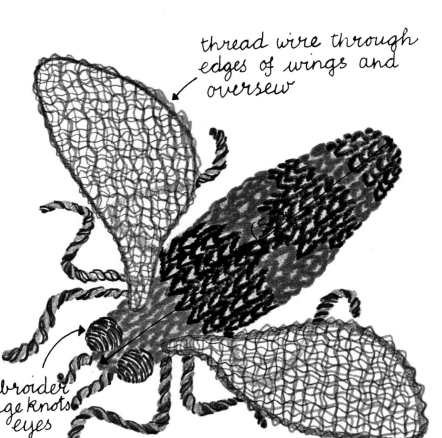

embroider large knots for eyes

Cushion collage

Instead of making single cushions, knit a complete set, filling them with abstract shapes, vibrant color and textural interest. Then use them separately or tie them together with lengths of French knitting for a most unusual floor cushion. Cushions give you the chance to experiment with many of the techniques described in this book. If you knit a basic square there are no worries about shaping and you can concentrate on incorporating as much color and detail as your ingenuity will allow. Combine textured stitches, motifs and different yarns with embroidery and three-dimensional effects. Extra strips, patches and strands of French knitting can be appliquéd onto the basic shape. Tease up areas of color with a wire brush for soft, fluffy effects and knit in beads, sequins or other objects as and where you please. The charts show how these cushions were made. You can follow them exactly or use them as starting-off points for your own ideas. They are all based on a 40cm (16in) square using no $10\frac{1}{2}$ (7mm) needles and the equivalent of double double knitting wool over 55 stitches and 65 rows. Knit both sides of the cushions or one side only and back them with felt. The latter is more practical and hardwearing, especially if you are intending to use them as floor cushions.

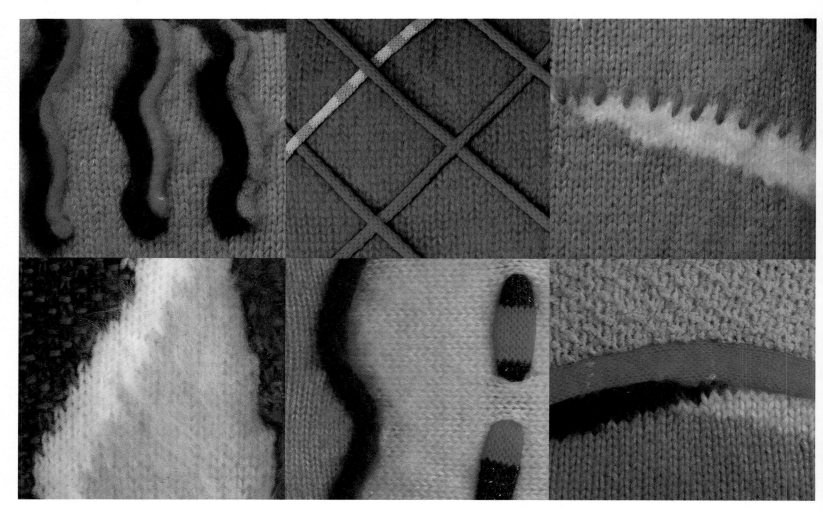

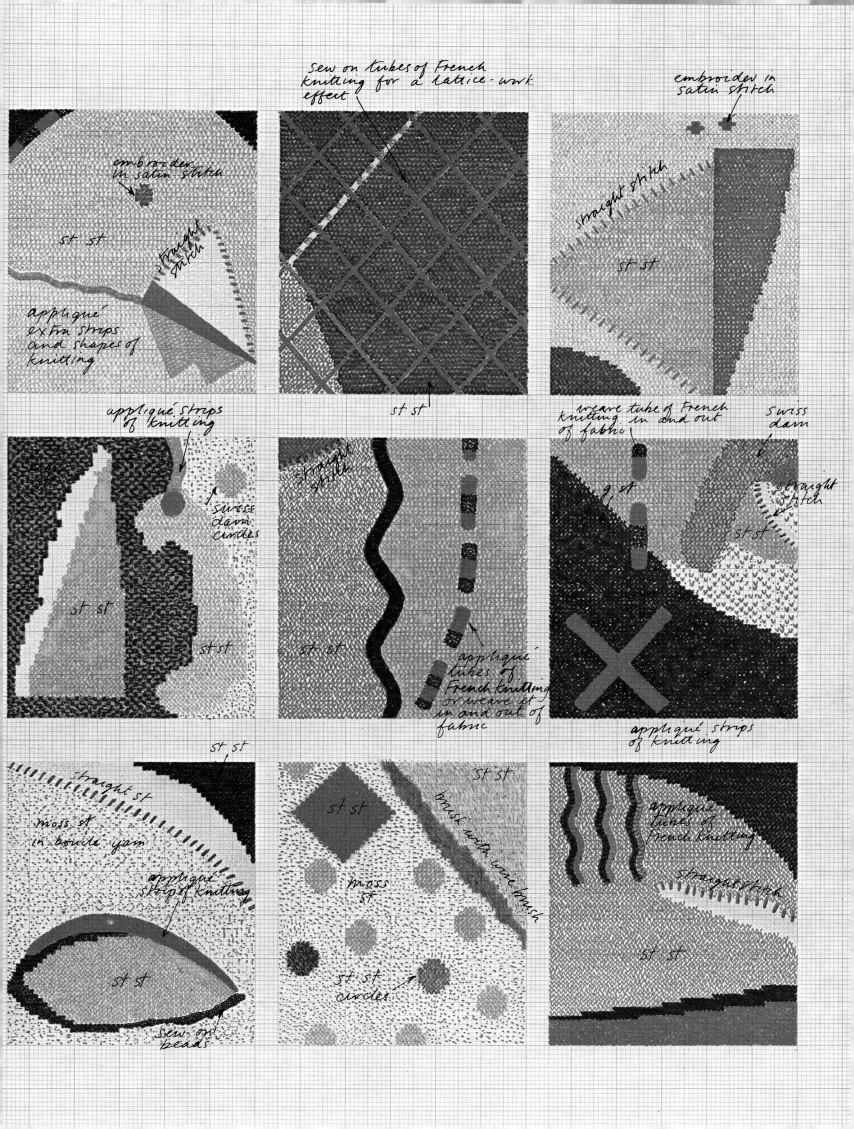

Rain drop

Window blinds can be designed to reflect the realities of the world outside. A rainy day inspired this one which is knitted in cotton yarn. The clouds are embroidered in mohair and the rain is represented by slanting lines of bugle beads, while strings of crystal beads, resembling raindrops, hang along the bottom edge. Spray the blind with stiffener to prevent it stretching and complete the scene with a puddle mat and several drips in sparkling mohair knitted in garter stitch and backed with toweling in a contrasting color.

Materials
300g (12oz) crochet cotton 3 ply equivalent (A)
Scraps of cotton yarns (B)
50g (2oz) mohair (C)
25g (1oz) DK (D)
1 pair no 5 (4mm) needles.
About 100 bugle beads in 2 colors
A quantity of pearly and crystal beads
2 wooden slats 87cm × 2.5cm
(34in × 1in)
Roller blind stiffener

Tension
22 sts and 44 rows to 10cm (4in) over st st on no 5 needles.

With A, cast on 200 sts.
Work in st st for 123cm (49in) or until work reaches desired length. Allow for 4cm (1½in) hem at each end and knit in B at random.
Bind off.

Finishing
1 Using C and D, embroider clouds.
2 Sew on bugle beads in slanting lines.
3 Turn under 4cm (1½in) hems at top and bottom of blind and insert wooden slats. Oversew ends of hems.
4 Decorate bottom of blind with a fringe of colored beads.
5 Spray blind with stiffener.

90 cm (36 in)

113 cm (45 in)

Make the clouds as large or small as you like

Thread wooden slats through top and bottom hems

Decorate the bottom of the blind with beads and crystals

1 square = 5 cm (2 in) for the same size as the mat in the picture

Puddle mat

Knit a puddle mat with sparkling mohair
or any other suitable yarn. You can either
follow the chart for shape or alter it
according to the size and design required.
If doing the latter, draw a paper pattern
and work as shown on p23. Make the
shape as curvaceous as possible and knit
droplets to continue the watery theme.

Materials
200g (8oz) sparkling mohair
1 pair no 7 (5mm) needles
Toweling

Tension
13 sts and 24 rows to 10cm (4in) over
g st on no 7 needles.

Mat
Cast on about 20 sts and work in g st,
follow chart for shape.

Drip (make several)
Cast on about 10 sts and work in g st,
follow chart for shape.

Finishing
Sew in any ends and back with toweling.

cm (39in)

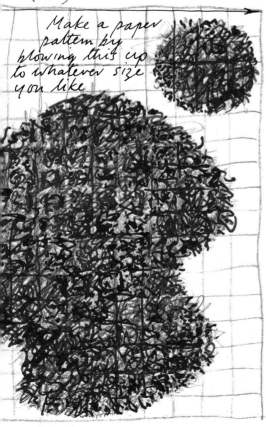

Make a paper
pattern by
blowing this up
to whatever size
you like

115

Four seasons' table mats

With matching coasters and napkin rings, each of these mats has been designed to represent a season. The background is worked in blocks of knit and purl stitches in contrasting colors to resemble a brick wall; it is then edged with a few lines of garter stitch which form the "flower bed".

Materials
Table mats 150g (6oz) brown DK (A)
50g (2oz) gray 4 ply (B)
25g (1oz) green DK (C)
1 pair no 5 (4mm) needles
Felt pieces in various colors
Coasters 25g (1oz) brown DK (A)
25g (1oz) gray 4 ply (B)
25g (1oz) green DK (C)
1 pair no 5 (4mm) needles
Napkin rings 25g (1oz) green DK
1 pair no 5 (4mm) needles
Cardboard tubing measuring 10cm × 4cm (4in × 1½in), cut into 4 pieces
The materials above make 4 of each item.

Table mat
With B, cast on 46 sts.

Apply appropriate flowers made from felt in a variety of colors; some ideas are given here. They can either be stitched on or threaded onto the yarn at 5cm (2in) intervals as shown on p40 and knitted in. Leave the coasters plain but carry the flower theme onto the napkin rings.

1st–3rd row K.
4th row K6A, *K2B, K6A; rep from *.
5th row P6A, *K2B, P6A; rep from *.
6th–9th row Rep 4th–5th row twice.
10th–11th row With B, K.
12th row K3A, *K2B, K6A; rep from * to last 3 sts, K3B.
13th row K3B, *P6A, K2B; rep from * to last 3 sts, P3A.
14th–17th row Rep 12th–13th row twice.
18th–19th row With B, K.
Rep 4th–19th row twice.
With C, work in g st for 7 rows.
Bind off.

Finishing
1 Darn in all loose ends and press well.
2 Trace pieces of flowers from drawings.

3 Cut out pieces in felt and join them.
4 Sew flowers at random onto last seven rows of work.

Coaster
With C, cast on 16 sts.
1st–2nd row K.
3rd–4th row With B, K.
5th row K4A, K2B, K4A, K2B, K4A.
6th row P4A, K2B, P4A, K2B, P4A.
7th–8th row As 5th–6th row.
9th–10th row With B, K.
11th row K2A, K2B, K4A, K2B, K4A, K2B.
12th row K2B, P4A, K2B, P4A, K2B, P2A.
13th–14th row As 11th–12th row.
15th–16th row With B, K.
17th–22nd row As 5th–10th row.
23rd–24th row With C, K.
Bind off.

Border
With C, pick up 14 sts down one side.
K 2 rows.
Bind off.
Rep along other side.

Napkin ring
Cast on 20 sts.
Work in g st for 27 rows.
Bind off.

Finishing
1 Darn in all loose ends.
2 Cover one piece of cardboard tube with knitting, join bottom edges and sew them together at join.
3 Trace pieces of flowers from drawing.
4 Cut out pieces in felt and sew them together.
5 Sew finished flowers at random around top of work.

Spring

Summer

Autumn

Winter

23cm (9in)

18cm (7in)

Trace the shapes on the left for seasonal flowers and foliage

Cut out shapes in colored felt and sew to edge of table mat

Add some mistletoe for Christmas!

Secret garden

Enjoy summer all the year round by knitting yourself a unique indoor garden. Construct a wooden frame to the required size of trellis, attaching 2.5cm (1in) wide wooden slats to its sides arranged in a lattice pattern. Before assembling the trellis, cover the frame and the slats with strips of knitting seamed at the back and remember to allow for the fact that the knitting will stretch when sewn round the wood. Decorate with knitted flowers, using the poppy pattern on p110 as a guide but varying the shapes of the leaves and petals as you please. Wire round the petals and leaves and attach them to stems made from French knitting (p38) which should also be wired. Then thread them in and out of the trellis together with a variety of insects and caterpillars and even a colorful bat. Refer back to pp108–11 for some ideas. Fill flower pots and window boxes with your favorite flowers. Complete the effect with colorful cacti in pots and a patio floor rug. The patterns for the last two items are given here.

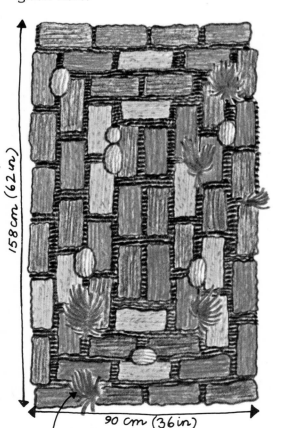

158cm (62 in)

90 cm (36 in)

sew grass tufts between bricks

Patio floor rug

Two rectangles knitted in garter stitch with bulky wool form the basis of this rug. Bricks knitted in stockinette stitch in three different shades are sewn on afterward as are the small pebbles and tufts of grass.

Materials

300g (12oz) black bulky wool (A)
300g (12oz) brown DK in each of 3 contrasting shades (B, C, D)
25g (1oz) green DK (E)
Scraps of gray DK (F)
1 pair no 9 (6mm) needles
1 pair no $10\frac{1}{2}$ (7mm) needles
1 pair no 15 (10mm) needles
Stuffing

Back rectangles (make 2)

With no 15 needles and A, cast on 45 sts.
Work in g st until work measures 156cm (62in).
Bind off.

Bricks (make 56)

With no $10\frac{1}{2}$ needles and B, C or D doubled, cast on 15 sts.
Work in st st until work measures 22cm ($8\frac{1}{2}$in).
Bind off.

Pebbles (make several)

With no 9 needles and F doubled, cast on 10 sts and work in st st for 12 rows.
Bind off.

Grass tufts (make several)

With no 9 needles and E doubled, cast on 20 sts.
Work in loop st as shown on p141 for 4 rows.
Bind off.

Finishing

1 Sew the two rectangles for back together.
2 Sew bricks to back following chart for pattern, leaving 0.5cm ($\frac{1}{4}$in) between bricks for cement.
3 Sew tufts of grass between bricks at intervals over rug. Cut through loops.
4 Run a gathering thread round the edge of each pebble square. Place a little stuffing in the center, pull up thread and fasten off.
5 Sew pebbles at intervals over rug.

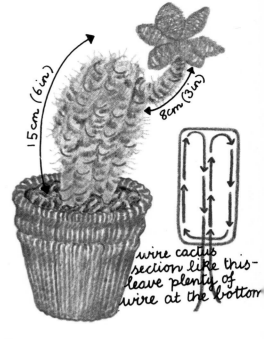

15cm (6in)

8cm (3in)

wire cactus section like this – leave plenty of wire at the bottom

Cactus in pot

This colorful cactus stands in a flower pot which is covered with a knitted strip and filled with Styrofoam, hidden by knitted earth. The cactus itself is made up of four sections with a flower at the top.

Materials

25g (1oz) green DK (A)
25g (1oz) green metallic yarn 4 ply equivalent (B)
25g (1oz) green mohair (C)
25g (1oz) pink crochet cotton (D)
25g (1oz) brown 4 ply wool (E)
25g (1oz) dark brown 4 ply wool (F)
1 pair no 3 ($3\frac{1}{4}$mm) needles
1 pair no 8 ($5\frac{1}{2}$mm) needles
1 12cm ($4\frac{1}{2}$in) plastic flower pot
Wire
Florist's Styrofoam to fit pot

Sections (make 4)

With no 8 needles and A, B and C together, cast on 10 sts.
Work in g st until work measures 15cm (6in).
Bind off.

Stem

With no 8 needles and A, B and C together, cast on 4 sts.
Work in g st until work measures 8cm (3in).
Bind off.

Flower petals (make 6)

With no 3 needles and D, cast on 4 sts.
Work in g st for 16 rows, inc 1 at each end of 5th and 7th rows and dec 1 at each end of 11th, 13th and 15th rows.
Bind off.

Pot
With no 3 needles and E, cast on
58 sts.
Work in st st until work measures 15cm
(6in).
Bind off.

Earth
With no 3 needles and F, cast on
40 sts.
Work in st st until work measures 8cm
(3in).
Next row K10, cast off 20 sts, K10.
Next row P10, cast on 20 sts, P10.

Work in st st for 8cm (3in).
Bind off.

Finishing
1 Sew pot piece into tube making a tuck
to simulate a ridge just below top edge.
Stretch tube over pot. Turn over 2.5cm
(1in) to inside of pot at top and glue in
place. Run gathering thread around
bottom and pull up under pot.
2 Wire cactus sections as shown in the
drawing leaving long ends at bottom of
each one. Place all four pieces together
and seam down the middle. Fan out

sections and bend them into shape.
3 Fold flower stem in half lengthwise and
stitch side seam.
4 Wire edges of each petal leaving long
ends of wire on each. Twist these ends
together and thread through center of
flower stem.
5 Attach stem to cactus and arrange
petals into flower shape.
6 Fill pot with Styrofoam and "plant"
cactus crushing the long wire ends to
help keep it in place.
7 Place earth over cactus through hole in
the middle and push it down into pot.

Fruit salad

Knitted fruits demonstrate the great potential for creating imaginative shapes in knitting. This banana, pineapple and bunch of grapes can be purely decorative, used as toys or put to a more practical use as giant floor cushions. Study the shape and texture of other fruits, vegetables and even animals for more ideas. Then experiment with different yarns and stitches on small samples until you achieve the right effect. Look back to pp42–3 to see how to stuff them so that they retain their shape.

Bunch of grapes

These grapes are knitted in stockinette stitch with bouclé wool, which helps convey the bloom of the fruit. They are then stuffed and sewn together to form a bunch. The leaf, complete with veins in stem stitch, is also knitted in bouclé.

Materials

1,350g (54oz) green bouclé (A)
200g (8oz) light green bouclé (B)
Oddments of olive green bouclé (C)
1 pair no 6 (4½mm) needles
Stuffing
50cm × 50cm × 2.5cm (20in × 20in × 1in) foam sheeting

Grapes (make 52)
With A, cast on 5 sts.
1st row Inc 1 in every st.
2nd row P.
3rd–6th row Rep 1st–2nd row twice (40 sts).
7th row K.
8th row P.
9th row K to last 2 sts, turn.
10th row Sl 1, P to last 2 sts, turn.
11th row Sl 1, K to last 4 sts, turn.
12th row Sl 1, P to last 4 sts, turn.
13th row Sl 1, K to last 6 sts, turn.
14th row Sl 1, P to last 6 sts, turn.
15th row Sl 1, K to end.
16th row P.
17th–48th row Rep 9th–16th row 4 times.
49th row K.
50th row P.
51st row K2tog to end.
52nd row P.
53rd–56th row Rep 51st–52nd row twice.
Bind off.

Fruit salad

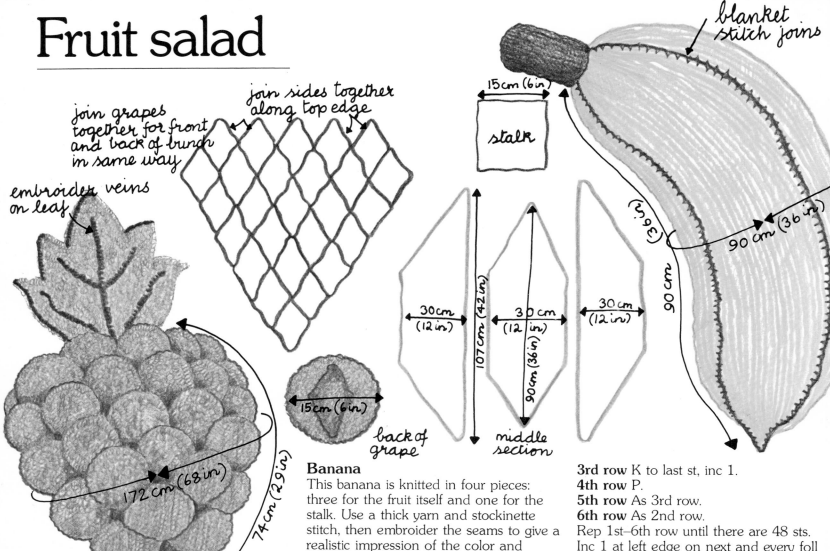

join grapes together for front and back of bunch in same way

join sides together along top edge

embroider veins on leaf

blanket stitch joins

15cm (6in)

stalk

172 cm (68 in)

74 cm (29 in)

15cm (6in)

back of grape

30cm (12in)

107cm (42in)

30 cm (12 in)

90cm (36in)

30 cm (12 in)

middle section

90 cm (36 in)

90 cm

90 cm (36 in)

Leaf (make 2 pieces)
With B, cast on 40 sts.
Work in st st, inc 1 at each end of first and every alt row until there are 100 sts, end with a P row.
   25 sts at beg of next 2 rows (50 sts).
Inc 1 at each end of next and every foll 3rd row until there are 120 sts, end with a P row.
   20 sts at beg of next 2 rows.
Dec 1 at each end of next and every alt row until 2 sts rem.

1 Join grapes as shown.
2 Join side seam leaving an opening at top for stuffing.
3 Using leaf piece as pattern, cut out foam sheeting 0.5cm ($\frac{1}{4}$in) larger all round than the leaf.
4 Join leaf pieces together round foam and blanket stitch round edge in C.
5 Embroider veins on leaf.
6 Stuff grapes, pushing filling well down into each section.
7 Join seam opening and sew leaf to seam at top of bunch.

Banana

This banana is knitted in four pieces: three for the fruit itself and one for the stalk. Use a thick yarn and stockinette stitch, then embroider the seams to give a realistic impression of the color and texture of the skin.

Materials
500g (20oz) yellow triple knitting wool (A)
50g (2oz) brown triple knitting wool (B)
1 pair no 5 (4mm) needles
1m × 1m (1yd × 36in) calico
61cm (24in) zipper
Stuffing
15cm × 15cm × 2.5cm (6in × 6in × 1in) foam sheeting

Front
With A, cast on 2 sts.
Work in st st, inc 1 at each end of first and every alt row until there are 48 sts, end with a P row.
Inc 1 at each end of next and every 4th row until there are 54 sts.
Continue without shaping until work measures 61cm (24in) from beg, end with a P row.
K2tog at each end of next and every 4th row until 48 sts rem, end with a P row.
K2tog at each end of next and every alt row until 2 sts rem.
Bind off.

Left side
With A, cast on 2 sts.
1st row K.
2nd row Inc 1 purlwise, P to end.

3rd row K to last st, inc 1.
4th row P.
5th row As 3rd row.
6th row As 2nd row.
Rep 1st–6th row until there are 48 sts.
Inc 1 at left edge on next and every foll 3rd row until there are 54 sts.
Continue in st st without shaping until work measures 70cm (28in) from beg, end with a P row.
Dec 1 at left edge on next and every foll 3rd row until 54 sts rem.
Rep 1st–6th row but dec instead of inc until 2 sts rem.
Bind off.

Right side
Work as for left side reversing all shaping.

Stalk
With B, cast on 30 sts.
Work in st st until work measures 15cm (6in), end with a P row.
Bind off.

Finishing
1 Using three main pieces as patterns cut out calico shapes, allowing for seam allowances of 5cm (2in) all round.
2 Seam calico to make bag and stuff.
3 Join left side to front along straight edge of left side.
4 Join right side to front in same way.
5 Insert zipper in remaining seam.
6 With B, blanket stitch over all joins.
7 Join sides and top of stalk, roll up foam sheeting and stuff stalk and sew on to one end of banana.

Pineapple

The scaly effect of a pineapple's skin is achieved by knitting all the segments separately in stockinette stitch with decorative increasing. They are then stitched together and backed with calico to prevent them from stretching.

Materials

900g (36oz) orange DK (A)
300g (12oz) green DK (B)
1 pair no 5 (4mm) needles
4m × 76cm (4½yd × 30in) calico
1.5m × 50cm × 2.5cm (1¾yd × 20in × 1in) foam sheeting
3m × 1m (3½ × 1yd) Dacron batting

Pineapple pieces (make 60)

With A, cast on 3 sts.
1st row Inc 1, K1, inc 1.
2nd row K1, P to last st, K1.
3rd row K1, inc 1, K1, inc 1, K1.
4th row As 2nd row.
5th row K2, inc 1, K1, inc 1, K2.
6th row As 2nd row.
7th row K to centre 3 sts, inc 1, K1, inc 1, K to last 2 sts, turn.
8th row Sl 1 purlwise, P to last 2 sts, turn.
9th row Sl 1 purlwise, K to centre 3 sts, inc 1, K1, inc 1, K to end.
10th row As 2nd row.
11th–30th row Rep 7th–10th rows 5 times (33 sts).
31st row K1, (sl 1, K1, psso) twice, K9, inc 1, K1, inc 1, K9, (K2tog) twice, P1.
32nd row As 2nd row.
33rd row Inc 1 purlwise, (sl 1, K1, psso) twice, K8, inc 1, K1, inc 1, K8, (K2tog) twice, inc 1 purlwise.
34th row K2, P to last 2 sts, K2.
35th row K1, inc 1 purlwise, (sl 1, K1, psso) twice, K8, MB, K8, (K2tog) twice, inc 1 purlwise, K1.
36th row K3, P to last 3 sts, K3.
37th row K1, P1, inc 1 purlwise, (sl 1, K1, psso) twice, K13, (K2tog) twice, inc 1 purlwise, P1, K1.
38th row K4, P to last 4 sts, K4.
39th row K1, P2, inc 1 purlwise, (sl 1, K1, psso) twice, K9, (K2tog) twice, inc 1 purlwise, P1, turn.
40th row Sl 1, K2, P to last 5 sts, K3, turn.
41st row Sl 1, P1, inc 1 purlwise, (sl 1, K1, psso) twice, K5, (K2tog) twice, inc 1 purlwise, P4.
42nd row K6, P to last 6 sts, K6.

43rd row P5, inc 1 purlwise, (sl 1, K1, psso) twice, K1, (K2tog) twice, inc 1 purlwise, P3, turn.
44th row Sl 1, K4, P to last 7 sts, K5, turn.
45th row Sl 1, P3, inc 1 purlwise, sl 1, K1, psso, K1, K2tog, inc 1 purlwise, P6.
46th row K8, P3, K8.
47th row P to 3 centre sts, P3tog, P to last 2 sts, turn.
48th row Sl 1, K to last 2 sts, turn.
49th row Sl 1, P to centre 3 sts, P3tog, P to end.
50th row K to end.
51st–58th row Rep 47th–50th row twice.
59th row P1, P3tog, P1.
60th row K3tog and fasten off.

Large leaves (make 4 pieces)

With B, cast on 50 sts.
Work in st st for 20cm (8in).
K2tog at each end of next and foll 4th row.
Work 3 rows.
K2tog at each end of next and every alt row until 2 sts rem.
Bind off.

Medium leaves (make 4 pieces)

With B, cast on 44 sts.

Work in st st for 15cm (6in).
Dec as for large leaves.
Bind off.

Small leaves (make 2 pieces)

With B, cast on 40 sts.
Work in st st for 10cm (4in).
Dec as for large leaves.
Bind off.

Finishing

1 Join pineapple pieces as shown.
2 Stuff each section with batting and back entire area with half the calico.
3 Quilt along seams of pineapple sections as shown on p45.
4 Join points together along top and bottom edges.
5 Insert zipper in side seam and make remaining calico into a bag and stuff.
6 Using leaf pieces as patterns cut out foam sheeting about 0.5cm (¼in) larger all round than the leaves; cut two large, two medium and one small piece.
7 Join leaves together round the foam.
8 Wrap two medium leaves around small leaf and then two large leaves around medium leaves, overlapping joins and stitching bunch firmly together at base.
9 Stitch bunch of leaves securely to top.

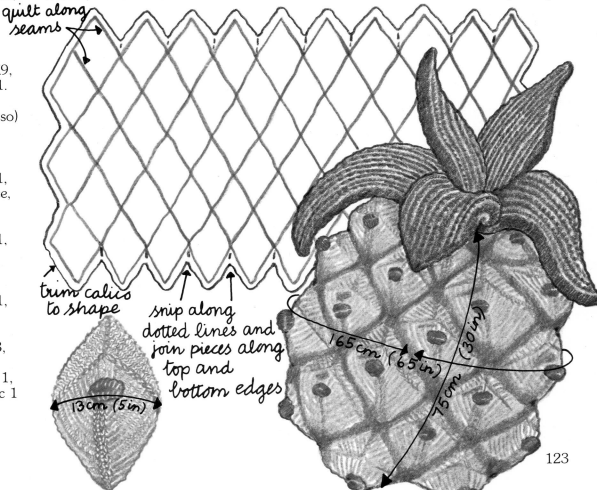

quilt along seams

trim calico to shape

snip along dotted lines and join pieces along top and bottom edges

13cm (5in)

165cm (65in)

75cm (30in)

123

Playtime

You can knit all sorts of interesting objects with your left-over scraps of yarn, such as the paint-box complete with brush, the bundle of brightly colored crayons, the clutch of ice pops and the ice cream with cone shown here. All are worked in simple stitches with the minimum of shaping and could be ideal starting-off points for teaching children to knit.

Paint-box and brush
This paint-box, worked open so that all the bright paints are on view, is lined with canvas to give it shape and body. The handle of the brush is lightly stuffed and the bristles are made from a thick yarn for a suitably hairy effect.

Materials
25g (1oz) 4 ply in main color (A)
Scraps of 4 ply in contrast color (B)
Scraps of 4 ply in a variety of bright colors (C,D,E,F,G)
Scraps of silver metallic yarn (H)
1 pair no 1 ($2\frac{3}{4}$mm) needles
Stuffing
1 piece of canvas 13cm × 18cm (5in × 7in)

Paint-box lid (make 2)
With A, cast on 53 sts.
Work in rev st st for 33 rows.
Bind off.

Lining
With B, cast on 46 sts.
Work in st st for 5 rows, beg with a P row.
Next row K3B, K8C, K8D, K8E, K8F, K8G, K3B.
Next row P3B, P8G, P8F, P8E, P8D, P8C, P3B.
Rep last 2 rows 6 times, then the first of them again.
With B, work 3 rows.
Next row Bind off 9 sts, K9, bind off 10, K9, bind off 9.
Work in st st for 3 rows on both sets of 9 sts, working each one separately.
Break off yarn.
With right side facing, cast on 9 sts.
Knit first set of 9 sts, cast on 10 sts, knit across second set of 9 sts, cast on 9 sts.
Next row P across all 46 sts.
Work in st st for 22 rows.
Bind off.

Finishing
1 Cut canvas into two pieces each measuring 6.5cm × 18cm ($2\frac{1}{2}$in × 7in).
2 Line each lid with canvas, leaving small allowance all round for turning. Tack canvas in place.
3 Using B, and chain stitch (p44), outline paint blocks and indicate mixing palettes on second half of knitted lining.
4 Turn under hems to a depth of about three rows on one long side of each lid and tack them down. Place hemmed sides of lids together with wrong side facing and place knitted lining on top.
5 Fold hem allowances of lids over edges of knitted lining and hem in place neatly all round edge except where 9 st sections cross over both lids. At these points join two lid sections together on right side to form hinges.

Brush
With H, cast on 5 sts.
Work in st st for 14 rows.
Next row With A, inc 1, K3, inc 1.
Next row P.
Continue in st st for 51 rows, inc 1 at each end of 7th row and dec 1 at each end of 17th, 33rd and 51st row (3 sts). Work 5 rows.
Next row Sl 1, K2tog, psso.
Break off yarn and thread through rem st.

Finishing
1 Cut several lengths of J the length of the brush plus 2.5cm (1in).
2 Wrap knitting around these lengths so that the ends project at the wide end and join brush lengthwise over them.
3 Wind length of H firmly around join between two colors and fasten off.
4 Twist "bristles" together to shape and trim if necessary.

Crayons
These are worked singly in stockinette stitch, then stuffed lightly and tied together in a bundle. They can easily be made longer or shorter.

Materials
Scraps of 4 ply in a variety of colors
1 pair no 1 ($2\frac{3}{4}$mm) needles
Stuffing

Cast on 12 sts.
Work in st st until work measures 9cm ($3\frac{1}{2}$in), end with a K row.
Next row K.
Next row *K2tog, K1; rep from * to end.
Next row P.
Next row (K2tog) 4 times.
Next row P.
Break off yarn and thread through rem sts. Draw up and fasten off.

Finishing
1 Join crayon lengthwise leaving opening at cast-on edge and stuff lightly.
2 Form opening into round shape and stitch carefully to close.

Ice pops

Knit a handful of ice pops in stockinette stitch in a range of glittering or pale ice cream colors, then decorate with beads to resemble confectionery.

Materials

Scraps of different-colored DK
1 pair no 4 (3¾mm) needles
Pop stick
Colored bugle beads
Dacron batting

With no 4 needles, cast on 18 sts.
1st row K.
2nd row Inc 1, P to end.
3rd row Inc 1, K to end (20 sts).
4th–30th row Work in st st, changing colours as required.
31st–40th row Work in st st, dec 1 at beg of each row (10 sts).
Bind off.
Make a second piece in the same way for the other side.

Finishing

1 Join side and top seams and stuff with Dacron batting.
2 Place pop stick in center and join bottom seam so that pop fits tightly around stick.
3 Sew beads on top.

Ice cream with cone

The cone is knitted in a lattice cable stitch which brilliantly conveys its wafer-like texture and is filled with ice cream made from two pompons and a knitted chocolate flake.

Materials

Scraps of yellow, pink, white and dark brown DK (A,B,C,D)
1 pair no 4 (3¾mm) needles
1 cable needle
Dacron batting

Cone

With A, cast on 38 sts.
1st–8th row Work in g st.
9th row *K2tog, K5; rep from * to last 3 sts, K2tog, K1 (32 sts).
10th row (Right side) P1, K1, *P4, K2; rep from * to last 6 sts, P4, K1, P1.
11th row K1, P1, *K4, P2; rep from * to last 6 sts, P4, K1, P1.
12th row P1, *sl next st to CN to front of work, P1, then K1 from CN, P2, sl next st to CN to back of work, K1, then P1 from CN; rep from * to last st, P1.
13th row K2, *P1, K2; rep from * to end.
14th row P2, *sl next st to CN to front of work, P1, then K1 from CN, sl next st to CN to back of work, K1, then P1 from CN, P2; rep from * to end.
15th row K3, *P2, K4; rep from * to last 5 sts, P2, K3.
16th row P3, *sl next st to CN to front of work, K1, then K1 from CN, P4; rep from *, end last rep P3.
17th row As 15th row.
18th–23rd row As 12th–17th row.
24th row As 12th row.
25th row K2tog, *P1, K2; rep from * to last 3 sts, P1, K2tog.
26th row P1, work as 14th row from *, end P1.
27th row K2tog, *P2, K4; rep from * to last 4 sts, P2, K2tog.
28th row P1, work as 16th row from *, end P1.
29th row K2tog, P1, *K4, P2; rep from * to last 7 sts, K4, P1, K2tog (26 sts).
30th–35th row As 24th–29th row (20 sts).
Work in g st for 16 rows, dec 1 at each end of every 3rd row (10 sts).
Continue in g st, dec 1 at beg of every row until 2 sts rem.
Bind off.

Chocolate flake

With D, cast on 20 sts.
Work in g st for 10 rows.
Bind off.

Finishing

1 Join side seam of cone and stuff with Dacron batting.
2 Using B and C, make two pompons for ice cream to a diameter of 5cm (2in) as shown on p37.
3 Place pompons in cone and thread pompon ties down back seam of cone.
4 Turn collar of cone up around pompons and sew round collar into middle of pompons to hold them in place. Turn collar down to hide stitches.
5 Join edges of flake and stitch it between pompons.

End games

Knitted props and accessories are essentially fun and have little practical purpose other than to amuse and to provide a talking point at parties and similar entertaining occasions. They also make interesting objects when displayed on shelves or in odd corners to surprise, and when used by children for dressing up and in games. Once you have grasped the idea that literally anything can be knitted, this lipstick, cigarette packet complete with cigarettes, lighter and mouse with cheese will simply become starting points for further forays into the world of soft craft.

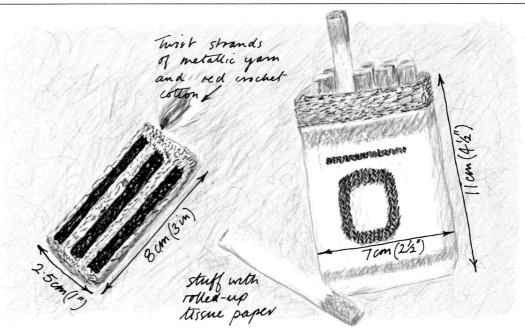

Twist strands of metallic yarn and red crochet cotton

stuff with rolled-up tissue paper

2.5cm (1")

8cm (3in)

11cm (4½")

7cm (2½")

Lipstick

This knitted lipstick can be used as a decorative accessory or as a toy. It is knitted in one piece; the case in silver metallic yarn and the actual lipstick in red crochet cotton.

Materials

Scraps of silver metallic yarn (A)
Scraps of red crochet cotton (B)
1 pair no 0 (2¼mm) needles
Stuffing

With A, cast on 12 sts.
Work in K1, P1 rib for 13 rows.
Next row With 5 strands of A, K.
Break off 4 strands.

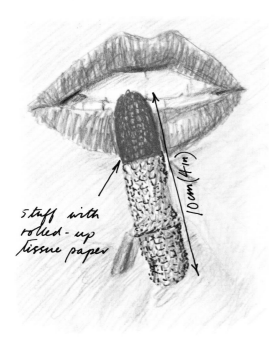

stuff with rolled-up tissue paper

10cm (4in)

Work in st st for 10 rows, beg with a K row.
With B, work in st st for 4 rows.
Next row *K2, K2tog; rep from * to end.
Next row P.
Next row *K1, K2tog; rep from * to end.
Next row P.
Next row K2tog to end.
Thread yarn through rem sts and fasten off securely.

Finishing
1 Join side seam.
2 Stuff lipstick with red fabric scraps and case with stuffing.
3 Gather up bottom opening and stitch.

Cigarette lighter
Make a cigarette lighter with silver and black metallic yarn and sew twisted strands of gold metallic yarn and red crochet cotton on the top for a flame.

Materials
Scraps of silver metallic yarn (A)
Scraps of black metallic yarn (B)
Scraps of gold metallic yarn and red crochet cotton (C)
1 pair no 0 (2¼mm) needles
Stuffing

With A, cast on 10 sts.
Work in rev st st for 7 rows.
Next row Cast on 18 sts, K to end.
Next row P.
Next row *K4A, K2B, K2A, K2B, K2A, K2B; rep from * to end.
Continuing the sequence of colors for vertical stripes, work in st st for 27 rows.
With A, work 2 rows.

Next row Bind off 18 sts, K to end.
With A, work in rev st st for 4 rows.
Bind off.

Finishing
1 Join side seam.
2 Sew end in place to form a box shape.
3 Stuff lightly.
4 Twist together short lengths of C to make flame. Sew in place at top edge.
5 Sew top of lighter in place.

Cigarettes
Knit a cigarette packet with a motif on the front to resemble your favorite brand and fill it with cigarettes knitted in fine crochet cotton and stuffed with rolled-up tissue paper.

Materials
13g (½oz) fine crochet cotton in white (A)
Scraps of fine crochet cotton in gray (B), blue (C)
Scraps of metallic yarn (D)
Scraps of beige 4 ply (E)
1 pair no 0 (2¼mm) needles
Tissue paper

Packet
With A, cast on 64 sts.
Work in st st for 10 rows.
With B, work 4 rows.
With A, work 10 rows.
Next row K10A, K6C, K26A, K6C, K16A.
This fixes the position of the motifs on front and back of packet.
Complete motifs, following chart above for pattern.
With A, work in st st for 4 rows.

chart for cigarette packet

work motif on front and back of cigarette packet

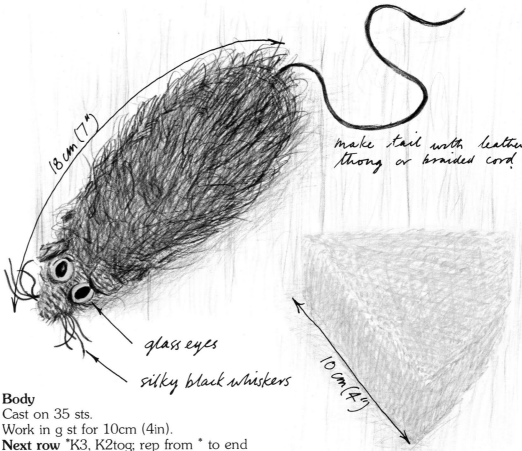

18 cm (7")

make tail with leather thong or braided cord

glass eyes

silky black whiskers

10 cm (4")

Next row K2A, K20C, K12A, K20C, K10A.
Next row P10A, P20C, P12A, P20C, P2A.
With A, work in st st for 2 rows.
With C, work in st st for 4 rows.
With A, work in st st for 2 rows.
With D, work in rev st st for 10 rows.
Bind off.

Cigarette (make several)
With A, cast on 10 sts.
Work in st st for 34 rows.
With E, work in st st for 8 rows.
Bind off.

Finishing
1 Join side and bottom seams of packet. Fold bottom corners and stitch to make box shape.
2 Line with cardboard or an empty cigarette packet to stiffen. Alternatively you could starch it.
3 Stuff cigarettes with rolled-up tissue paper and join side seams.

Mouse
This mouse is knitted with gray mohair in garter stitch. Its body is made in one piece. The ears are made separately and sewn on afterwards, as are the black crochet cotton whiskers.

Materials
25g (1oz) gray mohair
1 pair no 9 (6mm) needles
Black crochet cotton
Leather thong
1 pair glass eyes
Stuffing

Body
Cast on 35 sts.
Work in g st for 10cm (4in).
Next row *K3, K2tog; rep from * to end (28 sts).
Work 5 rows.
Next row *K2, K2tog; rep from * to end (21 sts).
Work 5 rows.
Next row *K2, K2tog; rep from * to last st, K1 (16 sts).
Work 5 rows.
Next row *K2, K2tog; rep from * to end (12 sts).
Work 3 rows.
Rep the last 4 rows once (9 sts).
Next row *K1, K2tog; rep from * to end (6 sts).
K 1 row.
Next row K2tog to end.
Break off yarn, thread through sts, draw up and fasten off.

Ears (make 2)
Cast on 3 sts.
Work in g st for 3 rows.
Next row Sl 1, K1, psso, K1.
Next row Sl 1, K1, psso.
Break off yarn and fasten off.

Making up
1 Brush body with a teasel brush.
2 Fold body in half lengthwise and join seam.
3 Stuff, then run a thread through cast-on edge and draw up for rear end.
4 Sew leather thong on for tail.
5 Sew on eyes and ears.
6 Sew on tufts of black crochet cotton below eyes for whiskers.

Cheese
This piece of cheese is knitted in a triangular shape in reverse stockinette stitch to resemble a slice and is stuffed with foam rubber.

Materials
25g (1oz) yellow crochet cotton
1 pair no 0 (2¼mm) needles
13cm × 13cm × 4cm (5in × 5in × 1½in)
Foam rubber

Top and bottom (alike)
Cast on 2 sts.
Work in rev st st for 2 rows.
Continue in rev st st, inc 1 at each end of next and every alt row until there are 40 sts, end with a K row.
Bind off 2 sts at beg of next 6 rows.
Bind off 3 sts at beg of next 6 rows.
Bind off rem 10 sts.

Side piece
Cast on 14 sts.
Work in rev st st until work measures 30cm (12in).
Bind off.

Finishing
1 Join side piece to top.
2 Join side seam.
3 Using bottom as pattern cut a piece of foam rubber to size of cheese.
4 Stuff foam rubber into cheese and sew on bottom.

Basics

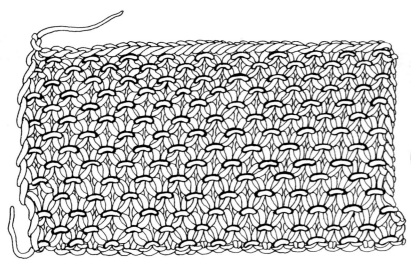

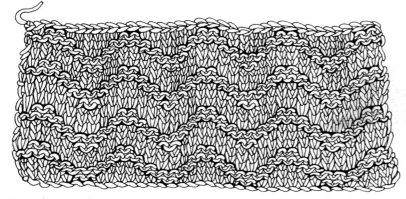

Moss stitch

Pattern repeats over 2 rows and an even number of sts. It is often confused with Irish moss stitch and is sometimes also called seed stitch or rice stitch. They are similar, the only difference being that in Irish moss stitch the pattern changes every other row and therefore repeats every 4 rows.

Cast on an even number of sts.
1st row *K1, P1; rep from *.
2nd row *P1, K1; rep from *.

Wager welt

Pattern repeats over 8 rows and any number of sts. The name wager refers to the puzzle of how many rows out of the 8 are in fact purled, the answer is 1. It is also known as puzzle stitch, dispute stitch and all fools' welt and looks most effective when the ridges are worked in a different color.

Cast on any number of sts.
1st row (Right side) K.
2nd row P.
3rd–8th row K.

Ripple stitch

Pattern repeats over 10 rows and 8 sts, plus 6 extra. It consists of g st zigzags against a st st background, which can look most effective when worked in a different color. This would involve working the P sts on right-side rows and the K sts on wrong-side rows in a contrast color.
Cast on a multiple of 8 sts, plus 6 extra.
1st row (Right side) K6, *P2, K6; rep from *.
2nd row K1, *P4, K4; rep from *, end P4, K1.

3rd row P2, *K2, P2; rep from *.
4th row P1, *K4, P4; rep from *, end K4, P1.
5th row K2, *P2, K6; rep from *, end P2, K2.
6th row P6, *K2, P6; rep from *.
7th row P1, *K4, P4; rep from *, end K4, P1.
8th row K2, *P2, K2; rep from *.
9th row K1, *P4, K4; rep from *, end P4, K1.
10th row P2, *K2, P6; rep from *, end K2, P2.

Escalator pattern

Pattern repeats over 24 rows and 16 sts. The use of purl stitch blocks results in an interesting diagonal pattern.
Cast on a multiple of 16 sts.
1st row (Right side) *K5, P11; rep from *.
2nd row *K11, P5; rep from *.
3rd row As 1st row.
4th–6th row Work in st st, starting with P.
7th row P4, *K5, P11; rep from *, end K5, P7.
8th row K7, *P5, K11; rep from *, end P5, K4.
9th row As 7th row.

10th–12th row Work in st st, starting with P.
13th row P8, *K5, P11; rep from *, end K5, P3.
14th row K3, *P5, K11; rep from *, end P5, K8.
15th row As 13th row.
16th–18th row Work in st st, starting with P.
19th row K1, P11, *K5, P11; rep from *, end K4.
20th row P4, *K11, P5; rep from *, end K11, P1.
21st row As 19th row.
22nd–24th row Work in st st, starting with P.

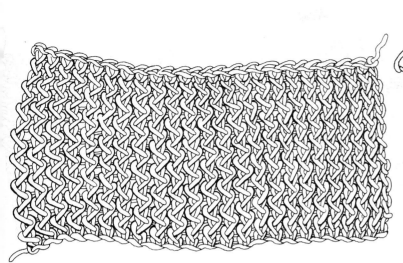

Twisted stockinette stitch

Pattern repeats over 2 rows and any number of sts. The right-side sts are knitted through the back of the loops, which twists the sts and gives a firm texture to the fabric. Cast on any number of sts.

1st row K each st tbl.
2nd row P.

Twisted rib

Pattern repeats over 2 rows and an odd number of sts. It creates a firmer and more elastic rib than the usual rib. It also makes the "ribs" stand out more than they do in an ordinary rib. Like ordinary rib it can also be varied by increasing the number of P and K sts, for example, K2 tbl, P2 or K3 tbl, P3 and so on.

Cast on an even number of sts.

1st row K1 tbl, *P1, K1 tbl; rep from *.
2nd row P1, *K1 tbl, P1; rep from *.

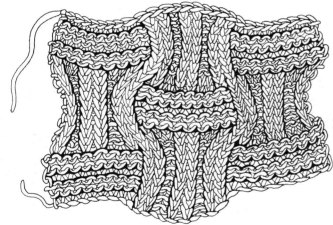

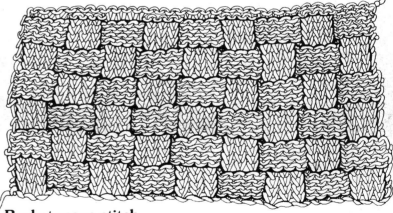

Double basketweave

Pattern repeats over 18 rows and 18 sts, plus 10 extra and is best worked in bulky yarns. Cast on a multiple of 18 sts, plus 10 extra.

1st row (Right side) *K11, P2, K2, P2, K1; rep from *, end K10.
2nd row P1, K8, P1, *P1, (K2, P2) twice, K8, P1; rep from *.
3rd row *K1, P8, (K2, P2) twice, K1; rep from *, end K1, P8, K1.
4th row P10, *P1, K2, P2, K2, P11; rep from *.
5th–8th row As 1st–4th row.

9th row K.
10th row (P2, K2) twice, P2, *P10, (K2, P2) twice; rep from *.
11th row *(K2, P2) twice, K2, P8; rep from *, end (K2, P2) twice, K2.
12th row (P2, K2) twice, P2, *K8, (P2, K2) twice, P2; rep from *.
13th row *(K2, P2) twice, K10; rep from *, end (K2, P2) twice, K2.
14th–17th row As 10th–13th row.
18th row P.

Basketweave stitch

Pattern repeats over 8 rows and 8 sts, plus 5 extra. It is often done with 7 sts across the horizontal band instead of 5 as given here. The basketweave effect can be enhanced by working the P blocks in a slightly lighter tone than the K blocks. Cast on a multiple of 8 stitches, plus 5 extra.

1st row (Right side) K.
2nd row K5, *P3, K5; rep from *.
3rd row P5, *K3, P5; rep from *.

4th row As 2nd row.
5th row As 1st row.
6th row K1, *P3, K5; rep from *, end last rep K1.
7th row P1, *K3, P5; rep from *, end last rep P1.
8th row As 6th row.

Stripes

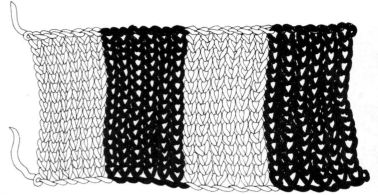

Horizontal stripes

Pattern repeats over 4 rows and any number of sts. The stripes are achieved by changing color at the beginning of a K row. This gives a continuous line of color on the right side of the fabric. The same number of rows can be used for each color, or varied to give an uneven striped effect. The purl side can also be used as the right side of the work; where each new color is introduced

it gives a broken line of color. Stripes can be worked in the same way in rib, but if you want an unbroken line of color on the right side of the work, K the whole of the color-change row.
Light color A, dark color B. With A, cast on any number of sts.
1st row With A, K.
2nd row With A, P.
3rd row With B, K.
4th row With B, P.

Vertical stripes

Pattern repeats over 2 rows and 30 sts. Stripes can be equal or unequal and of any width. When working narrow stripes, carry the yarn across or twist it at the back of the fabric. When working wider stripes of more than 5 sts, use separate balls of yarn for each color. They look best when worked in st st, but any of the other basic sts such as g st or rib can be used.
Light color A, dark color B.

Cast on a multiple of 30 sts as follows: 6A, 6B, 6A, 6B, 6A.
1st row K6A, 6B, 6A, 6B, 6A.
2nd row P6A, 6B, 6A, 6B, 6A.

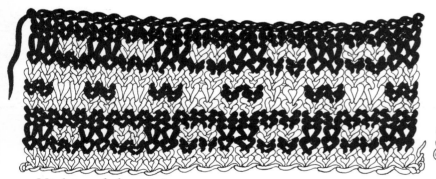

Night and day stripe

Pattern repeats over 12 rows and 4 sts, plus 2 extra. It consists of horizontal stripes of alternate colors, each stripe bearing touches of the opposite color. For a more textured effect you could work the B rows in rev st st.
Light color A, dark color B. With A, cast on a multiple of 4 sts, plus 2 extra.
1st row (Right side) With A, K.
2nd row With A, P.
3rd row With B, K1, sl 1, *K2, sl 2; rep from *, end K2, sl 1, K1.
4th row With B, P1, sl 1, *P2,

sl 2; rep from *, end P2, sl 1, P1.
5th–6th row As 1st–2nd row.
7th–8th row With B, as 1st–2nd row.
9th row With A, K2, *sl 2, K2; rep from *.
10th row With A, P2, *sl 2, P2; rep from *.
11th–12th row With B, as 1st–2nd row.

Zebra chevron

Pattern repeats over 12 rows and 24 sts, plus 2 extra.
Light color A, dark color B. With A, cast on a multiple of 24 sts, plus 2 extra.
1st row (Right side) With B, K1, *sl 1, K2; rep from *, end K1.
2nd row With B, P1, *P2, sl 1; rep from *, end P1.
3rd row With A, K1, *K1, sl 1, (K2, sl 1) 3 times, K3, (sl 1, K2) 3 times, sl 1; rep from *, end K1.
4th row With A, P1, *sl 1, (P2, sl 1) 3 times, P3, (sl 1, P2) 3 times, sl 1, P1; rep from *, end P1.

5th row With B, K1, *K2, (sl 1, K2) 3 times, sl 1, K1, sl 1, (K2, sl 1) 3 times, K1; rep from *, end K1.
6th row With B, P1, *P1, (sl 1, P2) 3 times, sl 1, P1, sl 1, (P2, sl 1) 3 times, P2; rep from *, end P1.
7th–8th row With A, as 1st–2nd row.
9th–10th row With B, as 3rd–4th row.
11th–12th row With A, as 5th–6th row.

Beaded stripe

Pattern repeats over 8 rows and 6 sts, plus 5 extra. A subtle use of colors means that this pattern can be seen in two ways: either as a line of dark beads against a light background or a line of light beads against a dark background. It forms a tweedy fabric and is most effective when worked in a fine yarn. Light color A, dark color B. With A, cast on a multiple of 6 sts, plus 5 extra.

1st row (Right side) With A, K.
2nd row With A, K1, *P3, K3; rep from *, end P3, K1.
3rd row With B, K1, *sl 3, K3; rep from *, end sl 3, K1.
4th row With B, P2, sl 1, P5; rep from *, end sl 1, P2.
5th row With B, K.
6th row With B, K4, *P3, K3; rep from *, end K1.
7th row With A, K4, *sl 3, K3; rep from *, end K1.
8th row With A, P5, *sl 1, P5; rep from *.

Chevron stripes

Pattern repeats over 4 rows and 14 sts, plus 1 extra. A zigzag striped effect can be achieved by the subtle use of stitch and color changes. The chevron shaping is formed by vertical lines of inc and dec sts. Light color A, dark color B. With A, cast on a multiple of 14 sts, plus 1 extra.

1st row With A, *K1, K into the loop below the next st on the left-hand needle, then K the st immediately above, K4,

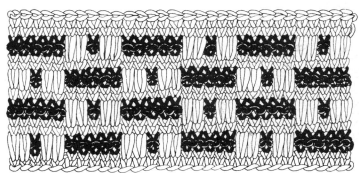

sl 1, K2 tog, psso, K4, K into the loop below the next st on the left-hand needle, then K the st immediately above; rep from *, end K1.
2nd row With A, P.
3rd row With B, as 1st row.
4th row With B, as 2nd row.

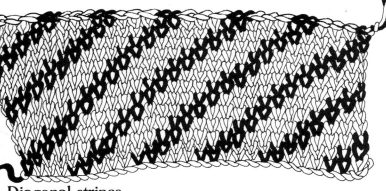

Diagonal stripes

Pattern repeats over 10 rows and 5 sts, plus 3 extra. The slant is obtained by moving the stripes 1 st to the right on K rows and 1 st to the left on P rows, but you can work more sts to the left and right, depending on the diagonal angle required.
Light color A, dark color B. With A, cast on a multiple of 5 sts, plus 3 extra.

1st row K3A, *2B, 3A; rep from *.
2nd row P1B, *3A, 2B; rep from *, end 2A.
3rd row K1A, *2B, 3A; rep from *, end 2B.

4th row P1A, 2B, *3A, 2B; rep from *.
5th row K1B, *3A, 2B; rep from *, end 2A.
6th row P3A, *2B, 3A; rep from *.
7th row K2A, *2B, 3A; rep from *, end 1B.
8th row P2B, *3A, 2B; rep from *, end 1A.
9th row K2B, *3A, 2B; rep from *, end 1A.
10th row P2A, *2B, 3A; rep from *, end 1B.

Dots and dashes

Pattern repeats over 8 rows and 10 sts, plus 7 extra. You can add a third color by using one color for the dots and another for the dashes. Purl the 4th and 8th rows for a smooth rather than textured effect or you could emphasize the dots with beads, sequins or crystals.
Light color A, dark color B. With A, cast on a multiple of 10 sts, plus 7 extra.

1st row (Right side) With A, K.
2nd row With A, P.
3rd row With B, K1, *K5, sl 2, K1, sl 2; rep from *, end K6.
4th row With B, K1, *K5, yf,

sl 2, yb, K1, yf, sl 2, yb; rep from *, end K6.
5th–6th row As 1st–2nd row.
7th row With B, K1, *sl 2, K1, sl 2, K5; rep from *, end last rep K1.
8th row With B, K1, *yf, sl 2, yb, K1, yf, sl 2, yb, K5; rep from *, end last rep K1.

Checks

Two-stitch check

Pattern repeats over 8 rows and 4 sts. It can be widened by working a four or six-stitch check. A different color can be introduced on the 7th–8th row for a three color checked pattern and two more K and P rows can be worked after the 2nd row to space the checks farther apart.
Light color A, dark color B.
Cast on a multiple of 4 sts.
1st row (Right side) With A, K.

2nd row With A, P.
3rd row With B, *sl 2, K2; rep from *.
4th row With B, *P2, sl 2; rep from *.
5th–6th row As 1st–2nd row.
7th row With B, *K2, sl 2; rep from *.
8th row With B, *sl 2, P2; rep from *.

Bricks

Pattern repeats over 8 rows and 4 sts, plus 3 extra. It consists of bricks worked in st st in one color which are set off by mortar worked in g st in another color.
Light color A, dark color B.
Cast on a multiple of 4 sts, plus 3 extra.
1st–2nd row (Right side) With A, K.
3rd row With B, K1, *sl 1, K3; rep from *, end sl 1, K1.

4th row With B, P1, *sl 1, P3; rep from *, end sl 1, P1.
5th–6th row As 1st–2nd row.
7th row With B, K3, *sl 1, K3; rep from *.
8th row With B, P3, *sl 1, P3; rep from *.

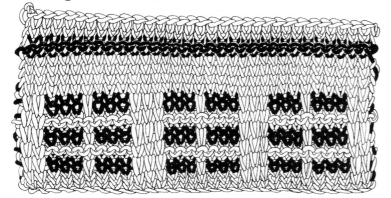

Windows

Pattern repeats over 14 rows and 10 sts, plus 3 extra. Simple checks are arranged into vertical and horizontal lines, the checks being grouped together into windows with six panes each. The ridges formed by the 6th and 10th rows give a textured effect.
Light color A, dark color B.
With A, cast on a multiple of 10 sts, plus 3 extra.
1st row (Right side) With A, K.
2nd row With A, P.
3rd row With B, K1, sl 2, *K3, sl 1, K3, sl 3; rep from *, end last rep sl 2, K1.
4th row With B, P1, sl 2, *P3, sl 1, P3, sl 3; rep from *, end

last rep sl 2, P1.
5th row With A, K.
6th row With A, P3, *K7, P3; rep from *
7th–10th row As 3rd–6th row.
11th–12th row As 3rd–4th row.
13th–14th row Rep 1st–2nd row.

Fair Isle check

Pattern repeats over 14 rows and 16 sts. This is one of many Fair Isle patterns and incorporates contrasting diamonds intersected by diagonal lines which are also in contrasting colors.
Light color A, dark color B.
Cast on a multiple of 16 sts.
1st row (Right side) *K1B, 7A; rep from *.
2nd row *P1B, 5A, 1B, 1A, 1B, 5A, 2B; rep from *.
3rd row *K3B, 3A, 1B, 3A, 1B, 3A, 2B; rep from *.
4th row *P3B, 1A, 1B, 5A, 1B, 1A, 4B; rep from *.
5th row *K3B, 1A, 1B, 7A, 1B, 1A, 2B; rep from *.

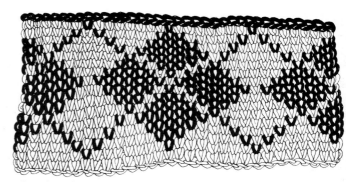

6th row *P1B, 1A, 3B, 5A, 3B, 1A, 2B; rep from *.
7th row *K1B, 1A, 5B, 3A, 5B, 1A; rep from *.
8th row *P7B, 1A; rep from *.
9th row As 7th row.
10th row As 6th row.
11th row As 5th row.
12th row As 4th row.
13th row As 3rd row.
14th row As 2nd row.

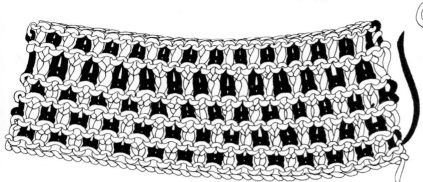

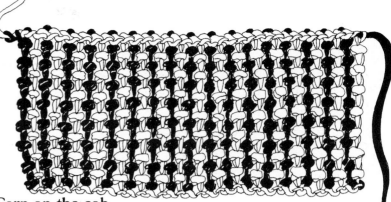

Waffle check

Pattern repeats over 8 rows and an odd number of sts and is worked in g st throughout. To arrange the checks in a vertical line instead of alternating them, repeat 1st–4th row only.
Light color A, dark color B.
Cast on an odd number of sts.
1st row (Wrong side) With A, K.
2nd row With B, K1, *sl 1, K1; rep from *.

3rd row With B, K1, *yf, sl 1, yb, K1; rep from *.
4th–5th row With A, K.
6th row With B, K2, *sl 1, K1; rep from *, end K1.
7th row With B, K2, *yf, sl 1, yb, K1; rep from *, end K1.
8th row With A, K.

Corn on the cob

Pattern repeats over 4 rows and an even number of sts. Knitted in narrow vertical lines it produces a thick, close, heavily textured fabric.
P rather than K the 2nd and 4th row for a simple variation.
Light color A, dark color B.
With B, cast on an even number of sts.
1st row (Right side) With A, K1, *K1, sl 1; rep from *, end K1.

2nd row With A, K1, *yf, sl 1, yb, K1; rep from *, end K1.
3rd row With B, K1, *sl 1, K1 tbl; rep from *, end K1.
4th row With B, K1, *K1, yf, sl 1, yb; rep from *, end K1.

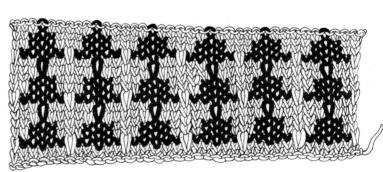

Bubble tweed

Pattern repeats over 12 rows and 3 sts, plus 2 extra. The subtle diagonal line running through this tweed is formed by moving 1 st to the right on every other row.
Light color A, dark color B.
With B, cast on a multiple of 3 sts, plus 2 extra.
1st row (Right side) With B, K1, *sl 2, K1, yf, p1sso; rep from *, end K1.
2nd row With B, P1, *P2, sl 1; rep from *, end P1.
3rd row With A, K2, *sl 2, K1, yf, p1sso; rep from *, end sl 1, K2.
4th row With A, P2, *sl 1, P2; rep from *.

5th row With B, K3, *sl 2, K1, yf, p1sso; rep from *, end sl 1, K1.
6th row With B, P1, *sl 1, P2; rep from *, end P1.
7th–8th row With A, as 1st–2nd row.
9th–10th row With B, as 3rd–4th row.
11th–12th row With A, as 5th–6th row.

Medallion check

Pattern repeats over 8 rows and 6 sts, plus 3 extra. Work each rep in two colors for multicolored triangles.
Light color B, dark color A.
With B, cast on a multiple of 6 sts, plus 3 extra.
1st row (Right side) With A, K1, *sl 1, K5; rep from *, end sl 1, K1.
2nd row With A, P1, *sl 1, P5; rep from *, end sl 1, P1.
3rd row With B, K3, *sl 3, K3; rep from *.
4th row With B, P3, *sl 3, P3; rep from *.
5th row With A, K1, sl 2, *K3, sl 3; rep from *, end K3, sl 2, K1.

6th row With A, P1, sl 2, *P3, sl 3; rep from *, end P3, sl 2, P1.
7th row With B, K4, *sl 1, K5; rep from *, end sl 1, K4.
8th row With B, P4, *sl 1, P5; rep from *, end sl 1, P4.

Cables

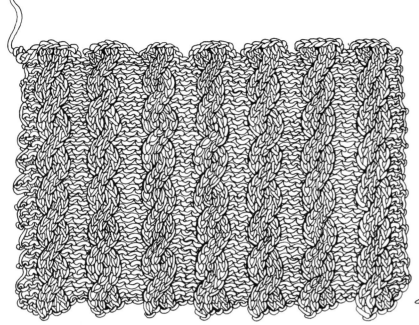

Four-stitch cable

Pattern repeats over 4 rows and 8 sts. There are many variations of this simple pattern, such as six-stitch cable, which is crossed every 6th row, or eight-stitch cable, which is crossed every 10th row.

Cast on a multiple of 8 sts.
1st row (Wrong side) K2, P4, K2.
2nd row P2, K4, P2.
3rd row As 1st row.
4th row P2, sl next 2 sts to CN to front of work, K2, then K2 from CN, P2.

Plait cable

Pattern repeats over 8 rows and 13 sts.
Cast on a multiple of 13 sts.
1st row (Right side) P2, K9, P2.
2nd row K2, P9, K2.
3rd row P2, sl 3 sts to CN to front of work, K3, then K3 from CN, K3, P2.

4th row As 2nd row.
5th–6th row As 1st–2nd row.
7th row P2, K3, sl 3 sts to CN to back of work, K3, then K3 from CN.
8th row As 2nd row.

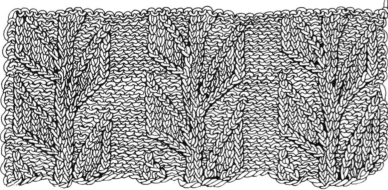

Banana tree

Pattern repeats over 12 rows and 18 sts. It produces a textured fabric and can be embroidered to great decorative effect.
Cast on a multiple of 18 sts.
1st row (Wrong side) K2, P3, K3, P4, BPC, K4.
2nd row P3, BKC, K1, BC, K2, P3, FC, K1, P2.
3rd row K2, P2, K4, P2, K1, P3, BPC, K2.
4th row P2, K3, BC, P1, K1, FKC, P3, FC, P2.
5th row K6, FPC, P2, K2, P4, K2.

6th row P2, K2, BC, P2, K1, (FKC) twice, P5.
7th row K4, FPC, P4, K3, P3, K2.
8th row P2, K1, BC, P3, K2, FC, K1, FKC, P3.
9th row K2, FPC, P3, K1, P2, K4, P2, K2.
10th row P2, BC, P3, BKC, K1, P1, FC, K3, P2.
11th row K2, P4, K2, P2, BPC, K6.
12th row P5, (BKC) twice, K1, P2, FC, K2, P2.

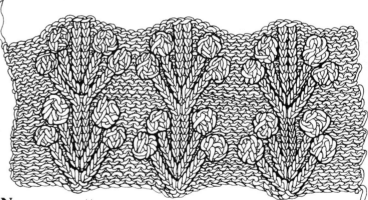

Nosegay pattern

Pattern repeats over 10 rows and 16 sts.
Cast on a multiple of 16 sts.
1st row (Wrong side) K7, P2, K7.
2nd row P6, BKC, FKC, P6.
3rd row K5, FC, P2, BC, K5.
4th row P4, BC, BKC, FKC, FC, P4.
5th row K3, FC, K1, P4, K1, BC, K3.
6th row P2, BC, P1, BC, K2, FC, P1, FC, P2.
7th row (K2, P1) twice, K1, P2, K1, (P1, K2) twice.
8th row P2, make bobble as

follows: (K1, P1) twice into next st, turn, P4, turn, K4, turn, (P2tog) twice, turn, K2tog, completing bobble; P1, BC, P1, K2, P1, FC, P1, make bobble, P2.
9th row K4, P1, K2, P2, K2, P1, K4.
10th row P4, make bobble, P2, K2, P2, make bobble, P4.

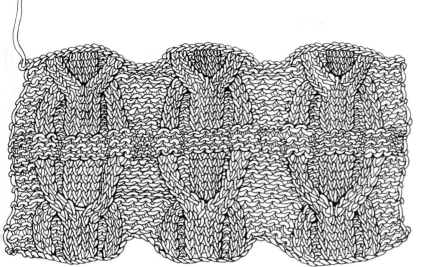

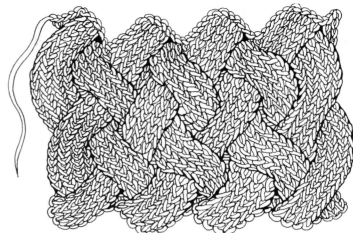

Box cable

Pattern repeats over 16 rows and 16 sts.
Cast on a multiple of 16 sts.
1st row (Right side) P2, K2, P2, K4, P2, K2, P2.
2nd row K2, P2, K2, P4, K2, P2, K2.
3rd–6th row Rep 1st–2nd row twice.
7th row P2, sl 4 sts to CN to back of work, K2, then P2, K2 from CN, sl 2 sts to CN to

front of work, K2, P2, then K2 from CN, P2.
8th row As 2nd row.
9th row As 1st row.
10th–11th row As 8th–9th row.
12th–16th row K.

Basket cable

Pattern repeats over 12 rows and 16 sts, plus 4 extra.
Cast on a multiple of 16 sts, plus 4 extra.
1st row (Wrong side) and all other wrong-side rows P.
2nd row K.
4th row As 2nd row.
6th row K2, *sl next 4 sts to CN to back of work, K4, then K4 from CN; rep from *, end K2.

8th row As 2nd row.
10th row As 8th row.
12th row K6, *sl next 4 sts to CN to front of work, K4, then K4 from CN; rep from *, end K6.

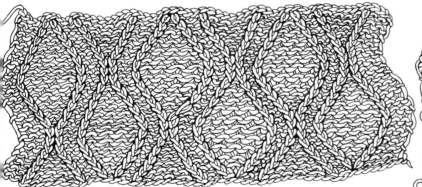

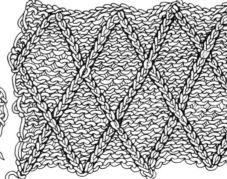

Double hourglass

Pattern repeats over 16 rows and 14 sts, plus 2 extra.
Cast on a multiple of 14 sts, plus 2 extra.
1st row (Wrong side) K1, *P1, K2, P1, K6, P1, K2, P1; rep from *, end K1.
2nd row P1, *FC, P1, FC, P4, BC, P1, BC; rep from *, end P1.
3rd row and all other wrong-side rows K all K sts and P all P sts.
4th row P1, *(P1, FC) twice, P2, (BC, P1) twice; rep from *, end P1.

6th row P1, *P2, FC, P1, FC, BC, P1, BC, P2; rep from *, end P1.
8th row K all K sts and P all P sts.
10th row P1, *P2, BC, P1, BC, FC, P1, FC, P2; rep from *, end P1.
12th row P1, *(P1, BC) twice, P2, (FC, P1) twice; rep from *, end P1.
14th row P1, *BC, P1, BC, P4, FC, P1, FC; rep from *, end P1.
16th row As 8th row.

Basic lattice

Pattern repeats over 16 rows and 8 sts.
Cast on a multiple of 8 sts.
1st row (Right side) P3, BKC, *P6, BKC; rep from *, end P3.
2nd row and all other wrong-side rows K all K sts and P all P sts.
3rd row P2, *BC, FC, P4; rep from *, end BC, FC, P2.
5th row P1, *BC, P2, FC, P2; rep from *, end BC, P2, FC, P1.
7th row *BC, P4, FC; rep from *.

9th row K1, *P6, FKC; rep from *, end P6, K1.
11th row *FC, P4, BC; rep from *.
13th row P1, *FC, P2, BC, P2; rep from *, end FC, P2, BC, P1.
15th row P2, *FC, BC, P4; rep from *, end FC, BC, P2.
16th row As 2nd row.

Eyelets

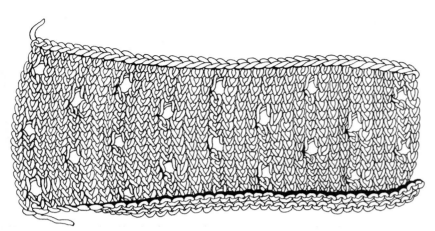

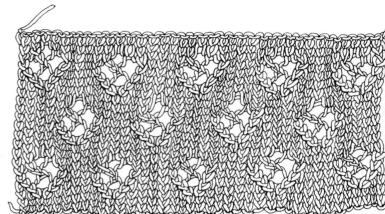

Simple eyelet pattern

Pattern repeats over 8 rows and 8 sts. Simple eyelets are either formed by yf, K2tog, or by yf, sl 1, K1, psso. The former method is explained here, but use the latter if you want a slightly more open eyelet. A simple eyelet may be used singly when a small buttonhole is required and the latter method is the best one for this. This pattern is for staggered rows; for vertical rows rep 1st–4th row only.

Cast on a multiple of 8 sts.
1st row (Right side) K.
2nd row and all other wrong-side rows P.
3rd row *K6, yf, K2tog; rep from *.
5th row As 1st row.
7th row K2, *yf, K2tog, K6; rep from *, end last rep K4.
8th row P.

Quatrefoil eyelet

Pattern repeats over 16 rows and 8 sts. It is worked on the same principle as simple eyelet stitch except the eyelets are grouped together in blocks of four.

Cast on a multiple of 8 sts.
1st row (Wrong side) and all other wrong-side rows P.
2nd row K.
4th row K3, *yf, sl 1, K1, psso, K6; rep from *, end last rep K3.
6th row K1, *K2tog, yf, K1,

yf, sl 1, K1, psso, K3; rep from *, end last rep K2.
8th row As 4th row.
10th row As 2nd row.
12th row K7, *yf, sl 1, K1, psso, K6; rep from *, end K1.
14th row K5, *K2tog, yf, K1, yf, sl 1, K1, psso, K3; rep from *, end K3.
16th row As 12th row.

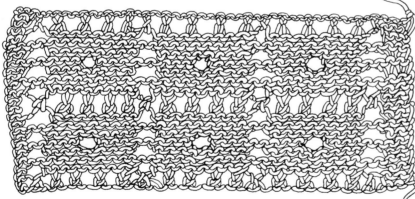

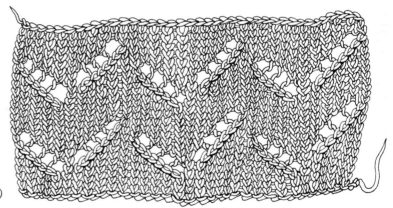

Snake eyes

Pattern repeats over 16 rows and 10 sts, plus 6 extra. It is a basic dice pattern consisting of g st blocks, divided by horizontal and vertical lines of eyelets with a single eyelet on each. Narrow ribbon could be threaded through the horizontal and vertical lines for a decorative effect.
Cast on a multiple of 10 sts, plus 6 extra.
1st row (Right side) K2, *yf, K2tog; rep from *, end K2.
2nd row K.

3rd row K1, *K2tog, yf, sl 1, K1, psso, K6; rep from *, end last rep K1.
4th row K2, *(K1, P1) into the yf of the previous row, K8; rep from *, end last rep K2.
5th–6th row K.
7th–8th row As 3rd–4th row.
9th row K6, *K2tog, yf, sl 1, K1, psso, K6; rep from *.
10th row K7, *(K1, P1) into the yf, K8; rep from *, end last rep K7.
11th–16th row As 3rd–8th row.

Zigzag eyelet pattern

Pattern repeats over 12 rows and 11 sts, plus 2 extra. Eyelets are grouped together in Vs to form lines of zigzags. Like many eyelet patterns this could provide a perfect background for beads and sequins.
Cast on a multiple of 11 sts, plus 2 extra.
1st row (Wrong side) and all other wrong-side rows P.
2nd row K6, *yf, sl 1, K1, psso, K9; rep from *, end last rep K5.

4th row K7, *yf, sl 1, K1, psso, K9; rep from *, end last rep K4.
6th row K3, *K2tog, yf, K3, yf, sl 1, K1, psso, K4; rep from *, end last rep K3.
8th row *K2, K2tog, yf, K5, yf, sl 1, K1, psso; rep from *, end K2.
10th row K1, *K2tog, yf, K9; rep from *, end K1.
12th row *K2tog, yf, K9; rep from *, end K2.

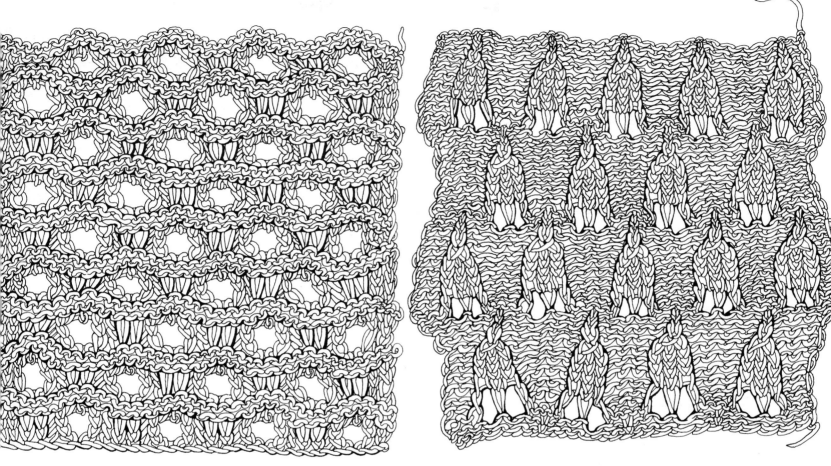

Eyelet honeycomb

Pattern repeats over 12 rows and 8 sts, plus 6 extra. It lends itself to threading with ribbons, strips of leather or plastic, braids or any other suitable material. Work vertically or horizontally in straight lines, weaving in and out of the holes. Various crisscross patterns can also be achieved.
Cast on a multiple of 8 sts, plus 6 extra.
1st row (Wrong side) K.
2nd row P.
3rd row P2, *sl 2, P6; rep from *, end sl 2, P2.
4th row K2, *sl 2, K1, K2tog, yf, yrn, sl 1, K1, psso, K1; rep from *, end sl 2, K2.
5th row P2, *sl 2, P2, (P1, K1) into the 2 made sts, P2; rep from *, end sl 2, P2.
6th row K2, *sl 2, K6; rep from *, end sl 2, K2.
7th–8th row As 1st–2nd row.
9th row P6, *sl 2, P6; rep from *.
10th row K3, yf, sl 1, K1, psso, K1, *sl 2, K1, K2tog, yf, yrn, sl 1, K1, psso, K1; rep from *, end sl 2, K1, K2tog, yf, K3.
11th row P6, *sl 2, P2 (P1, K1) into the 2 made sts, P2; rep from *, end sl 2, P6.
12th row K6, *sl 2, K6; rep from *.

Bluebell pattern

Pattern repeats over 20 rows and 6 sts, plus 5 extra. As an alternative it can be worked upside down so that the bluebells resemble tulips. Once the pattern has been mastered it is also possible to work individual flowers.
Cast on a multiple of 6 sts, plus 5 extra.
1st row (Right side) P2, *K1, P5; rep from *, end K1, P2.
2nd row K2, *P1, K5; rep from *, end P1, K2.
3rd row P5, *yon, K1, yrn, P5; rep from *.
4th row K5, *P3, K5; rep from *.
5th row P5, *K3, P5; rep from *.
6th–7th row As 4th–5th row.
8th row As 4th row.
9th row P5, *sl 1, K2tog, psso, P5; rep from *.
10th row K5, *P1, K5; rep from *.
11th row P5, *K1, P5; rep from *.
12th row As 10th row.
13th row P2, *yon, K1, yrn, P5; rep from *, end yon, K1, yrn, P2.
14th row K2, *P3, K5; rep from *, end P3, K2.
15th row P2, *K3, P5; rep from *, end K3, P2.
16th–17th row As 14th–15th row.
18th row As 14th row.
19th row P2, *sl 1, K2tog, psso, P5; rep from *, end sl 1, K2tog, psso, P2.
20th row As 2nd row.

Lace

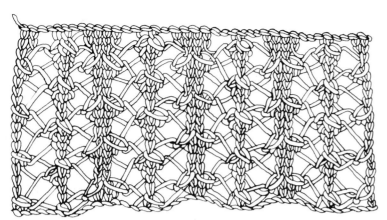

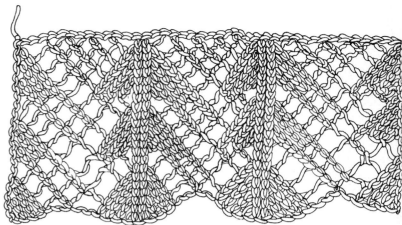

Bead stitch

Pattern repeats over 4 rows and 7 sts. Panels are repeated continuously on a multiple of 7 sts. You can add several K sts between the panels to make a firmer fabric. It is a traditional Shetland lace pattern and forms the basis of many more complicated laces. It is also similar to many Spanish lace patterns, reflecting the Spanish ancestry of many Shetland knitting patterns.

Cast on a multiple of 7 sts.
1st row (Right side) K1, K2tog, yf, K1, yf, sl 1, K1, psso, K1.
2nd row P2tog-tbl, yrn, P3, yrn, P2tog.
3rd row K1, yf, sl 1, K1, psso, K1, K2tog, yf, K1.
4th row P2, yrn, P3tog, yrn, P2.

Fan lace

Pattern repeats over 8 rows and 11 sts. This delicate openwork pattern is highly individual and consists of vertical columns of fan shapes, hence its name. It is most effective when worked in a fine wool such as 2 ply.
Cast on a multiple of 11 sts.
1st row (Wrong side) and all other wrong-side rows P.
2nd row *Sl 1, K1, psso, K3 tbl, yf, K1, yf, K3 tbl, K2tog; rep from *.

4th row *Sl 1, K1, psso, K2 tbl, yf, K1, yf, sl 1, K1, psso, yf, K2 tbl, K2tog; rep from *.
6th row *Sl 1, K1, psso, K1 tbl, yf, K1, (yf, sl 1, K1, psso) twice, yf, K1 tbl, K2tog; rep from *.
8th row *Sl 1, K1, psso, yf, K1, (yf, sl 1, K1, psso) 3 times, yf, K2tog; rep from *.

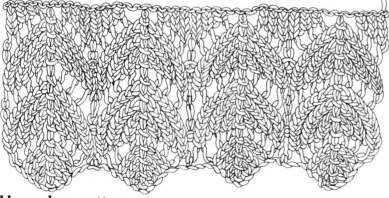

Horseshoe pattern

Pattern repeats over 8 rows and 10 sts, plus 1 extra. It is a traditional Shetland lace pattern that owes much of its popularity to its simplicity. The horseshoe shapes are formed from a simple yf, sl 1, K2tog, psso structure.
Cast on a multiple of 10 sts, plus 1 extra.
1st row (Wrong side) P.
2nd row K1, *yf, K3, sl 1, K2tog, psso, K3, yf, K1; rep from *.
3rd row P.

4th row P1, *K1, yf, K2, sl 1, K2tog, psso, K2, yf, K1, P1; rep from *.
5th row K1, *P9, K1; rep from *.
6th row P1, *K2, yf, K1, sl 1, K2tog, psso, K1, yf, K2, P1; rep from *.
7th row As 5th row.
8th row P1, *K3, yf, sl 1, K2tog, psso, yf, K3, P1; rep from *.

Fleurette

Pattern repeats over 12 rows and 6 sts, plus 5 extra. 1 st is added to each pattern repeat on rows 4 and 10 and taken off on rows 6 and 12.
Cast on a multiple of 6 sts, plus 5 extra.
1st row (Wrong side) and all other wrong-side rows P.
2nd row K2, *K1, yf, sl 1, K1, psso, K1, K2tog, yf; rep from *, end K3.
4th row K4, *yf, K3; rep from *, end K1.
6th row K2, K2tog, *yf, sl 1,

K1, psso, K1, K2tog, yf, sl 2 tog, K1, p2sso; rep from *, end yf, sl 1, K1, K2tog, yf, sl 1, K1, psso, K2.
8th row K2, *K1, K2tog, yf, K1, yf, sl 1, K1, psso; rep from *, end K3.
10th row As 4th row.
12th row K2, *K1, K2tog, yf, sl 2tog, K1, p2sso; rep from *, end K3.

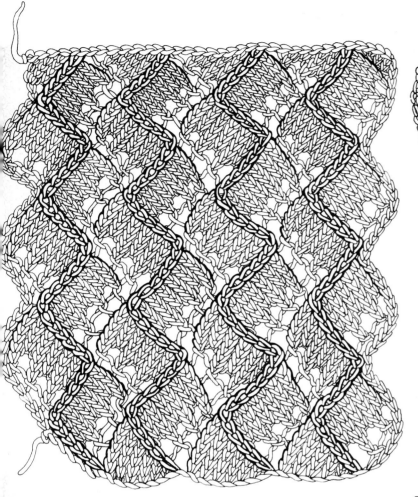

Traveling vine

Pattern repeats over 12 rows and 8 sts, plus 4 extra. 1 st is added to each pattern repeat on all right-side rows and taken off on all wrong-side rows. This pattern is of French origin and delicately curves first to the left and then to the right. It is formed on a simple, yf, K1, yf structure and the curves are constructed by placing the dec sts away from the yf sts for which they compensate.

Cast on a multiple of 8 sts, plus 4 extra.

1st row (Right side) K2, *yf, K1 tbl, yf, sl 1, K1, psso, K5; rep from *, end K2.

2nd row P6, *P2tog-tbl, P7; rep from *, end last rep P5.

3rd row K2, *yf, K1 tbl, yf, K2, sl 1, K1, psso, K3; rep from *, end K2.

4th row P4, *P2tog-tbl, P7; rep from *.

5th row K2, *K1 tbl, yf, K4, sl 1, K1, psso, K1, yf; rep from *, end K2.

6th row P3, *P2tog-tbl, P7; rep from *, end P1.

7th row K2, *K5, K2tog, yf, K1 tbl, yf; rep from *, end K2.

8th row P5, *P2tog, P7; rep from *, end last rep P6.

9th row K2, *K3, K2tog, K2, yf, K1 tbl, yf; rep from *, end K2.

10th row *P7, P2tog; rep from *, end P4.

11th row K2, *yf, K1, K2tog, K4, yf, K1 tbl; rep from *, end K2.

12th row P1, *P7, P2tog; rep from *, end P3.

Fern lace

Pattern repeats over 16 rows and 10 sts, plus 1 extra. It is of English origin and as an alternative is often worked over 12 sts, plus one extra and 20 rows. It is based on a yf, K1, yf structure, which forms veins on a st st background. Like many lace patterns this would be a perfect foil for delicate beading. For example, embroider tiny seed pearls to point up the tips of the fern fronds. It could also be used as an allover pattern or as an inserted vertical or horizontal panel set off by a plainer st on either side.

Cast on a multiple of 10 sts, plus 1 extra.

1st row (Wrong side) and all other wrong-side rows P.

2nd row K3, *K2tog, yf, K1, yf, sl 1, K1, psso, K5; rep from *, end last rep K3.

4th row K2, *K2tog, (K1, yf) twice, K1, sl 1, K1, psso, K3; rep from *, end last rep K2.

6th row K1, *K2tog, K2, yf, K1, yf, K2, sl 1, K1, psso, K1; rep from *.

8th row K2tog, *K3, yf, K1, yf, K3, sl 1, K2 tog, psso; rep from *, end K3, yf, K1, yf, K3, sl 1, K1, psso.

10th row K1, *yf, sl 1, K1, psso, K5, K2tog, yf, K1; rep from *.

12th row K1, *yf, K1, sl 1, K1, psso, K3, K2tog, K1, yf, K1; rep from *.

14th row K1, *yf, K2, sl 1, K1, psso, K1, K2tog, K2, yf, K1; rep from *.

16th row K1, *yf, K3, sl 1, K2tog, psso, K3, yf, K1; rep from *.

Texture

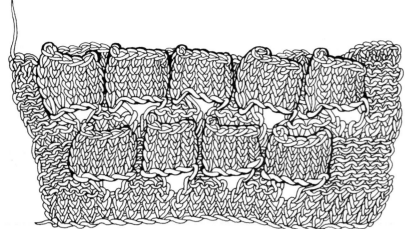

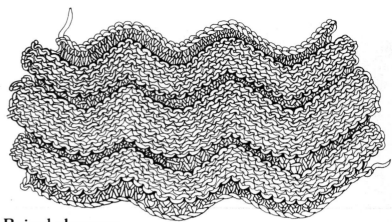

Barrel stitch

Pattern repeats over 12 rows and 4 sts, plus 4 extra. You can work a single row of barrels, align them vertically or stagger the spacing as above. To do this on every alt rep of the pattern K6 or P6 at beg of rows as appropriate and end K2 or P2. To increase the barrels in width or length, inc the number of sts or rows. Cast on a multiple of 4 sts, plus 4 extra.

1st row P4, *cast on 8 sts, P4; rep from *.
2nd row K4, *P8, K4; rep from *.
3rd row P4, *K8, P4; rep from *.
4th–9th row Rep 2nd–3rd row 3 times.
10th row K4, *bind off 8 sts, K4; rep from *.
11th row P.
12th row K.

Raised chevrons

Pattern repeats over 12 rows and 11 sts. The number of rows can be altered, however, to give a thicker or thinner band, as can the number of sts to give larger or smaller chevrons. If you work rows 1–6 on larger needles you will get a more pronounced chevron. These rows can also be worked in a different color. A few rows of raised chevrons can make an effective border for hems or sleeve edges.

Cast on a multiple of 11 sts.
1st–6th row Work in st st, starting with P.
7th row *K2tog, K3, yf, K1, yf, K3, K2tog; rep from *.
8th row P.
9th–12th row Rep 7th–8th row twice.

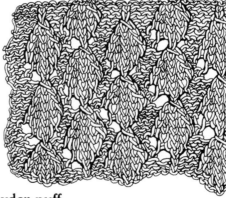

Bell motif

Pattern repeats over 14 rows and 4 sts, plus 4 extra.
Cast on a multiple of 4 sts, plus 4 extra.
1st row P4, *cast on 8 sts, P4; rep from *.
2nd row *K4, P8; rep from *, end K4.
3rd row P4, *K8, P4; rep from *.
4th row *K4, P8; rep from *, end K4.
5th row P4, *sl 1, K1, psso, K4, K2tog, P4; rep from *.
6th row *K4, P6; rep from *, end K4.

7th row P4, *sl 1, K1, psso, K2, K2tog, P4; rep from *.
8th row *K4, P4; rep from *, end K4.
9th row P4, *sl 1, K1, psso, K2tog, P4; rep from *.
10th row *K4, P2; rep from *, end K4.
11th row P4, *K2tog, P4; rep from *.
12th row *K4, P1; rep from *, end K4.
13th row P3, *K2tog, P3; rep from *, end P1.
14th row K.

Powder puff

Pattern repeats over 8 rows and 10 sts, plus 2 extra. It is based on a simple m1, K2tog structure to form vertical lines of powder puffs on a rev st st background.
Cast on a multiple of 10 sts, plus 2 extra.
1st row (Wrong side) K2, *P5, K2, P1, K2; rep from *.
2nd row P2, *m1, K1, m1, P2, sl 1, K1, psso, K1, K2tog, P2; rep from *.
3rd row K2, *P3, K2; rep from *.
4th row P2, *m1, K3, m1, P2,

sl 2tog knitwise, K1, p2sso, P2; rep from *.
5th row K2, *P1, K2, P5, K2; rep from *.
6th row P2, *sl 1, K1, psso, K1, K2tog, P2, m1, K1, m1, P2; rep from *.
7th row As 3rd row.
8th row P2, *sl 2tog knitwise, K1, p2sso, P2, m1, K3, m1, P2; rep from *.

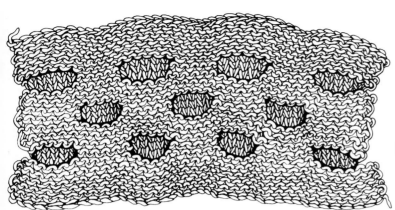

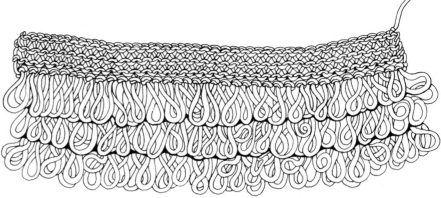

Buttonhole stitch

Pattern repeats over 20 rows and 10 sts, plus 2 extra.
Cast on a multiple of 10 sts, plus 2 extra.
1st–5th row Work in st st, starting with K.
6th row K6, *sl 5, K5; rep from *, end sl 5, K1.
7th row P1, *sl 5, P5; rep from *, end K1.
8th–9th row As 6th–7th row.
10th row As 6th row.
11th–15th row As 1st–5th row.

16th row K1, *sl 5, K5; rep from *, end K1.
17th row P1*, P5, sl 5; rep from *, end P1.
18th–19th row As 16th–17th row.
20th row As 16th row.

Loop stitch

Pattern repeats over 6 rows and any number of sts. It is based on the technique of winding yarn round the third finger to create a loop and is quick to work once mastered. The length of the loop can easily be increased by winding the yarn twice or more round the finger.
Cast on any number of sts.
1st–4th row K.
5th row (Wrong side) *Holding 3rd finger of left hand over yarn behind work, K1 (so that yarn forms loop around finger) but do not sl this st from needle, transfer the st just worked back on to left-hand needle and K2tog-tbl (the st just knitted and the original st), remove finger from loop to make another loop in the next st as before; rep from * into every st.
6th row K every st tbl.

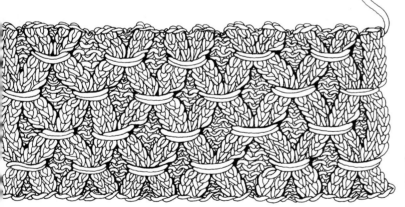

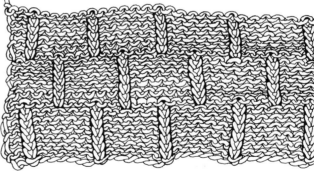

Smocking pattern

Pattern repeats over 8 rows and 8 sts, plus 2 extra. As an alternative smocking effects can be created by gathering the fabric and using any of the embroidery stitches shown on pp44–5.
Cast on a multiple of 8 sts, plus 2 extra.
1st row (Wrong side) K2, *P2, K2; rep from *.
2nd row P2, *K2, P2; rep from *.
3rd row As 1st row.
4th row P2, *insert right-hand needle from front between 6th and 7th sts on left-hand needle and draw a loop through, slip loop onto left-hand needle and K it tog with the first st on left-hand needle, K1, P2, K2, P2; rep from *.
5th–7th row As 1st–3rd row.
8th row P2, K2, P2, *draw loop from between 6th and 7th sts as before and K it tog with first st, K1, P2, K2, P2; rep from *, end K2, P2.

Piqué stitch

Pattern repeats over 12 rows and 6 sts, plus 5 extra. It is really a shallow rib pattern without the elasticity of an ordinary rib. It can be varied by increasing the width of the ribs or by working them in a different color.
Cast on a multiple of 6 sts, plus 5 extra.
1st row P2, *K1 tbl, P5; rep from *, end K1 tbl, P2.
2nd row K2, *P1 tbl, K5; rep from *, end P1 tbl, K2.
3rd–6th row Rep 1st–2nd row twice.
7th row *P5, K1 tbl; rep from *, end P5.
8th row K5, P1 tbl; rep from *, end K5.
9th–12th row Rep 7th–8th row twice.

Index

n00003 l00507 w01149 c05873
k06931

Acknowledgments

Designers
Val Moon 48–57
Esther Pearson 58–9
Edy Lyngaas 60–1
Katharine Blair 62–3
James Park 64–5
Sandy Black 66–7
Jennifer Kiernan 68–71
Rosie Tucker 74
Debbie Hudson 75
Rosie Tucker 76–8
Trevor Collins 79
Johanna Davis 80–1
Carolyn Cannon 82–3
Patsy North 84
Eleanor Hobbs 85
Lone Morton 86–7
Cherry Whytock 88–9
Roz Tosh 88–9
Helena Jedlinska 90–1
Debbie Hudson 92–3
Sandy Black 94–5
Debbie Hudson 96–7
Cec Merrigan 98–9
Fiona Cullen 100–1
Flea Davis 102–3
Helena Jedlinska 102–3
Esther Pearson 104–7
Debbie Hudson 108–11
Flea Davis 112–13
Diana Holmes 114–15
Ingrid Mason 114–15
Jayne Stewart 116–17
Debbie Hudson 118–19
Betty Barnden 120–3
Penny David 124–5
Caroline Sullivan 125
Anna Jones 126–7

Photographers
Simon de Courcy-Wheeler 1–9
Jim Lee 49–79
John Summerhays 80–5
Jim Lee 86–9
Peter Myers 89–99
Jim Lee 100–1
Peter Myers 103
Jim Lee 104–7
Red Saunders 108–9
John Summerhays 112–13
Peter Myers 115–19
Jim Lee 120–1
Peter Myers 124–5

Illustrators
Donna Muir 10–11
Sally Kindberg 12–15
Coral Mula 16–17
Carole Johnson 18–19
Donna Muir 18–19
Carole Johnson 20–1
Coral Mula 22–3
Clare Brooks 24–5
Coral Mula 26–31
Carole Johnson 32–3
Coral Mula 34–5
Sally Kindberg 36–41
Richard Phipps 42–3
Coral Mula 44–5
Carole Johnson 46–7
Donna Muir 48–55
Dorothy Ann Harrison 58–9
Donna Muir 60–1
Sally Kindberg 62–7
Terry Evans 68–71
Donna Muir 72–9
Johanna Davis 80–1
Dorothy Ann Harrison 82–7
Sally Kindberg 90–101
Dorothy Ann Harrison 102–3
Donna Muir 104–7
Sally Kindberg 108–11
Richard Phipps 112–13
Dorothy Ann Harrison 114–15
Sally Kindberg 116–23
Dorothy Ann Harrison 126–7
Sally Kindberg 128–41

The Publishers gratefully acknowledge the kind cooperation of the following suppliers: Jaeger Wool pp48–57, Pingouin Yarns pp88–91, Strawberry Studios pp94–5 and Top Shop pp96–7.

144